PORTFOLIO

THE PORTFOLIO BOOK OF
GREAT INDIAN BUSINESS STORIES

THE PORTFOLIO BOOK OF
GREAT INDIAN BUSINESS STORIES

RIVETING TALES OF BUSINESS LEADERS AND THEIR TIMES

PORTFOLIO
PENGUIN

An imprint of Penguin Random House

PORTFOLIO

USA | Canada | UK | Ireland | Australia
New Zealand | India | South Africa | China | Singapore

Portfolio is part of the Penguin Random House group of companies whose
addresses can be found at global.penguinrandomhouse.com

Published by Penguin Random House India Pvt. Ltd
4th Floor, Capital Tower 1, MG Road,
Gurugram 122 002, Haryana, India

Penguin
Random House
India

First published in Portfolio by Penguin Books India 2015

10 9 8 7 6 5 4 3 2

ISBN 9780143425243

Typeset in Adobe Garamond by Manipal Digital Systems, Manipal
Printed at Manipal Technologies Limited, India

www.penguin.co.in

This is a legitimate digitally printed version of the book and therefore might not
have certain extra finishing on the cover.

CONTENTS

RAHUL BAJAJ

Excerpts from *Business Maharajas* by Gita Piramal

Rahul was born on June 10, 1938, in Calcutta to Savitri and Kamalnayan (1915–1972) Bajaj, a Marwari businessman. The family was comfortably well off and in the process of moving from trade into industry. He schooled at Bombay's elite Cathedral and John Connon School, and graduated from Delhi's St Stephen's College with a BA (Hons) in Economics in 1958. Back in Bombay, Bajaj did a two-year stint at Bajaj Electricals, clocking in after morning lectures at the Government Law College. He spent most of 1961–62 as a junior purchase officer at Mukand and with some work experience under his belt, he left for Harvard. He passed out of the class of '64 with an MBA degree. In between (December 1961), he married Rupa Golap, a Maharashtrian beauty queen and an up-and-coming model. They have three children, Rajiv (b.1966), Sanjiv (b.1969) and Sunaina Kejriwal (b.1971).

Like his contemporary the late Aditya Birla, Rahul was raised in an intensely political family. Mahatma Gandhi treated his grandfather, Jamnalal Bajaj (1889–1942), as his fifth son. His grandfather was also a close friend of Jawaharlal Nehru. He contributed to the nationalist movement and the Congress Party, and was its treasurer for some years. The political tradition continued into the next generation. Between 1939 and 1947, most of the adult members of [the Bajaj] family found themselves behind prison bars in the cause of Indian freedom. Kamalnayan later became a Congress member of Parliament. When the Congress Party split in 1969, he left Indira Gandhi to join the Congress (O).

Though Bajaj has no personal political ambitions, he likes the company of movers and shakers. The Bajajs and the Nehrus have been family friends for over three generations. Kamalnayan and Indira Gandhi studied at the same school for a short time. Jawaharlal Nehru himself picked the name Rahul for Kamalnayan's first-born, a gesture which made 'Indira Gandhi hopping mad as she had wanted it for her own son,' recalls Rupa. (Coincidentally, Rahul and Rupa named their first-born Rajiv, and Rajiv and Sonia Gandhi named their son Rahul.) As prime minister, Rajiv Gandhi reportedly turned to Bajaj for advice. Closer home, Bajaj has been in the kitchen cabinet of Sharad Pawar, four times chief minister of Maharashtra.

Unlike Birla, however, Bajaj was brought up in a spartan atmosphere, unusual for a business family. Kamalnayan grew up in Gandhi's ascetic ashram at Wardha. His children (Rahul, Suman and Shishir) grew up in relatively more luxurious surroundings, in the leafy bylanes of Bombay's posh Carmichael Road. Rahul's upbringing and values owed more to Mahatma Gandhi than Jawaharlal Nehru, being more middle class than aristocratic. Holidays were often spent playing with the workers' children in the family's factories. Given this background, the idea of living inside an industrial complex did not appear as ludicrous to Bajaj as it would to his peers in the Marwari aristocracy. 'Actions speak louder than words. I did not and do not believe in absentee landlordism,' Bajaj is fond of declaring.

Bajaj's first office was simple: a Godrej table, a Godrej chair, and not much else. 'Though I was an MBA from Harvard, I didn't have any fancy ideas that I must have staff, or a secretary,' he remarks virtuously. His no-nonsense, hard-nosed, direct approach soon created an aura around India's king of the road. It is an image which affords Bajaj immense satisfaction.

His efforts at projecting a 'middle-class' image are, at times, a touch ridiculous. Such as the superfluous identikit badge dangling from the pocket of his half-sleeved safari suit. Why does a gold stripe embellish Bajaj's laminated mugshot when those of his executives are mere silver? Would any of the security personnel have the temerity to question, let alone check, the boss's walkabouts?

Rupa chuckles at the thought. They have been living in the factory complex for almost three decades. On shifting from Bombay to Pune, they were allotted a 10' by 12' room in a Bajaj guest house. The rest of it was reserved for the general manager of Bajaj Electricals, a group company now run by Shekhar Bajaj. Dussehra 1965 saw them finally in a house of their own. Rupa has no complaints. Like her husband, she enjoys colony life despite tense moments such as those following the police firing in 1979.

'That night we hardly slept. We received a couple of crank calls saying it would be better if the children and I go away, maybe to Bombay. Rahul and I thought about it. I said no. I wanted to be with Rahul and I didn't want people in the colony to think that Rahul's wife and children could just take off for Bombay when things became difficult. I also thought that if I went away, it would be a long, long time before I could come back. Once you go away in such a situation, it is very difficult to feel secure enough to come back. Since there was firing, an inquiry would take place which would be a long drawn out thing. The workers were in a mood to fight the management for a long time. I wanted to stay here with him,' Rupa recalls.

But times change. The next generation has its own views. 'I don't think one should be rigid. There are business families who live in big cities, away from their factories. I believe it is important to know how the company works and the kind of management systems it follows,' says Sanjiv. Sanjiv might have thought differently had he been in his father's black Bally sandals on November 26, 1964, the day a twenty-six-year-old Rahul joined Bajaj Tempo Ltd.

TEMPO TANTRUMS

His first job was as a deputy general manager. 'I had to see the commercial side which included purchasing, marketing, sales, accounts, finance, audit, everything but the production.' His boss was Naval K. Firodia (b.1910), then chief executive of Bajaj Auto and managing director of Bajaj Tempo.

Thin and ascetic-looking, his starched white khadi Nehru topi proclaiming his Gandhian convictions, Firodia was a lawyer from Ahmednagar who had spent time in Yerawada prison during the 1942 Quit India Movement, and got to know the Bajaj family in the '20s through the Congress Party. Following Independence, Firodia joined the Bajaj Group, and helped them tie up joint ventures to manufacture auto-rickshaws and scooters in India. In August 1957, Bajaj Tempo was promoted to make three-wheelers using German technology. The first Indian Vespa from Bajaj Auto operated out of a garage shed at Goregaon, on Bombay's outskirts, and Bajaj Auto had its manufacturing facility at Kurla. Later both plants were shifted to Akurdi, with a grass strip separating them. Today there's a wall on this strip.

The wall is a constant reminder of the rift between the Firodias and the Bajajs. Earlier, members of either family would simply stroll across the strip whenever they felt the need of company or advice. Today, even if the wall hadn't been there, neither would dream of casually walking over to the other side as in the past. The earlier friendship between the two families deteriorated into a cold war and by September 1968, a twenty-year-old partnership lay in tatters. Rahul Bajaj resigned from Bajaj Tempo and N.K. Firodia from Bajaj Auto. The Firodias walked off with Bajaj Tempo and the Bajajs held on to Bajaj Auto. The sales of the two companies were roughly Rs 70m apiece. Small beer even in those days.

Neither side wants to talk about why the fight broke out but each feels it got the short end of the stick. 'I felt they had taken away our company. Of course, they have their side of the story,' is all that a reticent Bajaj is willing to say. The Firodias were equally unhappy. Though they had Bajaj Tempo, they felt they should have got Bajaj Auto, a company which they felt they had built up, which was in a monopolistic market, and which had great potential, while they considered that Bajaj Tempo's 'immediate prospects were not very bright'.

According to a friend of both families, the relationship between the Firodias and the Bajajs began to sour shortly after Rahul Bajaj joined Bajaj Tempo. 'You have to view the fight in the correct perspective,' he said. 'Even the Bajajs accept that N.K. Firodia played a crucial role in establishing both Bajaj Auto and Bajaj Tempo and that he and his brother, HK, are very good managers and have done a lot for the two companies. But you have to remember that for many years, Firodia had been working for Bachraj Trading at Rs 500 a month. Later when Bajaj Tempo and Bajaj Auto were promoted, the Bajaj Group provided the financing though the Firodias held a quarter share in the managing agency firm. But after Rahul joined the business, the Firodias began buying shares in the market, possibly from mid-1967 onwards, trying to quietly strengthen their position in Bajaj Auto. When they found out, naturally the Bajajs took umbrage, especially young Rahul. Ironically, he was looking after the commercial side of the business, and so the shares which the Firodias had bought came to him for transfer, which of course he refused to do. I believe this was the genesis of the fight.'

Before the parting of the ways, the battle for Bajaj Auto—fought first in the boardroom, then on the stock market with both the Bajajs and the Firodias trying to acquire its shares—was fierce. Initially, the Firodias had 13 per cent of Bajaj Auto's issued share capital of 104,250 shares but by the end of February 1968, they had managed to hike it to 23 per cent. The Bajajs started out with 28 per cent and gradually built this up to 51 per cent. One of the better-known skirmishes in this battle was a bid to acquire a critical 4 per cent block held by financial institutions such as the LIC and the UTI. Basing their calculation on the share's market price of Rs 260, the Firodias offered Rs 262.50 per share for the block. Rahul Bajaj, on the other hand, was much more aggressive and boldly submitted an offer of Rs 411. Outflanked, the Firodias walked out of the auction disdainfully, saying 'they didn't have money to throw'.

From the boardroom and stock markets, the war progressed to the courts. In round one, the Firodias moved the Supreme Court in an attempt to arm-twist Rahul into transferring the shares they had bought from the stock market. The Supreme Court refused to oblige. In 1988, antagonism flared publicly. The *Sunday Observer* carried an interview where an angry Bajaj declared his 'firm conviction that Bajaj Tempo will one day be a part of the undivided Bajaj Group'. 'A bullock does not die as a result of a crow's curse,' Firodia countered, quoting a Maharashtrian proverb.

The mud-slinging and the legal actions didn't subside for two decades after the war's outbreak and even today the tension between the two families threatens to blow up any time. The conflict is partly due to the fact that both families continue to hold significant chunks of stock in each other's companies even after the divorce.

The problem was, the Firodias held 23 per cent in Bajaj Auto, which ensured that Rahul couldn't get a special resolution passed without their permission. However, in the early '90s, in order to fund an ambitious expansion programme, the Firodias gradually sold off some of their Bajaj Auto shares, bringing down their holding to 13 per cent. While this move considerably eased the pressure on the Bajaj camp, the Firodias found their position worsening in Bajaj Tempo.

After the split, the Firodias had carefully built up their stake in Bajaj Tempo from 13 per cent to 26 per cent, but their expansion plans forced them to make a number of rights issues which diluted their holdings. As their stake plummeted, for a brief moment in 1991–92, the possibility of a hostile bid arose and cash-rich Bajaj gleefully seized the tempting opportunity. Initially, the Bajaj group held 23 per cent in Bajaj Tempo. Now Rahul acquired a dangerous extra 3 per cent so that the Germans, the Firodias and the Bajajs each held 26 per cent with the balance 22 per cent scattered among the public. The opportunity vanished, however, when Bajaj Tempo made yet another issue (in 1993) and persuaded Daimler Benz to renounce their rights in favour of the Firodias.

Currently the Firodias probably have 36 per cent, Bajaj 26 per cent, and Daimler Benz 16 per cent and Rahul admits there's no possibility whatsoever of acquiring Bajaj Tempo (sales 1995: Rs 5.65bn). So why does he hold on to these shares? What are his intentions? Bajaj offers a tongue-in-cheek reply: 'It is a good investment. The Firodias run Bajaj Tempo very well. Their track record shows that. Whenever I want to sell my shares, I will make a good profit on them.' This attitude combined with Rahul's ability to block special resolutions is an Achilles heel which has left the Firodias feeling vulnerable. So long as that sentiment endures, and Bajaj doesn't appear to feel any desire to allay or dispel it, there is unlikely to be a thaw in the cold war between two of Pune's giants.

Bajaj has an equally tempestuous relationship with another scooter maker, Piaggio, owned by the Agnellis of Italy. The powerful Turin-based family runs an industrial empire which, according to David Lomax, author of *The Money Makers*, is 'so big and influential that no Italian government would dare either to ignore it or to adopt policies which would damage its overall interests'.

Piaggio and the Bajaj group tied up in early 1960 to assemble scooters in India. Vespa in India was as loved as Vespa in Europe, the first wheels alike of the rich and the poor. A young Sir Terence Conran, the British designer, scooted round London on his. In New Delhi, the college-going Bajaj found that his Vespa boosted his popularity. The technical collaboration ended in 1971 when the Indira Gandhi government refused permission to extend its term. Some analysts felt this was a blessing in disguise. 'With Rahul's tough and disciplined approach, the company soon found its footing in the market and Bajaj Chetak and Super became legends,' commented one.

On the day the collaboration officially ended, Piaggio wrote to Bajaj, thanking him for years of 'really friendly cooperation' and wishing Bajaj Auto 'the most successful future'. It was dated April 1— All Fool's Day—an unintended irony. A decade later, Piaggio would accuse Bajaj of pilfering Piaggio designs in a California district court.

Piaggio's move appears to have been a knee-jerk reaction to Bajaj's export thrust. Pune's scooter king had started dreaming of becoming a global player. Between 1978 and 1981, Bajaj Auto's export sales jumped from Rs 63.5m to Rs 133.2m. A euphoric Bajaj even ran a campaign in *Time* magazine, perhaps the first Indian advertiser to do so. But he was still just a country cousin. Piaggio's production in 1981 was 905,000 vehicles, that of Bajaj Auto, 173,000. Piaggio's sales were L626bn (about Rs 4.7bn at the then current rates). Bajaj Auto's were Rs 1.16bn.

Bajaj's euphoria evaporated as Piaggio initiated legal action against him in the USA and West Germany. The Italians claimed that Bajaj had violated the terms of their collaboration, had not returned Piaggio's original drawings and so had no right to manufacture scooters.

Bajaj claims he had Piaggio's tacit permission. 'How else could it have been? We couldn't be expected to invest crores of rupees in plant and equipment and then one fine day cease to manufacture and let our investment go to seed. And, if Piaggio had not acquiesced in our action, it should have taken legal action *then*, not ten years later.' Piaggio's lawyers—Indian—took a rather dim view of this attitude. 'It's a matter of national importance that Indian companies abide by the agreements that they enter into with foreign companies. We want a greater inflow of foreign technology. How can we inspire confidence if we violate agreements?'

Bajaj brushes aside the argument. 'I remember a whole week in Genoa with four of my colleagues in 1975. A deal was about to be finalized. Everything was done. Without charging any royalty and fees, without any equity in our company, Piaggio would give the plans of their scooters and three-wheelers. In return we would give them the worldwide right for exporting our vehicles. We fixed the minimum value they would export each year for the next ten years. It got stuck on one small point. We wanted R&D cooperation. They wouldn't agree to that. But we broke amicably as we had done in 1971. Later our exports increased a little bit. They were still chicken feed. But Piaggio thought it was a threat.'

Hiring Baker-McKenzie, one of the largest international law firms in the world, Bajaj poured $1m into his defence. It was a huge figure for an Indian company at the time.

The great scooter war ended on a whimper. In the USA, Piaggio offered an out-of-court settlement. The millions of dollars compensation demand was scaled down to $50,000. Bajaj 'refused to budge and in the final settlement only gave a promise that he would not sell Bajaj scooters of Piaggio design in the US. By then there was no demand for the scooters in the US anyway.' In Germany, Bajaj Auto lost in the lower courts but won in the supreme court.

If Bajaj didn't lose, neither did he win. 'The case took four to five years during which our exports suffered. Piaggio succeeded in their aim to that extent. Our Indonesian and Taiwanese exports, our two major markets at that time, did not stop. They stopped later on for other reasons, local economic and political reasons.' Bajaj is philosophical.

'Journalists like to dramatize but quite frankly there was no hate. It was a serious business fight. In their position I might have done the same bloody thing.' What really hit Bajaj between the eyes, however, was the sight of Piaggio nonchalantly scooting into his lane. And he couldn't do a thing about it.

In the mid-'80s, following the relaxation of constraints in the light commercial vehicles (LCV) industry, the government reluctantly permitted fresh investments in the two-wheeler industry. The move led to a wave of foreign collaborations. Piaggio was quick to put its foot into the crack in the door by signing a technical collaboration with Deepak Singhania of Lohia Machines (better known as LML) and with Andhra Pradesh Scooters.

Bajaj was and is still sore. Piaggio came here claiming they had better technology, a better vehicle and a better deal for the Indian customer. 'If they were so much better than us, they could have easily beaten us in America and Germany. Why did they take recourse to the courts? But then, they are in business. We are in business. My anger was directed against the government of India for allowing them to enter again. It made my blood boil. This was a wrong policy. I was not afraid of competing with them, and time has shown [this]. They should have been told to withdraw their cases against an Indian exporter and *then* come to India.'

October 1989 brought signs of an accord. Piaggio's home turf was under attack from the Japanese. In India, LML was doing badly. The Italians began to wonder whether the LML investment had been such a good idea after all. Giovanni Alberto Agnelli, nephew of the legendary Gianni Agnelli, the heir to the Fiat empire and Piaggio's vice-president, brokered a secret visit by Bajaj and his team to Piaggio headquarters in Pisa to work out a strategic alliance. A key element was a 10 per cent cross-holding in each other's companies. Also on the negotiating table was a collaboration for spare parts and the ending of a few remaining bits of the long-running German court battle.

As before, this attempt too fizzled out. Meanwhile LML slipped deeper in the red. To rev up its image, Piaggio picked up 25.5 per cent of its equity for Rs 80m in 1990. The fresh fuel injection soon got used up. In 1993, LML's losses hit Rs 360m. From the sidelines, *Business India* smirked: 'Piaggio tried to dent Bajaj's growing market share but only got its nose bloodied.' September 1993 saw a third futile attempt at reconciliation. Agnelli junior flew from Turin to Pune. Piaggio wanted to replace the Singhanias with a new Indian partner. Would Bajaj consider this? Bajaj instead revived the idea of a 10 per cent cross-holding between their companies. The talks came close to success, but broke down when Piaggio apparently started talking of raising the cross-holdings. Suddenly LML's asking price began to look too high. If Bajaj gave in to Piaggio's demand for more equity, he would expose his soft underbelly. In 1993, of Bajaj Auto's Rs 370m share capital, about 51 per cent was controlled by the Bajaj family, roughly 10 per cent by company dealers, and around 20 per cent by the Firodias. If Bajaj gave away more than 10 per cent, his biggest foe could use it as a dangerous lever if things didn't work out with Piaggio later.

Scenting an opportunity, other Indian industrialists immediately made a beeline for Italy. Among them were the Nandas of Escorts and the Munjals of Hero Motors. At one point it looked as if Rajan Nanda, Escort's vice-chairman, had clinched the deal. Eventually, Piaggio decided not to separate from the Singhanias. Since the Agnellis and Bajaj continue to keep careful watch over each other, this chapter is still open.

YOU CAN'T BEAT A BAJAJ

Driving through the cavernous manufacturing facilities at Akurdi and Waluj (near Aurangabad), it is difficult to imagine that this company has frequently been the victim of government paranoia. The '70s and '80s were particularly difficult. The Bajaj family has had close connections with the Congress Party since the '20s, but the goodwill evaporated abruptly when Kamalnayan spurned Indira Gandhi during the party's 1969 split. Subsequently, her administration stubbornly refused to allow Bajaj Auto to expand its manufacturing facilities on socialistic grounds as Bajaj Auto was a monopoly.

'My blood used to boil. The country needed two-wheelers. There was a ten-year delivery period for Bajaj scooters. And I was not allowed to expand. What kind of socialism is that?' asks Rahul Bajaj.

His vociferous criticism of economic policy cost Bajaj—who has always voted Congress—more brownie points. Outwardly, the relationship between the Nehru–Gandhi dynasty and the Bajajs was cordial, but 'my family never had the kind of contacts you are talking about. We were very much in the freedom struggle but we never used those contacts for our business purposes. Maybe some others have. In any case I don't think such contacts would have meant anything to the then government in power, either the Congress government under Madam Gandhi, or when the [1979 Akurdi] strike took place, the Janata government under Mr Morarji Desai.'

What about money power? 'Even if giving money could have bought any licences, I can categorically say we did not give any ministers or any senior bureaucrat a single penny to get us a licence.'

Despite its straitjacket, Bajaj Auto prospered. In its start-up year (1962), it manufactured 3995 scooters. It immediately initiated a successful indigenization process which sheltered it when the Gandhi administration refused permission to extend the Piaggio collaboration. By 1971, the Bajaj scooter was a completely local product without any imported Italian parts. Since 1994, it has been producing over a million two-wheelers annually.

It's generally accepted that Bajaj Auto's success is largely due to Rahul Bajaj. In 1970, after the managing agency system was abolished, he became managing director, moving up to chairman on his father's death in 1972. He made the Bajaj scooter so popular that a flourishing black market developed. A customer fortunate enough to be allotted a Chetak or Super could sell it the next moment at double the price. Dealers charged customers huge premiums— unofficially to jump the queue. A Bajaj scooter is still a regular dowry demand among middle-class families. In Indian movies, scooter chases were as popular twenty years ago as computer-generated images are today.

Bajaj refused to exploit the situation. Holding the price line became an ethical issue, a modern twist to Gandhian trusteeship concepts imbibed during childhood. 'Ensuring that the consumer obtains the best possible product at the lowest possible price and the employee gets a fair wage for a day's work is the criterion of ethics in business,' he insisted. The government admitted that Bajaj had not taken 'any undue advantage of its dominant position', but it still refused to relax production restrictions. Lobbying by competitors like UP Scooters Ltd and Automobile Products of India fanned official anxiety about the power of big business.

For Bajaj, the Licence Raj was a 'nightmare' and a time of 'great difficulties'. 'I know how difficult it can get to chase someone in New Delhi for a licence. Then some fool delays the whole project by procrastinating, because he wants something for himself.' India is probably the only country in the world which threatens to penalize management for overproduction. Bajaj thumbed his nose at such rules, 'but thank goodness I was never actually penalized though I was quoted often for saying that I was ready to go to jail for excess production just as both my parents had for the freedom struggle.'

Interestingly, the long-desired permission for major capacity expansion came during the Janata Party administration (1977–79). George Fernandes, as industries minister, allowed Bajaj Auto to double its licensed capacity to 160,000 two-wheelers.

There was to be a question mark about this permission. Rahul Bajaj's *Congresswala* image and his personal friendship with Sharad Pawar is well known. Why did the Janata Party grant something which the Congress had withheld for years? Was there a quid pro quo? Rumours centred round Fernandes, a close friend of Viren Shah. Shortly before the end of the Emergency (1975–77), an arrest warrant was issued for Fernandes for his alleged role in the Baroda Dynamite Case (1977). Shah claims he 'did not shelter Fernandes', but admits that he knew where Fernandes was hiding and that he organized interviews with the international media for Fernandes while he was underground. Sensitive to international disapproval about the excesses of the Emergency, Indira Gandhi called for elections in 1977. After she lost and the Janata Party came into power, did a grateful Fernandes repay the debt?

'Rubbish,' says Viren Shah. 'Petty Indians will think and say such things, but George is just not that kind of man. He is a man of principles. He genuinely believes that we have to have more industry, more factories. Just look at his record. During that time, he permitted so many companies to expand.' Unfortunately for Shah's protestations, Fernandes is better remembered as the minister who forced Coca-Cola and IBM to leave India, thereby alienating the international business community and choking off foreign direct investment for years, and for comparing the Indian business community with rats.

Bajaj Auto received its second major permission to expand capacity on October 7, 1982. By this time Indira Gandhi had begun to heed her son Rajiv's views on the need to open up the economy. 'It's true that Rajiv could not dismantle the industrial licensing system, but he gave us as many licences as we desired,' said Bajaj. Narain Dutt Tiwari, who was industry minister, allowed Bajaj Auto to build a 300,000 unit at Waluj. The Rs 2bn plant was built in a record fourteen months. President Zail Singh inaugurated it on November 5, 1985. Three years later, during Rajiv Gandhi's prime ministership, capacity was upped to a massive one million scooters.

The last permission came just in time. In the last decade, local and international competition has been hotting up, and the fact that Bajaj Auto has a world-size plant gives it a vital edge. Economies of scale help make it an extremely profitable operation. 'Our scooters are 20 per cent cheaper than that of the nearest competitor *and* we enjoy a 20 per cent profit margin,' says Rajiv Bajaj smugly.

'POLITICAL VENDETTA'

Government sleuths keep a watchful eye on these hefty profit margins. Twice they suspected that government coffers weren't getting their fair share of them and instituted 'search and seizure' proceedings.

The first, conducted on May 18, 1976, during the Emergency, was carried out on the entire group. The second, on December 17, 1985, when Vishwanath Pratap Singh was finance minister, was limited to Bajaj Auto. Each time the raiders went away empty-handed. On both occasions, instead of the Bajaj family being feathered and tarred, it was the government which came under flak for using its muscle to harass businessmen for their political convictions.

Ironically, both times, a Congress administration authorized the raids though ever since the party was formed, the Bajajs have always voted for it. So why did they fall out of Indira Gandhi's favour? Why did she order the mammoth three-day raid in 1976 where 1100 income tax sleuths simultaneously swooped on 114 Bajaj establishments across the country? They questioned even Jankidevi, Rahul's eighty-four-year-old grandmother, who had renounced all worldly possessions after Jamnalal's death in 1942 and who lived in an ashram at Wardha.

Eighteen months later, Rahul and his uncle Ramkrishna (1923–1994) aired their suspicions to the Shah Commission, a committee set up by the Janata Party to examine the misuse of political power during the Emergency. In a written note read out by Ramkrishna to the Commission, the Bajajs claimed that the raid was 'an act of political vendetta'. Outlining the background of the raid, Ramkrishna deposed that the family's relationship with the Gandhi dynasty started deteriorating with his brother Kamalnayan's opposition to Indira Gandhi's first bid for prime ministership in 1966. 'Ever since then the previous regime had assumed that our family was against them, especially as it was their stand that those who were not with them were against them.'

Ramkrishna had lost favour because he refused to allow the government to take over the Vishva Yuvak Kendra in Delhi of which he was the managing trustee. The fact that Viren Shah, an accused in the Baroda Dynamite Case, was their partner didn't help the situation. The relationship nose-dived after Jayprakash Narayan (1902–1979), a respected socialist freedom fighter, condemned the Emergency and urged the public to protest against it from his death-bed in Bombay's Jaslok Hospital. The links between Narayan and the Bajajs were strong and several Bajaj members had visited Narayan during the Emergency, buttressing Mrs Gandhi's belief that the family was against her.

If further kindling was needed, it was provided by the family's relationship with Acharya Vinoba Bhave (1895–1982), a staunch Gandhian and a leader of the Sarvodaya movement for social reform. In January 1976, Ramkrishna's brother-in-law, Shriman Narayan, organized a *sammelan* for the high priest which was partly funded by the Bajaj Group. Bhave, who initially had indirectly supported the Emergency, now turned against Mrs Gandhi and used the *sammelan* as a forum to protest against the Emergency, calling for its revocation and the release of all political detenues. As preparations began for a second *sammelan*, the Gandhi regime tried to get it postponed or cancelled. Describing the incident to the Shah Commission, Ramkrishna told an enthralled audience of how a common friend contacted him to 'use' his influence over Shriman Narayan and Bhave himself. Ramkrishna excused himself. It would be neither right nor proper. He could not help the government. Delhi was not amused.

Ramkrishna Bajaj's deposition provoked a spat in the income tax department over who had ordered the raid. Under persistent grilling by Justice Shah, part of the truth emerged with the needle of suspicion pointing to S.R. Mehta, the chairman of the Central Board of Direct Taxes. In March 1976, an assistant director of inspection had been despatched to Bombay to collect dirt on the Bajaj group. The mission was unsuccessful, but his advice was ignored and a raid was ordered by Harihar Lal, the director of inspection (investigation). Gradually, more sordid details tumbled out about procedural 'lapses' and a messy 'smirch' Bajaj campaign but very little extra came to light about who and what exactly triggered off the raid.

Rupa has her own suspicions. 'Rahul had gone to Ahmedabad where he made a speech at some meeting where he criticized Sanjay Gandhi or made a negative comment about him. Afterwards we were told—but it has never been confirmed—that perhaps that sparked the raid.' Rahul is noncommittal: 'This is all conjecture. We don't know anything for sure. At the Shah Commission hearings the income tax officers concerned gave evidence that there was no justification for the raid, and everyone knew we were against the Emergency.'

If political vendetta lay behind the 1976 raid, the reasons for the 1985 raid are even murkier. Authorized by V.P. 'Mr Clean' Singh, then Rajiv Gandhi's finance minister and prime minister-in-waiting, the income tax investigation on Bajaj Auto was part of Singh's campaign to clean up corporate India. During this campaign, 6000 raids were conducted, about 100,000 residences searched and almost half a million people subjected to interrogation.

Apparently keen to demonstrate total impartiality, Singh's victims were selected from a broad spectrum: from noted industrialists like S.L. Kirloskar, a visionary Pune-based entrepreneur, to doctors, lawyers, film stars, drug barons and smugglers. The scale of attacks and the humiliating media coverage engineered by Singh's team culled from the Directorate of Revenue Intelligence, the Directorate of Enforcement and the Directorate of Anti-evasion, initially froze businessmen into numbness. Once this wore off, mass hysteria set in, to be replaced by roars of resentment, ultimately leading to Singh's transfer from the finance ministry to defence (on January 24, 1987).

As word spread of the nationwide income tax raid on Bajaj Auto, the initial reaction was one of disbelief. After all, this was the company of which the government itself had declared that 'despite its dominant position, the company has not tried to take undue advantage of its dominant position'. Barely a few years after the endorsement, the government was claiming that it was committing income tax fraud. With their backs to the wall, the government officials tried to justify themselves, the thrust of their argument being the high premiums commanded by Bajaj vehicles. For example, Bajaj Auto produced nearly 33,000 three-wheelers. On an official price tag of Rs 27,000, the premium ranged between Rs 10,000 and Rs 20,000. In this situation, tax officials felt there was considerable scope for under-reporting income.

According to government sources, their suspicions were aroused when a raid on a Bajaj Auto dealer in Patna led to the recovery of duplicate books showing that Rs 1.2m had been paid to a top company executive. The raid report was sent to the finance ministry which authorized further research and a more detailed report. The investigation was entrusted to D.N. Pathak, Bombay's newly appointed director of investigation who had just arrived from Uttar Pradesh (Singh's home state). For five months, Pathak and his team studied the market, gathering information piecemeal, collecting lists of Bajaj dealers.

One day before the raid, a deputy director of intelligence visited the Bajaj plant disguised as a schoolteacher to check out the various entry points and sensitive locations. The Pune commissioner of income tax was requested in a letter sent in a sealed cover to collect a hundred people at his office and also to arrange buses and taxis. On December 17 at 7.45 a.m., 285 income tax officials in Pune and Bombay fanned out to sixty-five locations. Pathak had signed a hundred and one search warrants.

But when the party reached Bajaj's residence, its owner wasn't there. He had left the previous night for Bombay. Caught off-guard by this elementary gap in their information, the party recovered enough to call Bombay and request a local team to be despatched immediately to Mount Unique, a skyscraper off busy Peddar Road. The Bombay–Pune lines hummed with anxious inquiries until the tax sleuths finally caught sight of the tycoon engaged in his favourite activity—chatting on the telephone. Once Bajaj had satisfied himself about the correctness of their identity, he agreed to their 'request' to accompany them to his office at Bajaj Bhawan at Nariman Point. There he was interrogated for six hours.

After three days of exhaustively searching Rahul Bajaj's house, office and bank lockers as well as those of his executives and dealers, the raiders called a press conference where they triumphantly announced the 'seizure of unexplained cash of nearly Rs 20 lakhs, jewellery and other valuables of Rs 80 lakhs, 1500 US dollars and a few other currencies'. The press note added that 'a substantial part of the seized assets have been admitted by the concerned persons to be their concealed incomes and wealth'. Significantly, the note did not mention any names.

Up in arms against the income tax department's press note, Bajaj issued his own. Denying any wrongdoing by Bajaj Auto, he claimed that the premiums were collected by dealers and not by the company. If he were allowed to increase capacity and meet consumer needs, the premiums would automatically disappear. Asked to counter Bajaj's allegations, the income tax department sheepishly admitted that the company's book-keeping was indeed clean as a whistle and that whatever seizures had been made, were from the dealers.

Ironically, barely five months after his finance minister raided Bajaj, Rajiv Gandhi invited him to be chairman of Indian Airlines (IA). It was the first time someone from the private sector had been selected. Was the appointment a gesture of atonement? Bajaj scoffs at the idea: 'No, no, it had nothing to do with the raid. It might have been a bit of an embarrassment for Mr V.P. Singh, but I don't think my appointment had anything to do with the raid at all.'

VIJAY MALLYA

Excerpts from *The Vijay Mallya Story* by K. Giriprakash

BUILDING BRAND KINGFISHER

Vijay Mallya deserves credit for the revival of Kingfisher beer. Today, it is the leading beer brand in the country with a market share of about 50 per cent. There is an interesting tale to the launch of Kingfisher beer and its resurgence. Mohan Meakin's Golden Eagle was the leading brand in the beer segment when Vittal Mallya and Srinivas Rao decided to launch a brand which could take on the competition. While scouting around, they found that one of their top officials had a letter pad with the logo of a kingfisher bird on it. They persuaded the executive to part with the logo, and so the Kingfisher brand was born. Over time, the logo has evolved from depicting a sitting kingfisher to one in mid-flight.

The brand went into hibernation for sometime until Vijay Mallya decided to revive it. He is believed to have conducted his own survey by standing near the gates of several colleges interviewing students on what they thought would work for a brand. The survey yielded some interesting facts: youngsters aspire for brands which enhance their lifestyle as well as those they can connect with. Within months, Kingfisher beer was relaunched and marketed in several parts of the country. However, the biggest problem the brand faced was that it was not pan-Indian. Its distribution network was restricted and, as beer is a seasonal drink, its sales in the north were muted.

During those days, the breweries of United Breweries in north India were shut down because of poor sales in the winter months and in the south, where Kingfisher was popular, it was in short supply because the breweries did not have the capacity to cater to the increased demand. The company decided to rationalize production: those breweries which were shut down during the off season in a particular region would be used to manufacture beer and supply to those states where there was a shortfall.

Another issue United Breweries encountered in its retail business was regarding packaging, especially bottles, a key raw material for any liquor company. The packaging costs for a liquor company are huge and if they are not controlled well, they can shave off a large portion of its profits. In the case of United Breweries, even though the invoice included the cost of the bottles, the dealers would either forget to return them or return broken bottles. Therefore, United Breweries had to constantly produce new bottles, which involved a large expenditure.

To arrest this trend, the company management decided to impose a new rule for dealers: they would get a fresh supply of beer cases only when they returned an equal number of bottles. The local 'kabadiwallas', or those who trade in used bottles, play a crucial role in the liquor trade. They are the ones who collect used bottles from those who retail as well as those who consume liquor. In turn, the liquor distributors or dealers buy the used bottles from these kabadiwallas and return them to the manufacturers, thus completing the cycle.

The cycle is broken if the distributors fail to buy bottles from the retail traders, and that was what was happening in the case of United Breweries. But once the new rule was imposed strictly, the company started benefitting from it.

Several years later, the same issue cropped up in a different manner. The traders of used bottles started forming a cartel to extract more money from the distributors, which again hit the manufacturers hard. Therefore, manufacturers started patenting the design of the bottle apart from printing the name of the brand or that of the company on these bottles. Obviously, the traders were forced to sell the bottles only to those companies whose name was printed on them.

In addition to these measures, the price of Kingfisher beer was made uniform so that the landed cost of the beer to the dealer would be the same everywhere irrespective of where it was sourced from.

This exercise was begun in 1984 and by the late 1980s, most of UB Group's breweries had turned profitable.

By early 1986, Golden Eagle had started yielding ground to Kingfisher. By March the same year, Kingfisher was officially declared the largest-selling beer brand in the country.

There were still pockets of the market where Kingfisher beer was still way behind the competing brands. One such market was Bombay. During the late 1980s, Associated Breweries' London Pilsner was the biggest brand in the city, so much so that five-star hotels didn't even bother to offer other brands to their customers.

Once, during his stay at the Taj Mahal hotel, Vijay Mallya happened to order a bottle of Kingfisher beer but was politely informed that the only beer available there was London Pilsner. Not being someone who took no for an answer, he is believed to have summoned one of his top marketing executives to fly down to Bombay to ensure that the Taj started serving Kingfisher as well.

The executive immediately took the next flight to Bombay and sought a meeting with the food and beverage manager, Camellia Punjabi. After some intense negotiations, the hotel agreed to start offering Kingfisher beer to its guests. In turn, United Breweries offered to fund the cost of printing the hotel's menu cards. Ironically, London Pilsner now is in the same position Kingfisher was in before it entered the Taj, having dropped to an insignificant market share. (United Breweries later went on to acquire Associated Breweries, the makers of London Pilsner.)

While United Breweries kept increasing its market share as well as expanding its portfolio of brands, it failed to recognize the potential of strong beer in the country. The initial hesitancy cost the company several crores as well as leadership in that segment. Some of the top executives did make the company aware of the opportunity strong beer offered but either ego issues or the inability to keep pace with emerging trends made the management completely ignore the suggestions.

According to one of the insiders, a top executive in the company made a strong pitch for launching a strong beer in the market at one of the company's meetings held in Kathmandu in Nepal, but his suggestion was rejected as the management felt that it was ahead of its time and would fail. After all, the idea behind drinking beer was not to get drunk, and there was a chance that any change in its alcohol content might turn out to be counterproductive.

But the executive felt that since various state governments in India do not have separate tax structures for beer and spirits, consumers were likely to prefer liquor with higher alcohol content at similar prices.

Some of the domestic liquor companies were able to see the potential strong beer had to offer long before United Breweries realized it and launched brands with higher alcohol content. Brands like Haywards 5000, Thunderbolt and Bullet, which had 8 per cent v/v alcohol content (compared with about 5 per cent v/v for normal beer), were launched with great success in the market.

Meanwhile, Mallya started acquiring companies unrelated to his core liquor business—such as Mangalore Chemicals & Fertilisers (MCF) and Best & Crompton Engineering—while exiting those his father had bought like UB Mec, a battery venture, and Kissan. His only major success amidst the mountain of failed acquisitions was Berger Paints. His venture into soft drinks started off with a bang with brands like Rush, Thrill and Sprint that were supposed to take on the multinationals, but these went bust after a short time, forcing the group to write off about Rs 33 crore in losses, a huge amount of money in those days.

But in the breweries business, Mallya confidently strode ahead. While Vittal's legacy to his son was supply-led solidity, which meant that the company could supply as well as distribute better than any other company could, what Vijay Mallya brought to the table was his ability to convert supply-led dominance to demand-led dominance.

Mallya has always maintained and zealously promoted the idea that the consumption of liquor is part of one's lifestyle. Therefore, he regularly hired movie actors to promote his brands through surrogate advertising. Some of those who were in charge of such promotions say that several crores were spent in advertising and, initially, even they didn't know what the outcome of such expenditure would be. For example, several lakhs would be spent in sponsoring the Derby in Bombay, even though there was no direct connection between the sport and the liquor business. But Mallya always backed such investments in brand building, saying that in the long term this approach would pay off, and ultimately it did.

One of the biggest assets Mallya created to promote his brands was the Kingfisher swimsuit calendar. The limited-edition calendar is much sought after by the who's who in the fashion world. It was launched in 2003 and features various models in swimsuits who are photographed on the beaches of Goa, the French Riviera and other such exotic destinations. Ace photographer Atul Kasbekar is involved with the production of the calendar. Those selected to feature in the calendar are seen to receive a huge boost to their careers. Actors Deepika Padukone and Katrina Kaif modelled for the calendar before they were launched in movies.

THE BATTLE FOR SHAW WALLACE

Vijay Mallya spent an entire night at the police commissioner's office on Infantry Road in Bangalore. He had been arrested on his way back from Calcutta on the night of 5 June 1985 for violating the Foreign Exchange Regulation Act (FERA).

With the exception of Allen Mendonca, an intrepid reporter who wrote about the incident in the *Indian Express*, the Bangalore press did not carry the story—either they did not get wind of the arrest or they chose not to report it. By the time the *Express* was out for circulation the next morning, the thirty-year-old Mallya had already been released with surety from one of his managers who had to furnish his home-ownership papers to get his boss out of the police commissioner's office.

All transactions involving foreign currency at that time were put under a microscope because India didn't have a deep enough forex reserve to boast about. Such transactions had to be approved by the

Reserve Bank of India and any violations were treated as criminal offences. Mallya had fallen afoul of the regulators, but few knew what was going on behind the scenes until he was arrested. (The second time Mallya faced arrest was in October 2012 when a cheque issued by his airline, Kingfisher Airlines, to the GMR Group, which operates the Hyderabad airport, bounced. A non-bailable arrest warrant was issued against Mallya and four others for failing to pay the user charges levied by the airport. Surprisingly, the charges were dropped and Mallya flew into India in time to be physically present to cheer his racing team, Sahara Force India, at the Formula 1 racing event.) Once the news of Mallya's night at the police commissioner's office broke, the national press was all over the story, trying to dig more and find out how Mallya got into this mess.

What unfolded was a sensational tale of corporate intrigue, double-crossing and family feuds—all centred on Shaw Wallace & Company. The battle for Shaw Wallace is an important chapter in the life of Vijay Mallya. He spent the best part of his youth, and over two decades, fighting to gain control of a company which he had coveted since the day he took over the reins from his father. What is unique about this battle is that Mallya is perhaps one of the few corporate czars who bought the same company twice: once for Rs 55 crore and two decades later for a whopping Rs 1545 crore.

Shaw Wallace & Company was started in 1886 by UK-based Robert Gordon Shaw and Charles William Wallace, in Calcutta. The company owned tea gardens in east India, operated gas stations for Burmah Oil Company and even owned a few distilleries and breweries. Old-timers say that Shaw Wallace was one of the most ethical companies in its heyday and was very well managed. Long before employee stock-option plan became a buzzword, Shaw Wallace had introduced a similar scheme called the SW Staff Participation Trust for its employees. About 5–6 per cent of the company's profits was set aside for the trust. Shares from the trust were given out to senior employees to retain their services.

Such focus on employees and stakeholders had turned Shaw Wallace into a blue-chip company. Its return on capital was as high as 165 per cent during the 1970s and its debt on the books never lasted more than fifteen days. The first Indian chairman of Shaw Wallace was S. Panduranga Acharya who took over from Sir Anthony Hayward, after whom some of the brands were named.

Acharya began his career with Shaw Wallace as an assistant accountant, eventually becoming the chairman and managing director (CMD). He ran the company competently, though people who worked with him reckoned he was more of an accountant than a businessman. It is believed that even when there was enough cash for the company to expand and diversify, Acharya would tell his managers who routinely tipped him off about acquisition opportunities that he would rather put all the extra money in banks than invest it in acquiring assets. What worked for Shaw Wallace, however, was an enviable portfolio of liquor brands such as Royal Challenge, Haywards, Director's Special, Officer's Choice, Antiquity and Antiquity Blue, all of which have stood the test of time. It had everything going for it—a clean record, high returns to shareholders, marquee brands and piles of cash—making it the perfect acquisition for the ambitious.

Shaw Wallace initially had multiple owners through cross holdings among the promoters. Sime Darby, based out of Malaysia, was one of the owners while R.G. Shaw Company, based in London, was another which held 40 per cent stake in Shaw Wallace. Both Sime Darby and Shaw Wallace had interlocking shares. In 1971, Sime Darby decided to take over R.G. Shaw's operations and did so through a reverse merger. The result was that Shaw Wallace came under the control of Sime Darby. But when Sime Darby decided to acquire the tyre-maker Dunlop in Malaysia, it decided to sell off its 40 per cent stake in Shaw Wallace to raise money for the acquisition. At that time, Shaw Wallace had assets of around Rs 6 crore and its turnover was Rs 200 crore.

Mallya, who had been eyeing Shaw Wallace for a long time, was thrilled to find out that the company's foreign shareholding was up for sale. But, according to domestic laws, since he was an Indian citizen, he was not allowed to acquire a company based abroad. To overcome the hurdle, he decided to rope in a business partner who was a non-resident Indian and hence was eligible to acquire the foreign shareholding of Shaw Wallace. As he didn't know any businessmen who were NRIs, he decided to tap into the network of his friend Brijesh Mathur who used to work at Grindlays Bank.

The brief to Mathur was simple: rope in an NRI businessman who would be willing to buy the foreign shareholding of Shaw Wallace and, once Mallya was able to get NRI status, transfer the shareholding to him. But then even the best-laid plans can sometimes go horribly wrong and in this case, they did. Of all the businessmen in the world, Mathur chose Manohar Rajaram Chhabria, a Sindhi businessman who had interests in electronics and a few other companies, to collaborate with Mallya. A non-resident Indian, the lanky Chhabria was as pugnacious as they come and was known for acquiring Indian companies which had foreign shareholding.

It is not known whether Mallya performed a background check on Chhabria before agreeing to partner with him; he seems to have had implicit faith in Mathur's judgement. Chhabria and Mallya met several times to go over the plan before deciding to put it into operation. They decided to float a joint venture which would be registered in Hong Kong for the purpose of acquiring Shaw Wallace. The company in turn would float a special purpose vehicle—Carrasco—in which the partners would have equal shareholding.

But Mallya was not the only businessman to know about the potential sale of Shaw Wallace. The Canadian liquor major, Seagram Company, and the US-based cookie company, Nabisco, were also in the race to acquire Shaw Wallace. But at some point of time, Seagram either lost interest or delayed taking a firm decision on the bid even though it was a hot favourite to win the deal. Nabisco for some reason was not considered a serious contender. Eventually Sime Darby approached Mallya, asking him whether he was willing to raise the bid price. In his eagerness to buy Shaw Wallace, Mallya agreed to increase the price. Meanwhile, there were enough rumours doing the rounds that certain interests had paid off top executives at both Sime Darby and Seagram in an attempt to bag Shaw Wallace. But such rumours and more were bound to circulate because of the nature of the transaction, and were never substantiated.

Mallya had made two assumptions here: one that he would get his NRI status soon, which would ensure that he was not violating the laws of the land. The second assumption was that he would not face much resistance from the Indian management of Shaw Wallace or his proxy.

By now it seemed fairly certain that Mallya would win the bid. But what unfolded after this was a series of events which left Mallya wondering what on earth had made him partner with Chhabria. Sime Darby either did not know Indian regulations or didn't care for them. Acharya, the CMD of Shaw Wallace at the time the company was being sold, is believed to have received a call from one of the directors of Sime Darby informing him that they had sold off their entire stake to a company run by an Indian resident and an NRI. The news left Acharya stunned. He had nurtured Shaw Wallace to a position of strength and perhaps assumed that Sime Darby would offer the company to him first. Once it became clear that he had been completely sidestepped in the decision-making process, he decided that he wouldn't let go of the company without a fight. He also assumed that with the help of the financial institutions who were key shareholders in the company, he would be able to retain control of Shaw Wallace.

As per the deal with Sime Darby, all Mallya had to do now was raise about $26 million to buy the foreign shareholding in Shaw Wallace, which would give him majority control of the Calcutta-based company. To fund the acquisition, both Mallya and Chhabria decided that they would raise part of the money through debt while the rest—about $6 million each—would come from their own contributions.

Here is where several versions emerge about the nature of the deal. According to one version, as the entire process of acquiring Shaw Wallace was conceived and executed by Mallya, the onus of paying the entire amount rested with him and not with Chhabria. But Mallya's hands were tied because he was yet to be granted NRI status. But mysteriously, the required funds were raised and Carrasco became the 40 per cent owner of Shaw Wallace. How did that happen? Around the same time, rumours started circulating in corporate circles that Mallya might have actually managed to pump in the $6 million.

There are also unsubstantiated rumours that it was Acharya and his men who had actually tipped off the police in India about Mallya's alleged violation of forex laws. The police decided that a prima facie case could indeed be made against Mallya and he was promptly arrested when he arrived in Bangalore from Calcutta while Kishore Chhabria, Manu's brother who was also a director of the joint venture, was arrested in Delhi.

Though both of them were released on bail, Mallya's secret deal was now out in the open. But did Mallya actually pay the money required to buy Shaw Wallace? If he did, then it was in clear violation of FERA rules.

Until Mallya roped him in, Manu Chhabria did not realize how lucrative and important a company Shaw Wallace was. Had it not been for Mallya, the Sindhi businessman wouldn't have got even a whiff of such a big company going abegging, as a close relative of Chhabria revealed later. It was pretty obvious that Chhabria would not let such a company slip out of his hands. He also realized that Mallya could never publicly admit that he was in bed with Chhabria for this deal.

Sensing a huge opportunity, the canny businessman did not leave it to Mallya to raise the additional money required to buy Shaw Wallace. He himself started approaching banks, and by January 1985, had managed to raise the required finances to acquire Shaw Wallace on his own.

With the officials from the Enforcement Directorate chasing him, Mallya had to eventually backtrack and let go of his stake in Carrasco, thereby handing over full control of the company to Chhabria.

The story might have ended with Chhabria gaining control of Shaw Wallace had it not been for the tough legal battle put up by Acharya. Not to be left behind, Chhabria filed a counter case with the department of company affairs under Section 397 of the Companies Act alleging that Acharya should be removed from his position as CMD because of allegations of misappropriation and diversion of funds and for stripping of assets of the company.

The battle between the two lasted for over two years. During that period, Acharya managed to mop up about 17 per cent extra stake in the company; now he just needed the support of the financial institutions to topple Chhabria.

But at a crucial shareholders' meeting in 1987, which was called to decide the ownership issue, the financial institutions, which had always supported Acharya in the past, decided to abstain from voting for reasons best known to them. Chhabria won the vote and the company was in the bag. Acharya went back to his office and put in his papers, bringing to an end his more-than-three-decade-long association with Shaw Wallace. Subsequently, Acharya revealed to a journalist that Chhabria had graciously offered to let him continue as the CMD but he had declined the offer. Acharya now lives in Bangalore and is associated with several non-governmental organizations there.

Years later, expressing his condolences over the demise of Manu Chhabria in 2002, an *Economic Times* report quoted Acharya as saying that he fought to wrest back control of Shaw Wallace on the issue of principles. The acquisition of such a substantial stake should have taken place in a transparent manner, though he claimed that Sime Darby had informed him that the stake was in fact sold to a Bengali lawyer.

Once Chhabria was in the saddle, it was Mallya's turn to stake his claim. He demanded that Chhabria give him 50 per cent of the ownership of Shaw Wallace. But Chhabria declined, stating that since Mallya had not paid his part of the money fully, he could not assert part-ownership. Chhabria also reminded him that not only had Mallya maintained that he did not have any knowledge of the transaction and denied being a part-owner of Carrasco, he had also declared to the Enforcement Directorate in Bombay in August 1985 that he had no connection with either Chhabria or with Shaw Wallace.

Mallya wasn't chagrined with the fact that he had misjudged Chhabria. It was becoming increasingly clear that Mallya had not done his homework before launching his bid to acquire Shaw Wallace. When Chhabria refused to give him his share in Shaw

Wallace, Mallya is believed to have asked him to return his money instead. But Chhabria told him that Mallya's share had been used up for paying legal fees.

There was no documentary evidence that could support Mallya's claim. Apparently, Chhabria used this loophole to inform Mallya that he had never received any money from him.

A desperate Mallya is believed to have rushed to Delhi to seek intervention from politicians, hoping they would counsel Chhabria, but nothing came of it.

Mallya had no other option but to bide his time till he was declared an NRI and, once economic reforms hit the country in the early 1990s, readied himself to fight the battle to wrest control of Shaw Wallace.

The court battle was fought in Hong Kong as that was where the takeover vehicle, Carrasco, was registered. It turned out to be a no-holds-barred corporate battle. Chhabria by then had increased his stake in Shaw Wallace to around 55 per cent. Of the remaining, 22 per cent was with the financial institutions, 7 per cent with foreign institutional investors and 16 per cent with the public. According to *Corporate Takeovers in India* by Vijay Kumar Kaushal, the shares of Shaw Wallace were held by R.G. Shaw and its three subsidiaries: Thomas Rice Milling Co. Ltd, Shaw Scott & Co. Ltd and Shaw Darby & Co. Ltd.

Kaushal claims that in order to acquire Shaw Wallace, Chhabria actually bought Carrasco through his Singapore company, Keysberg Ltd. In turn, Carrasco took a $15-million loan from the American Express Bank. The balance of $11.14 million was loaned to Carrasco by Chhabria with $9.67 million being given by Keysberg and $1.47 million directly funded by him. Carrasco, according to the books, was half owned by Chhabria, but the identity of the other part-owner was not known even then. It is believed that Mallya's stake apparently reflected in the transaction. American Express Bank, which had extended a loan of $15 million to Carrasco, had done so based on the cash deposits Mallya made to the bank. But when the case came up for scrutiny after Mallya took Chhabria to court, Chhabria is believed to have disputed it by producing before the Indian Company Law Board a letter written by the vice president of the bank stating that the loan was arranged on a personal guarantee from R.R. Chhabria, a relative of Manu Chhabria's.

Now that the trail regarding the $15 million had been established, the next component of the money—$9.67 million from Chhabria to Keysberg—came under scrutiny. Allegations were made that the money may have come to Carrasco from a $10.3-million loan that a Singaporean firm, Tentura Ltd, which has a management contract with a Far Eastern subsidiary of Mallya's United Breweries, took from the State Bank of India, Singapore.

Mallya denied that such a transaction had taken place and pointed out that $9 million out of the $10.3 million was drawn against letters of credit. He also claimed that he was being needlessly drawn into matters concerning Tentura and he had no financial links with the company. United Breweries' link to the firm was simply through a management contract.

Shaw Wallace was not Chhabria's only acquisition. His success emboldened him to acquire more companies, one of which was Dunlop Tyres which he bought in collaboration with R.P. Goenka, but later, he fell out with him just as he had with Mallya.

This was how Indian corporate battles were fought then: under the cover of darkness and by exploiting the poor regulatory environment in India.

Though Chhabria had successfully managed to ward off the threat from Acharya and was now in the saddle, he constantly worried about how Mallya would mount a bid to regain control of Shaw Wallace. After all, the entire takeover operation had been Mallya's brainchild and Chhabria was merely a part of the supporting cast.

But Mallya knew it would not be easy to wrest control of Shaw Wallace because of the inherent complications in the way the deal was structured and executed. Therefore, he and the strategy cell of the company decided that wisdom lay in bidding for Shaw Wallace's key brands. But this approach was not all that simple. After all, why would Chhabria part with marquee brands? Mallya persisted in the belief that there was no harm in trying either. A hostile bid for brands would create some amount of turbulence and raise suspicion in the rival's camp.

In 1999, Mallya made an offer to buy Royal Challenge, Director's Special and Haywards whiskies for about Rs 250 crore. These three were among the leading brands in their segments. Put in perspective, in 1985, Mallya was willing to pay Rs 55 crore ($27 million) to buy out Shaw Wallace itself and now he was willing to pay nearly five times more for just three brands in Shaw Wallace's portfolio. In fact, it was good money if Chhabria had agreed to sell the brands as he would have been able to wipe off some of the losses his group of companies had incurred.

But being an astute businessman, Chhabria realized what Mallya was up to. Now it was his turn to make a counter offer.

According to a report in the *Economic Times*, he hired an advertising agency to launch a campaign which would put Mallya in his place. The ad firm came out with a television commercial mocking Mallya's rather audacious offer. The commercial shows a bar in a club where a set of people are outshouting each other to buy different brands of liquor. A man walks in with a pronounced swagger, crushes a cigarette butt with his heel and goes up to the bartender, and says: 'I want to buy RC, DSP and Haywards.' Taken aback, the bartender blinks and exclaims: 'Vijay sahib, aap bhi?'

Then the camera zooms in on the cartons of Director's Special and Royal Challenge placed near the bar, and the voiceover declares: 'India's most wanted'.

The ad apparently did dent Mallya's hopes of bagging the brands, though Chhabria later claimed that United Breweries Ltd never wanted to put money on the table. He confided to a journalist that if Mallya had been really keen, he would have considered the offer seriously.

Mallya's animosity towards Manu Chhabria was well known, but the liquor tycoon also had a falling out with Manu's brother, Kishore, later.

Even though Kishore and Manu Chhabria were siblings, there was no love lost between the two because of certain family misunderstandings. As a result, Kishore decided to part ways with his brother and walked away with one of the subsidiaries of Shaw Wallace, BDA Distilleries, a company with total revenues of about Rs 120 crore, after he had raised his stake in the subsidiary by buying shares in the market. Mallya, who was closely watching the developments in the Chhabria family, decided to approach Kishore, offering him a 26 per cent stake in one of his companies, Herbertsons, if he agreed to merge BDA with the company. Mallya had been eyeing BDA for some time because one of its brands, Officer's Choice whisky, was the largest-selling whisky in its segment.

There was another, much bigger, design behind his offer to Kishore Chhabria. Even though Kishore had walked away with BDA, Manu had filed a case against his brother to get back the company. Mallya realized that if Kishore were to lose the case, then BDA would go back to Manu, and Herbertsons would get a toehold in Chhabria's empire. Kishore took up Mallya's offer and was appointed vice chairman of Herbertsons. As per the deal, Mallya transferred 25.52 per cent of his 46.9 per cent stake in Herbertsons and 75,000 convertible debentures to Kishore Chhabria.

However, the friendship between Mallya and the younger Chhabria didn't last long, for Mallya learnt that Chhabria had started increasing his stake in Herbertsons by purchasing shares in the open market.

But Kishore Chhabria had a different take on the dispute with Mallya. He claimed that Mallya had gone back on his promise of delegating more powers to him even though he was made the vice chairman of Herbertsons. Therefore, the only way for him to get a firm hold in Herbertsons was to increase his stake in the company through the open market. Between 1994 and 1997, Kishore Chhabria ended up acquiring another 20.27 per cent stake in Herbertsons. When Mallya learnt that Kishore was quietly buying more shares of Herbertsons, he increased his stake from the 21.38 per cent he had held earlier to 37.88 per cent through the open-market route.

Some of these transactions were allegedly carried out in a manner frowned upon by regulators and lawmakers.

The matter was taken to court and, at one point, Mallya was battling both the brothers in different cases. Kishore Chhabria did offer a way out by stating that he would return the stake he held in Herbertsons if Mallya paid Rs 120 crore as well as cash against the stake that Chhabria owned. Obviously, Mallya would have none of it. The case continued and even went to the Supreme Court. SEBI then asked both of them to divest the wrongfully acquired stakes through a sale in the public. But by early 2005, both Mallya and Kishore Chhabria realized that their long dispute would only drain them further and both of them went back to the negotiating table and settled their differences.

Kishore Chhabria withdrew from Herbertsons, selling his entire stake of slightly over 49 per cent to United Breweries, while Mallya handed back BDA Distilleries to Chhabria. The deal was finally settled for Rs 131 crore in favour of Kishore Chhabria. In turn, Mallya decided to consolidate his entire liquor business into one entity, United Spirits, while Kishore Chhabria decided to restructure BDA.

By 2000, the Chhabria brothers started reconciliation efforts and ended their decade-long rivalry. Shaw Wallace and Manu Chhabria withdrew all the 200 cases against Kishore Chhabria except one, which came back to haunt Kishore Chhabria later.

But tragedy struck the Chhabria family soon after. Manu Chhabria, who had been ailing for some time and had undergone a bypass surgery, passed away suddenly on 6 April 2002. Days before Chhabria passed away, Mallya is rumoured to have visited him at the hospital to inquire about his health.

Chhabria left his entire empire, the $1.5-billion Jumbo Group, to his wife, Vidya, and their three daughters, Kiran, Komal and Bhavika. India's first corporate raider was dead, but the conflict between Shaw Wallace and Mallya was not over. It took another three years and innumerable pitched battles fought in courts and boardrooms for it to come to an end.

Though Vidya Chhabria became the chairman of Shaw Wallace after her husband passed away, she did not have the experience required to run such a large business empire and her daughters too staked a claim for bigger shares for themselves. The family finally decided to exit several of their businesses and hive off Shaw Wallace into two entities: beer and liquor; and seek joint-venture partners for both.

As soon as Mallya learnt that Shaw Wallace was seeking a joint-venture partner, he decided to sue the company as the dispute over the ownership issue was still pending in the Hong Kong court. Also, one of his companies, McDowell, held a small stake in Shaw Wallace, which allowed him to file a case seeking to restrain the Chhabrias from hiving off the assets. He followed it up with an open offer for Shaw Wallace's liquor business.

In the case of Shaw Wallace's beer business, Mallya approached the Bombay High Court to restrain South African Breweries (SABMiller), one of the bidders and the second-largest beer company in the world, from entering into any deal with Shaw Wallace.

Though Mallya received flak for filing these cases, he maintained that he was doing so to protect the shareholders and creditors of Shaw Wallace. But why the UB Group would want to protect their interests was beyond one's imagination.

Mallya was clearly set to disrupt the business empire of Shaw Wallace and he hoped that repeated attempts to do so would unsettle the company's new bosses, including the chairperson Vidya Chhabria and the new managing director (MD) Komal Vazir Chhabria.

But the joint venture did happen and both Shaw Wallace and SABMiller entered into a 50–50 partnership. The South African company bought 50 per cent in the venture as well as management control for $132.8 million. At that time, Shaw Wallace had 22 breweries in its fold and sales of 32 million cases—about 36 per cent of the total market.

The reason SABMiller was allowed to proceed with the joint venture, which it eventually took over, was the fact that both Mallya and Vidya Chhabria decided to call a truce.

Two developments brought on their decision to shake hands: One, Mallya had won a major legal battle in the Hong Kong high court in January 2004, which upheld his contention that he was in fact an equal partner in Carrasco, the joint venture which had been floated to acquire Shaw Wallace. And, two, the Jumbo Group, which also owned Shaw Wallace, decided to challenge the order and refer the matter to a court of appeal as it felt that it 'clearly constitutes criminal breach of the Indian law'.

In view of these interminable cases, Vidya Chhabria decided to use her discretion and end one of the biggest corporate battles in India by agreeing to a settlement with Mallya. So, in 2004, both United Breweries Ltd and Shaw Wallace made a public announcement that all disputes between them had been resolved. The case in the Hong Kong court was dismissed in June 2004 once they filed consent terms.

But what had not been resolved yet was who would get to partner with Shaw Wallace in their liquor business.

As Shaw Wallace had already found a partner for its beer business, it decided to call for bids for its liquor business in 2004. Mallya was quick to realize that though both he and the Chhabrias had agreed to settle all legal disputes, he was not exactly welcome in their fold. The settlement was to ensure that Mallya never again troubled the Chhabrias. But having lost the initial battle to take over Shaw Wallace, Mallya could not let go of the opportunity to have another shot at acquiring it. This time, he also had the added advantage of not having Manu Chhabria as an adversary.

He put in a bid for the liquor business for Rs 1251 crore. The other bidders were Newbridge Capital in partnership with Ramesh Vangal, the former head of Seagram India, and Whyte & Mackay. As it turned out, United Breweries' bid was the highest, a fact which Mallya claimed had been orally conveyed to him by McKinsey, advisers to Shaw Wallace. He also claimed that he was informed that the bid was for the 55 per cent stake held by the Chhabria family and not for the liquor business.

But the last thing the Chhabrias wanted was to let the company go to Mallya after putting up a stiff resistance for over two decades. Even though the bid was accepted, Shaw Wallace decided that it would delay the sale of the business for as long as possible.

However, Mallya was not one to give up easily. He returned the following year, in February 2005, with an open offer to acquire

25 per cent of the stake at a price of Rs 250 per share. It meant shelling out a total of Rs 300 crore if the offer was fully subscribed, valuing the company at Rs 1200 crore. It was an audacious move but one that would give him rich dividends if it paid off.

Shaw Wallace was quick to respond to the open offer, terming it as a hostile bid that did not have the consent of the promoters. But Mallya clarified that as the bidding process was taking a long time, he had decided to make the open offer through his three companies—United Spirits, McDowell & Co., and Phipson Distillery.

Of course, one obvious benefit for Mallya was that if he acquired Shaw Wallace, his company would emerge as a major spirits company in the world with total sales of 53 million cases, including 15 million cases of Shaw Wallace. Also, even if Mallya owned part of the 25 per cent he had made, he would be an indirect owner of Shaw Wallace's beer business, partly owned by SABMiller, and be a significant minority shareholder with the power to prevent Shaw Wallace from initiating the sale of the liquor business to anyone without his approval.

As the days went by, Mallya's pressure tactics via the open offer started working. His stance that he would talk only to Vidya Chhabria and not to her daughters also worked in his favour.

In March 2005, he received word from the Vidya Chhabria camp suggesting that she was ready to give in. Mallya arrived in Dubai and, after several meetings with her, managed to convince her to part with Shaw Wallace.

It is believed that the then ICICI Bank chief, K.V. Kamath, brokered the deal which was finalized for $300 million—Rs 1300 crore. Soon after the deal was signed, Mallya called his mother who was living in London at the time to inform her that he had finally bagged the Shaw Wallace liquor business.

A very pleased Lalitha Mallya congratulated her son on his latest conquest.

The final outgo for the UB Group was Rs 1545 crore, including Rs 312 crore for the 25 per cent stake through the open offer. ICICI Bank facilitated the entire funding.

As Mallya had already made it clear that he was not interested in Shaw Wallace's beer business, SABMiller later bought the remaining stake of 50 per cent by paying another Rs 158 crore ($36 million) to acquire 99 per cent of the beer business.

Shaw Wallace was later merged with United Spirits. This ended one of the biggest battles in corporate India.

'It's been twenty years, three months and four days, to be precise, since I set my sight on Shaw Wallace. It was a battle worth it and today, I have handsomely won it,' Vijay Mallya declared at a press conference later.

But Mallya had a few more scores to settle still. This time, he trained his guns at his foe-turned-friend-turned-foe Kishore Chhabria. In 2006, a year after he acquired Shaw Wallace, he filed a case against the Kishore Chhabria-owned BDA Distilleries, seeking the return of its Officer's Choice whisky.

Now how could he do that when he had already allowed Kishore Chhabria to take BDA Distilleries with him in return for shares in Herbertsons? It was because, out of the 200-odd cases which Manu Chhabria had filed through Shaw Wallace against his brother, Kishore, the one relating to Officer's Choice was still pending in the court. It was either an oversight or deliberate, but Mallya made use of it once Shaw Wallace was in his kitty.

After a series of long-drawn battles which stretched for a decade and a half, Mallya decided to end his dispute with Kishore Chhabria. More because he was set to finalize the deal with Diageo (which would take over United Spirits) and did not want any litigations to delay the process.

In October 2012, Mallya agreed to withdraw all cases relating to the legal dispute over the brand. In return, he received a sum of Rs 8 crore—approximately $2 million—from Kishore Chhabria for doing so.

That ended all disputes with the Chhabria family. Unless Mallya chooses to spring another one.

RATAN TATA

Excerpts from *Business Maharajas* by Gita Piramal and *TATAlog* by Harish Bhat

TUSSLE FOR THE CROWN

Some months before Ratan's appointment as the deputy chairman of Telco, in July 1988, JRD[1] had finally made up his mind over the succession issue, and his choice fell on Mody.[2] To ensure a smooth transition, JRD drew up an elaborate plan. He was already Tisco chairman. Mody would become Telco's chairman, taking over from Moolgaokar,[3] its ailing chairman. This would make Mody head of the two biggest companies in the Tata group, with a combined sales muscle of Rs 30bn, or a little more than half the group's total sales at the time, and would put him in a strong position to stake a claim to the group chairmanship after JRD retired. In JRD's game plan, once Mody was Telco's chairman, Ratan would become his deputy.

When JRD played the first move in this grand game of chess, Mody was overjoyed. Had he but restrained his glee, he could have had it all. Instead, Mody allowed himself to prematurely gloat in an interview to the *Business Standard*. His supporters went one step further by crowing about how easily Mody would sort out Telco's problems. Telco was then passing through a rough patch with a dip in profits due to its ambitious expansion programme (in March 1987, Telco made a meagre profit of Rs 29.3m on sales of Rs 12bn). Mody's gung-ho attitude alarmed several Telco executives who began to fear a putsch once he took over.

---

[1] JRD—JRD Tata.

[2] Mody—Russi Mody.

[3] Moolgaokar—Sumant Moolgaokar, chairman of Telco.

On hearing the whispers, an incensed Moolgaokar refused to step down. He would carry on in the saddle. He insisted that Ratan be immediately inducted into Telco as executive deputy chairman, giving him the portfolio of handling Telco's day-to-day operations. Palkhivala, then deputy chairman, voluntarily resigned but continued as a director. Mody tried to wriggle out of the tight situation by blaming the faux pas on 'speculative' and 'mischievous' reporting but the damage had been done.

Both Mody and JRD tried to persuade Ratan to resign and publicly state that he would only accept the position under Mody's chairmanship, but he refused to do so. Among the values he had learnt from his grandmother was the sanctity of promises. He would not denigrate Moolgaokar, who had built Telco over the years.

Mody tried to put a good face on a sticky situation but inside he was seething. News of a strike at Telco, therefore, may have acted as a soothing balm to his sore spirit.

CORPORATE SPURS

Trouble at the truck manufacturer's Pune plant had started brewing even before Ratan Tata entered the scene. It gradually developed into one of the bloodiest strikes in recent history. On April 7, 1988, the day Ratan was appointed Telco's deputy chairman, everything appeared normal. By December 1988, when he formally took over the chairmanship from the fragile eighty-two-year-old Sumant Moolgaokar (1906–1989), the tension was palpable.

Nonetheless, few expected the situation to snowball as it did. Most people had their eyes on Russi Mody, wondering how he would react to Ratan's stepping up the ladder leading to JRD's throne. Nobody anticipated that an assault on Ratan's position would come not from an autocratic Tata executive but an unknown trade union leader.

His name was Krishnan Pushparajan Nair, better known as Rajan Nair. The son of a trade union leader and the eldest in a family of eight, Nair worked in Philips before joining Telco as a machine miller in

September 1976. Six years later he became the general secretary of the Telco Kamgar Sanghatana (TKS). Though a Keralite, Nair was fluent in Marathi and has been described as a 'first-rate demagogue with a penchant for drama'. In March 1988 he was suspended for allegedly threatening to murder a security guard and sacked a few months later.

The day Nair was sacked, he left Telco vowing 'to bring the Telco management to its knees'. He tried his best to keep to his word. The unresolved wage agreement became his rallying point with the management. Nair insisted on Tata's recognition of his status as the workers' leader as a starting point for any negotiation. The management's view was that a dismissed worker with a criminal record could not be accepted as the leader, and while it was willing to talk with other members of the TKS on Telco rolls, Nair had no locus standi. At the time, there were 8525 blue-collar workers at the Pune plant and two major unions. From November 1988, antagonism between the workers and the management worsened. Rumours of a lockout fuelled the tension. Ratan was not new to tackling labour problems, having warded off a sticky situation in his Nelco days. But this was hardly the sort of welcome he needed in Telco. As a strong believer in the principles of transparency and fairness, he was willing to negotiate, but Nair's ego had the better of him and he thought he could put it across to the new, amiable-looking chairman of the company. He was mistaken. Behind the soft exterior of Ratan was a determination toughened by many years of hard experience in the corporate world.

Matters reached a flashpoint on January 31, 1989. Tata's visit to the Pune plant was greeted on the shop floor with a tool-down strike. On the same day, the local authorities saw fit to take Nair into preventive custody. On hearing this, the second shift workers hijacked buses which were supposed to take them to the plant at Pimpri (just outside Pune), and diverted them to the city where they besieged the district court. Nair was released. Tata says that he was unaware of what was happening in the city as he was huddled in a meeting at the plant with Powar, one of Nair's closest aides, and others. 'Nair chose to make out that he was arrested because I said so [but] I didn't get him arrested. It happened totally independently. If there was an issue of getting him arrested, I wouldn't be meeting his people. But that was the last time I met with them because when they went out, they misrepresented the meeting.'

All through the summer and monsoon, the situation inched inexorably towards a strike despite mediation attempts by Sharad Pawar, Maharashtra's chief minister, and others. Nair was not interested in parleying for peace. On March 15, Nair's men selected about twenty-two managerial personnel and rival unionists, and assaulted and stabbed them, in various parts of the city. Asked about this, Nair said 'the provocation was from the management because the previous day one of the TKS members was slapped on the shop floor'.

This was as much as Ratan could take. From then on his resolve hardened and he refused to give in to any intimidatory tactics of Nair and his men. Meanwhile, Ratan launched measures to build bridges between the management and the workforce. Telco had been contributing silently to the development of the Pimpri–Chinchwad belt. Now, at the time of its worst industrial crisis, it needed the support of the local community the most to correct the impression of the image of an exploitative corporation which Rajan Nair's campaign had sought to project. Telco shed its conservative image for the first time and utilized the media to create a public opinion; the managers initiated a one-to-one contact with the workforce to convince them of the management's intentions, and slowly the tide began to turn.

On September 19, in a shrewd move to woo away support from Nair, the management signed a three-year retrospective agreement with TKS's rival, the Telco Employees Union (TEC), offering a wage hike of Rs 585 and a lump sum arrears of Rs 7000. There was a stick attached to the tempting carrot. Tata wrote to every Telco employee in the Pimpri and Chinchwad units, warning that 'the company would have to reconsider its plans for further investments in Pune if the trend of labour unrest continued'. The management claimed that 1570 workers had accepted the offer and more were expected to follow. Seriously worried, Nair mulled over his options.

Two days later, Nair announced that he and his supporters would go on an indefinite fast at the Shaniwarwada Fort. With red bandannas tied round their foreheads, 3000 or so workers trooped into the fort to begin their fast. Significantly, the initials RNP (for Rajan Nair Panel) and not TKS were printed on the bandannas. Clearly, this was not just a management–union issue, but one involving a personal agenda. A one-day bandh was organized in the Pimpri–Chinchwad areas as a display of strength as also to convey the impression of Nair's growing influence in the region. From Bombay, Datta Samant rushed to Pune to express his support.

By the third day, workers were fainting from hunger. At the end of a week, there was a real fear that a fatality could trigger off uncontrollable violence. Pawar stepped up the pressure on both sides to break the deadlock and meet. They agreed.

On the morning of Wednesday, September 27, Tata flew into Bombay from the USA. Nair had arrived from Pune the previous evening. A tripartite meeting between Tata, Nair and Pawar was arranged for the afternoon at Varsha, the chief minister's official residence. Before that, Samant led a morcha to Bombay House while Nair held rallies and press conferences. These vitiated the already charged atmosphere. In an obvious bid to slight Tata, Nair and his team deliberately arrived very late. Scheduled for 4 p.m., the meeting finally opened at 5.30 p.m. It proved to be inconclusive. Nair was unwilling to concede ground.

Meanwhile, Pawar was becoming increasingly worried about the strike's political repercussions. The Pimpri–Chinchwad area was a crucial vote bank, home to over 2000 industrial units with an annual turnover of Rs 35bn and nearly a quarter million workers. Opportunistic politicians of every hue had jumped onto Nair's bandwagon. The Janata Dal leader, Sambhajirao Kakade, was backing Nair. George Fernandes and Madhu Dandavate, socialist leaders, were in constant touch with the strikers. And in the shadow of the Lok Sabha elections scheduled for November 24, Pawar was getting flak from Delhi politicians and Pune industrialists for the state government's kid-glove treatment of Nair. Moreover, Telco was the largest company in the region and any prolonged dispute would have a tremendous economic fallout. He had to do something.

Under cover of darkness, at 2.30 a.m. on September 29, the State Reserve and Pune city police launched Operation Crackdown. Eighty buses stopped outside the Shaniwarwada Fort's quadrangle. Pouring out of the buses, the police cordoned off the fort, stormed inside, and rounded up the workers.

The evacuation went on in batches until 4 p.m. While the workers were taken to police stations in Pune, a separate vehicle took Nair and his lieutenants to the nearby Ratnagiri jail where they were charged with attempting to commit suicide and defying prohibitory orders. Nair was released on bail the next day but it was clear to everybody that the strike had been effectively smashed.

For Ratan, the Telco crisis became a test of his managerial abilities. Because Nair so obviously lost, the media trumpeted Tata's victory. Tata believed it was a vindication of the principles and values which the group had so zealously protected and propagated all along.

In hindsight, Ratan takes heart from a new spirit of teamwork which emerged during the strike. 'Intimidation led to a hunger strike [but] workers came back to work during the strike. Fearing intimidation, they stayed in the plant. Office staff were manning machines, and people in the accounts department were moving materials. Some people were fed up and they came back, as an "enough is enough" kind of situation emerged. We started producing vehicles with about 800 people. I think that the kind of spirit that was created in Pune then would never have been created were it not for that conflict. So there were winners. They were caused by circumstances which were, ironically, created by Rajan Nair.

'Today there is a sense of friendliness. I can walk around the shop floor and talk to people. They come and talk to me. We smile and shake hands. I think the union has become a very productive and constructive organ of the company. Perhaps, we took our workers for granted. We assumed that we were doing all that we could for them when probably we were not. We gave a Rajan Nair—or any name—a chance to come and do what he did.'

In Jamshedpur, Russi Mody brooded over the Rajan Nair crisis. Mody was the acknowledged labour expert of the Tata group.

Under his helm, there hadn't been a single tremor of labour unrest at Tisco for almost half a century. The media's portrayal of Ratan as a tough manager capable of handling difficult labour situations posed a subtle threat to the ageing baron.

Indifferent or unaware of the forces around him, Ratan concentrated on patching up the shredded labour relations and building up trust between the management and the workers. March 31, 1991 was a red-letter day. Despite the strike, Telco overtook Tisco to become India's biggest company in the private sector by sales. Telco's sales shot up by almost a third to Rs 26bn and profit before tax grew by 58 per cent to Rs 2.35bn. Vehicle production rose by 26 per cent to 81,931 units. Tisco's sales were Rs 23.3bn. Telco's excellent results established Ratan's credentials as a top-notch manager. Reason enough for Mody to feel even more threatened.

RUSSI MODY

At Tisco, Mody took every opportunity to declare he would leave only when the board kicked him out. Which it summarily did on April 19, 1993, closing a mordant chapter in the group's history. As an outstanding man-manager in his heyday with a hands-on style which earned him a Padma Bhushan, Mody had set many precedents. His last was not particularly illustrious. Before this, no Tata chairman had ever been fired, let alone been forced to resign. The sacking came barely days before he was to officially retire on May 21. It was a pathetic comedown for a rare man who was once the 'toast' of industry.

The bespectacled bon vivant was appointed Tisco's managing director in 1974 and became the chairman in 1984 of India's biggest company in the private sector. His large ego often prompted him to say, 'There are only three great men who have come out of Harrow in this century—Jawaharlal Nehru, Winston Churchill and Russi Mody.'

So why did JRD sack a man who once was thought to be one of India's most astute managers? He didn't have a choice: Mody forced it upon himself. He displayed a singular lack of finesse during his last few years with the Tatas. Had he behaved with greater decorum, he could have had a much more graceful exit and assured himself pride of place in Tata history.

The last straw was an interview published in *The Hindu* in which Mody accused Ratan (Tisco's then deputy chairman) and Jamshed J. Irani (its managing director) of mismanaging Tisco's affairs and causing its share prices to crash. He also threatened to launch a campaign to mobilize support for himself from shareholders and financial institutions.

At an emergency meeting on April 19, 1993, there was a great deal of anger and resentment at Mody's statements. As Ratan pointed out, 'The main issue is that a chairman either agrees with his management's policies, or he leaves the board.' Coming as it did after a series of Mody misdemeanours and with tempers running high, it was a foregone conclusion that the board would fire Mody. And when the resolution was put to the vote, it was unanimously passed. Ratan Tata would be 'chairman of the company as from today'.

Earlier, Mody had avoided the March 25, 1991 Tata Sons board meeting which appointed Ratan as chairman of Tata Sons, but the day JRD handed over his crown to Ratan, Mody began to worry in earnest. Ratan had become Tisco's deputy chairman on January 31, 1985, and as group chairman would undoubtedly take over Tisco's chairmanship from Mody whenever Mody chose to retire. However, his term as managing director was due to expire on June 14, 1993. Mody was anxious that his protégé, Aditya Kashyap, should succeed him. The only hitch was that there was already a number two—Irani.

On the afternoon of November 26, 1991, a circular signed by Mody quietly announced sweeping managerial changes. Tisco would now have four managing directors. In the new pecking order, Irani was demoted from being the joint MD to additional MD, Kashyap moved up from executive director (corporate) to Irani's former position as joint MD, and Ishaat Hussain, the executive director in charge of finance, was designated a deputy MD. Mody continued as chairman and MD. Despite the intentional fuzziness of the designations, Mody's strategy was transparent. He wanted to move up Kashyap and Hussain, both in their mid-forties, and position Kashyap as Tisco's future chairman with Hussain as his number two.

Mody was so confident that his diktat would be obeyed that he flew off to Europe with Kashyap for a month-long holiday the next evening.

In designing his coup, Mody had totally neglected to take Ratan's reaction into account. And Ratan was upset. 'In the largest professionally managed corporation in the private sector, when changes in the senior management structure at the board level and/or succession plans are drawn up, then surely it should be a subject for collective decision-making rather than the decision of any single individual,' he stressed.

Pointing out that neither at or after Tisco's November 27 board meeting did Mody make an attempt to get the board's approval or leave room for discussion, Ratan reiterated his stand that 'the board of directors constitute a collection of independent individuals and each one has the right to express his independent judgement without being accused of being pro or anti'.

There were other arguments stacked against Mody. A professionally-run company had to take more than ordinary care not to show favouritism. It was true that the divorced Mody had never hidden the fact that Kashyap was his constant companion and legal heir, yet others on the Tata Steel board were perturbed by the impropriety of the methods adopted to suddenly elevate Kashyap. Mody had overreached himself and had to be curbed. Furthermore, it was not as if Irani lacked experience or was incompetent. On the contrary, the government had once sounded him out for the chairmanship of the Steel Authority of India. Palkhivala[4] and Nusli Wadia endorsed Ratan's hard line. Palkhivala, the group's legal expert, discovered that Mody had violated Tisco's articles of association by not informing the board of the changes prior to sending out the circular.

Mody's friends lost no time in updating him in London, but he failed to fully appreciate the vigour of the forces building up against

---

[4] Palkhivala—Nani Palkhivala.

him in his absence. On December 29, he flew into Delhi from London where he tried unsuccessfully to meet Narasimha Rao, the prime minister, and Manmohan Singh, the finance minister. On the afternoon of December 31, Mody arrived in Bombay and drove straight to Bombay House for a private meeting with JRD. Mody also began hectic lobbying of the outside directors, but it was apparent to him that he did not have a case to be backed.

By 2.30 p.m. on January 1, a compromise had been hammered out. Mody would apologize to the board, Irani would be clearly number two, there would be only two managing directors—Mody and Irani. The rest would be executive directors. The expected discord at the Tisco meeting did not materialize. By 4.55 p.m., the show was over. It was a clear victory for Ratan.

Heroically, Mody wrapped a few tattered shreds of black humour around him. At Tisco's EGM the next day, when a shareholder asked what award Mody should get when *Business India* had named Ratan Businessman of the Year and Irani was Steelman of the Year, Mody promptly quipped: 'I got the Bamboo of the Year.'

From this moment, Mody's star began to set. At about the same time Ratan pushed through with his retirement policy which called for Tata directors to give up their executive powers at sixty-five years and for non-executive chairmen to retire at seventy-five. Framed in the larger interests of the Tata Group to promote succession planning, it affected Mody directly as he was on the verge of turning seventy-five.

Mody started to feel insecure and sounded out whether he would be allowed another five-year term as executive chairman if he resigned as managing director. The response from Bombay House was a firm 'no'.

Mody accepted the 'no' with considerable ill grace and was forced to change his position only after Nusli Wadia told him during the lunch recess that if he did not fall in line, he (Wadia) would personally move a resolution at the board's post-lunch session to sack Mody as managing director. Mody then caved in and a formula was quickly hammered out. Wadia woke up JRD who had been taking a post-lunch nap, and an agreement was reached. When the board reconvened at 2.45 p.m., Mody began by calling for champagne.

According to the agreement, Mody was offered two concessions in view of his past contributions as also his long association with the group. He would remain chairman until June 1993 and he would retain charge of Tisco's international operations. And Tisco would hold off the Tata Sons' policy on the retirement age of Tata chairmen and managing directors for the time being. But far from ending the feud, the compromise prolonged the uneasiness within the company. The feuding grew into a low-intensity warfare and, predictably, the company's operations suffered. Mody accepted the compromise unwillingly and continued to create problems for Irani in the discharge of his responsibilities as the new managing director.

In March 1993, at the Founder's Day celebrations in Jamshedpur, JRD and Ratan once again brought up the issue of Tisco's acceptance of Tata Sons' retirement policy, with Mody. Mody had crossed seventy-five on January 17, 1993. Instead of taking the hint, Mody suggested that the policy, if introduced in Tisco, should exempt present incumbents. His predecessor, JRD, had had a long innings. Why should Mody be deprived of his?

Ratan pointed out that JRD's was a special case when the retirement policy was not in place. It was now important to depersonalize structures and remove subjective elements, such as the granting of extensions, in the tenure of the group's directors. Mody asked for the details of his retirement package in case he agreed to step down. Once he had them, he said, he would finalize things.

By all accounts the severance package was very generous but Mody kept hedging the question of his retirement. During the March 11 board meeting, JRD eventually introduced the retirement policy, at which point Mody rose, picked up his papers and walked off, saying, 'I declare the meeting closed.' The meeting continued after a few moments of silence, this time presided over by the deputy chairman, Ratan. Badly upset by Mody's walkout, some directors strongly objected to Mody's behaviour. The retirement policy was adopted unanimously. The board agreed that Mody should retire before the next AGM (which would be held in July) but that he should be allowed to choose and announce the actual date. Mody was lucky to be allowed the choice. Later, when JRD phoned him to communicate the board's decision, Mody preferred to have his severance package approved before he announced the date.

At the next meeting, on April 13, which Mody avoided by going to Delhi, the protests grew shriller. Mody had taken to vociferously bad-mouthing Tisco's performance in the press and on Doordarshan. The board retaliated by passing a resolution that Mody would have to go by May 1 and not July 17. It took two and a half hours of debate to come to this decision. When JRD phoned Mody to convey the board's decision, he requested time till May 21 as it was an auspicious day for him. Then came the fatal *Hindu* interview. And the sacking. Ratan's perseverance and commitment to principles had managed to bring down Mody from the high pedestal that he had assumed for himself.

INDIA'S FIRST INDIGENOUSLY DEVELOPED PASSENGER CAR

THE UNVEILING

Today cars have become items of intense desire. Consequently, auto shows have begun to rival fashion shows as far as the glamour quotient is concerned. Auto Expo 1998, held in New Delhi, was extra special because Tata Motors was launching an Indian car for the first time in history. Hundreds of children happily waving the Indian flag made the occasion festive rather than businesslike. To drive home the point further, the pretty car girls at the Tata pavilion were dressed in Indian attire, unlike the other pavilions where Western skirts were the norm. Cleverly gauging the mood that this car would be the showstopper at the Auto Expo, the organizers dressed up in smart sherwanis as well. And there, under the spotlight in the centre, stood the Tata car.

The Auto Expo is a biennial event that is held in the vast Pragati Maidan grounds. *Pragati* means 'progress' in Hindi—the arrival of the Tata car in January 1998 ensured that the grounds lived true to its name. An indigenously built Indian car was not merely a symbol of progress but an act of faith: few people had ever imagined that India would make its own car. The minister of commerce and industry, the late Murasoli Maran, saw the car at the expo and immediately called it 'The Kohinoor of India'. Like the legendary Kohinoor diamond, the car sparkled, attracting huge crowds.

The car itself had not yet been christened, but seeing the five prototype vehicles on display, the guest columnist for Rediff.com, Veeresh Malik, wrote about the car: '"like Zen" would be the best description, except for the fact that, unlike Zen, it has an excellently roomy rear seat. Test drives, however, were out for the moment. For those of you wondering, yes, it is likely that Telco [as Tata Motors was known then] will make, and sell, a world class car. It appears to be, frankly, like a cross between the Maruti Zen/Alto and the Mercedes-Benz A-Class small car with cheaper specs.'

Vikram Sinha, who now heads the car-manufacturing plant at Tata Motors, recalls being present at the unveiling. 'There was exceptional euphoria all over,' he says, and his eyes light up even today. 'There were endless queues to see India's first car, and I even met people who had come all the way from Mumbai just to take a look. What struck all of us was the feeling of patriotism and pride which flowed through that hall!'

Girish Wagh, who is now in the senior management team at Tata Motors, and who has played a key role in spearheading the development of the latest small car, Nano, was a young engineer in Tata Motors at that time. He recalls with pride that his father, who was a member of the Indica project team, was there at the auto show launch. 'My father called it one of the most fulfilling and satisfying days of his life,' he says, 'and that means everything to me.'

PATRIOTISM, PRIDE AND COURAGE

Cars have always been symbols of patriotism and pride. Famous auto brands such as Toyota, Rolls-Royce, Mercedes-Benz, Ford, Fiat and others have virtually been flag bearers for their respective countries. Yet, in the early 1990s, India, despite having launched missiles and spacecraft, did not have a car it could call its own, a car that had been designed and produced within the country. In 1993, Ratan Tata, chairman of Tata Motors, addressed the Automotive Component Manufacturers' Association of India in New Delhi, and suggested the possibility of component and car manufacturers in India getting together to produce an 'Asian car'. His intent was to emulate the Japanese and deliver a project worthy of national pride.

It was a good time to launch a brave new effort, because the Indian government—headed by P.V. Narasimha Rao, along with able economist Manmohan Singh as finance minister—had announced a slew of liberalization measures just a couple of years earlier, designed to take the country into a fast-paced growth trajectory, and eventually into the league of First World nations. History has shown that cars are often an engine of rapid economic growth all over the world. Speaking on the reaction to this address, Ratan Tata said, several years later:

> Needless to say, there was considerable criticism and cynicism about my suggestion. In the absence of a positive reaction, I decided that if we were not going to do this as a collaborative national effort, Tata Motors would undertake the lead effort. In 1995, we formally undertook a programme to develop a new Indian car. Two types of reactions were forthcoming at that

stage: one was that we were being very brave but, the other, which came more often, was that we were being very foolish.

Both of these extreme reactions stemmed from two facts. First, Tata Motors had achieved fame and success as a maker of trucks and commercial vehicles—it had never made cars. Second, the venture was very expensive, entailing investments of around Rs 1700 crore, and could make or break the company's fortunes. Of course, this was not the first time that the chairman of the Tata Group was being faced with intense cynicism regarding a pioneering new venture, or being labelled 'foolish' for pursuing a courageous dream.

In a classic example of history repeating itself, here is a relatively ancient anecdote that took place more than ninety years ago, as told in *The Creation of Wealth*. This was when Jamsetji Tata, then chairman of the Tata Group, was pursuing steel manufacturing for the first time. Till 1903, India had never made its own steel. Lala recounts: '[When he heard about the Tata Steel venture] the Chief Commissioner for the Indian Railways, Sir Frederick Upcott, said—Do you mean to say that the Tatas propose to make steel rails to British specifications? Why, I will undertake to eat every pound of steel rail they succeed in making.'

A few years later, when the Tata Group had made a big success of the steel venture, Mr Dorab Tata, who succeeded Jamsetji as chairman, commented dryly, 'If Sir Frederick had carried out his undertaking, he would have had some slight indigestion.'

This time, while there was once again no dearth of naysayers who refused to believe in an Indian car, there are no reports of any of them offering to eat the car. Since the Indica weighs 995 kg and contains over 2000 steel components, it may have caused severe indigestion. On the other hand, many sceptics would have fit into this car with ease, because Ratan Tata was clear that the new car had to provide ample space for the typical Indian family. In his own words:

We started out to design an Indian car from scratch. We felt that the Ambassador, much as it is maligned, is the ideal size for the travelling Indian public. So we decided to design a car with the internal volume of an Ambassador, the size of a Maruti Zen, and ease of entering and exiting, particularly for the rear seats. We thought of pricing it close to the Maruti 800, which is a very successful car, and adding the economy of diesel. Finally, we packaged this into a contemporary design.

These famous words became a clarion call to everyone in Tata Motors, as the company commenced the exciting and arduous journey of building India's first indigenous car, rising to the chairman's challenge.

FUTURISTIC DESIGN

The first task was to finalize a design concept for the car, because most other things flow from the basic design. Ratan Tata led this path-breaking effort from the front. In this effort, he was perhaps also propelled by his own deep and abiding love for aesthetics and design.

The only cars that were seen in India those days were the Ambassador, the Premier Padmini and the Maruti 800. The original concepts for these cars had been created several years ago in countries outside India. None of these vehicles could be described as having exciting, contemporary designs. The first two vehicles looked and felt prehistoric when compared with the sleek modern cars one saw in Hollywood movies, but these dinosaurs stubbornly refused to go into extinction. Occasionally, a few beautiful but expensive imported cars also made it to Indian roads, and received envious glances from people who could never even think of owning or travelling in one of them.

If the Indica had to be world class, its design had to be comparable with the best in Europe and America. It had to be contemporary, appealing and so distinctive that it would sweep Indians off their feet. This task was assigned to the company's designers at the Engineering Research Centre located in Pune, commonly called the ERC. The designs were then refined and finalized in association with the famous Turin-based design house, IDEA. The ERC is a formidable facility, with a brilliant team of engineers. The designing process was completely automated at the centre using computer-aided design (CAD) and computer-aided manufacturing (CAM) stations, a novelty in those years. Tata Motors invested a massive sum of over Rs 120 crore on 225 CAD stations for its 340 engineers to work on.

When I visited the ERC during the writing of this book, it was buzzing with activity, as it must also have been during those early days of the Indica development, beginning in 1995. Several smart, young design engineers in the company got the rare opportunity to work on India's first car project. One of them was Ravindra Rajhans, a member of the core development team. Rajhans had graduated with a master's degree in industrial design from one of India's most-reputed engineering colleges, the Indian Institute of Technology (IIT), Mumbai. He had earlier worked on the styling of a light commercial vehicle (LCV) called the Tata 709, and also on the Tata Safari, a sports utility vehicle (SUV) that appeared to be a crossover between an LCV and a car. When he was asked to join the Indica team, he says he nearly fell off his chair.

Those were heady days. We had the privilege of presenting our sketches and designs directly to our chairman, Ratan Tata. We were told that the design of the car would be developed by us, and finalized in collaboration with IDEA, a design house in Turin, Italy.

I remember a meeting in Pune during September 1995, where some of us asked the chairman—'Sir, why are we going to Italy? Can't we do the design here, entirely in our own facilities in Pune?'

His answer told us what the quest for world class meant. Mr Tata looked us in the eye, and said—'I believe totally in our own capabilities. But when we visit motor shows abroad, we see the great strides which global car companies have made, the excellent designs they have already launched in

Europe and other Western countries. Our effort should be to leapfrog into the future. For this to happen we should work in the design environment of Europe, where the design ethos is well ahead of India. Then we can hope for a car which is ahead of its time.'

Turin was, therefore, a perfect choice; it is the design capital for the stylish Italian car industry, housing firms such as IDEA, and the headquarters of brands such as Fiat, Lancia and Alfa Romeo. It is also breathtakingly beautiful, surrounded on the western and northern fronts by the majestic snow-clad Alps. Natural beauty has always been a source of inspiration for intensely creative people such as designers.

Meanwhile, back home in Pune, a mammoth exercise in creativity and execution was under way: over 3800 components, 700-plus dies and 4000 fixtures for the Indica were being designed. These parts were also being simultaneously tested and validated, which was made possible by CAD systems that had been installed just in time for this project. In fact, paper drawings were done away with completely, which was an achievement in its own right.

Between Pune and Turin, the engineers at Tata Motors had to address several complicated design challenges. The car had to rise to Ratan Tata's challenge, and provide the space large enough for an Indian family. A typical Indian family has five or six people—husband and wife, two children and one or two grandparents who live in the same home. On long drives, the family also travels with a significant amount of luggage. One must not forget to mention here that this luggage will include tasty, freshly cooked home-made or local food. From personal experience, I can confidently say that this matter of food receives a lot of attention while planning a car journey.

For a product from the house of Tatas, which enjoys the trust of millions of Indians, safety had to be a zero-compromise feature. A colleague who lives in Europe, once commented on the car driving experience in India: 'How do you drive safely on roads where, on one side, autorickshaws are zipping by madly like Formula 1 cars, while on the other side, cows are ambling as if the roads were their favourite meadows?'

The engine, which is at the heart of the car, had to provide excellent performance and mileage. Here, the Tata Motors team worked with Le Moteur Moderne (LMM), France, for engine testing and evaluation. The transmission system was designed entirely in-house, adding new capabilities to a company that had no background in cars. Accelerated learning became the mantra of the hour in all areas, simply because there was no in-house expertise of manufacturing cars to fall back on.

When the first prototype of the Indica was unveiled several months later, in some secrecy within Tata Motors, it was clear that this design effort had succeeded brilliantly. Everyone agreed that here was a car clearly ahead of its time; it looked very distinctive compared to other Indian cars of that period, and had an unmistakable international appeal. Everyone agreed that the car offered incredible space when compared to any vehicle of similar class. And the Indica met global crash test standards with ease. But at its heart it was an Indian car.

Rajhans recounts an interesting 'Indianness' story from his days in Turin.

I remember the day the first design prototype of the Indica was finally ready, and it looked so beautiful. My colleague and I, who were deeply involved in the design effort, wanted to celebrate the occasion before shipping the prototype car to India. In Italy, they celebrate with champagne. But we were so proud of the Indianness of the car that we wanted to celebrate with a puja (prayer) to God Almighty, for having guided us in making our design so successful, so wonderful. To perform this traditional puja ceremony, we needed a coconut, *haldi* (turmeric) and *kumkum* (vermilion). But where do you find these in a place like Turin? We roamed virtually every road and cobbled street of Turin for an entire day, hunting for these three essential items. It was difficult, but we eventually found them. We conducted our Indian puja and left the broken coconut in the car, as a symbol of the Almighty's blessings.

> I am told that our colleagues back in India were most
> surprised to find the coconut, when they opened the shipment
> and unveiled the car!

Everyone who saw the prototype car remembers their first reaction even today.

Girish Wagh says that he first saw the purplish-blue Indica when he strolled into the prototype shop on some other work.

'Wow, what a wonderful new Toyota car!' was his first thought. It was only when he got closer that he realized it was not another vehicle from the Japanese Zen master of cars, but the new Tata car.

Some other reactions from the Tata Motors shop floor were equally euphoric. 'The first sight of the car was a "wow" moment for us. This was breakthrough styling, and we knew it as soon as we saw it!'

'The final design was chosen by Mr Tata, out of a few shortlisted concepts. We fell in love with it; we knew instinctively that we were backing a winning horse.'

COMPONENTS OF A WORLD-CLASS CAR

Even as the design concept was constantly being refined in collaboration with IDEA, work had also commenced on another big area—manufacturing or sourcing of components and vendor development.

The 3885 discrete designed components of the car now had to be locally developed and manufactured, either by Tata Motors or by capable vendors. Quick decisions were taken on which parts would be made internally and which outsourced. Either way, most of these were being made for the first time ever within the country. Global car companies such as Ford Motors and General Motors have grown on the back of strong vendor partners such as Visteon and Delphi, built over several decades. Tata Motors, on the other hand, did not have a vendor base for car parts. It had to develop this vendor community from scratch. It had to ensure that vendors met the global quality standards required, making it a task of Herculean proportions.

One man who recalls this vividly is Dilip Huddar, who is now the general manager of strategic sourcing for the company. He was a key member of the Indica ancillary development team.

Our mandate was to develop the supplier base for the new car. A special team was created, called SQIG—the Supplier Quality Improvement Group. We were told that over 500 cars would be made per day.

Until then, our plant was manufacturing around 100 trucks or Sumo vehicles per day, so this was a huge mindset shift! We used to begin work at 6.30 a.m. to make this possible, and end the day pleasantly exhausted but never before midnight. There was so much to do and so little time. This was such a large and prestigious investment for us; we were determined to make it happen really well.

Another member of this team was Atul Chandrakant Bhate, who heads product development for the cars business today. He had joined Tata Motors in 1992, fresh from graduate school where he had studied mechanical engineering.

'I was terribly excited when I was selected for the cars project. On the very first day, we were told that we would be given intensive training by an expert named A.J. Agnew, on development of parts for cars. The message was very clear—this is a different ball game from trucks and commercial vehicles.'

A.J. Agnew had been worldwide director of supplier quality at the Cummins Engineering Corporation in the USA. It was clear that the Tata Group was sparing no effort to ensure a world-class car. Agnew made it clear that everything had to be aligned perfectly with the final quality of the car, which is what mattered to people buying the vehicle. He emphasized that even the smallest compromises were not to be accepted, that tolerances had to be very strict and narrow. A detailed thirteen-step quality improvement programme was immediately put in place.

Dilip Huddar recalls: 'Our vendors were initially shocked that they had to carry out so many big quality improvements. Some of them began asking, why invest so much money into improving quality when Indian consumers will be happy with less? We had to convince them that Indian consumers deserved more, and Indica was determined to provide them the best.'

Nonetheless, several entrepreneurs were very keen to supply parts to the first Indian car. This was a matter of real pride for them. Some of them had even unofficially seen drawings of the new car, which had fuelled their interest further. They were now insistent that they would supply, and they did. In the midst of such exciting work with individual vendors, yet another major development was pioneered by the company, which would soon become instrumental to the future of the Indian car industry. Tata Motors decided to float a holding company for manufacturing car components, called Tata AutoComp Systems Limited. This company then formed joint ventures with global giants for specific components, thus bringing the best possible expertise into the country from different parts of the globe.

A joint venture with Johnson Controls of the United States was established to produce car seats. A partnership with Ficosa of Spain produced rear-view mirrors. Radiators were produced by a third company that was formed in collaboration with Toyo, Japan. These are some of the countless partnerships that Tata Motors formed with various global players. These joint venture companies, under the umbrella of Tata AutoComp Systems, today supply to a range of Indian and global vehicle brands, including Tata Motors, Ashok Leyland, BMW, Mercedes-Benz, Ford, Mahindra & Mahindra, and Honda. Indica had not merely given India its first indigenous car; it also helped establish in the country a global supply chain for cars!

Apart from Tata AutoComp Systems, more than 300 vendors were developed, which supplied over 1000 high-quality parts. In turn, this created a stream of 12,000 jobs. Nearly 98 per cent of all parts used in the Indica were made in India, an amazing statistic for a country that had never before made its own car.

'We created the entire sheet-metal vendor fraternity around Pune,' says Atul Bhate. 'Sheet metal used in cars is large and voluminous, so vendors had to be close to our car-manufacturing plant.'

He goes on to add:

Many vendors have also gained handsomely from the Indica car project. Several thousand jobs have been created at their units, and small fledgling factories have now become large, profitable enterprises with revenues running into hundreds of crore of rupees. They are today large, sophisticated units catering to an array of brands. Some of them are listed on the stock exchange, and even have styling studios of their own!

WHERE SHOULD THE INDICA BE MANUFACTURED?

While components were being developed, thought was also being given to where the Indica would eventually be manufactured, bringing together thousands of these components and shaping them into a complete car.

As the story goes, the team at Tata Motors Pune had initially concluded that Indica cars should be manufactured inside a building called the E-block. This is a set of buildings located within the existing commercial vehicles factory of the company, where trucks and LCVs had been manufactured for several years. The managers who came to this conclusion were also ready with all supporting details and charts, and felt their decision was the most efficient approach. Then, Ratan Tata visited the plant and discussed the subject. He is reported to have asked for a pair of binoculars, which were duly given to him. Clutching these binoculars, he walked up to the terrace of this block and surveyed the surrounding areas. Standing there, he saw the barren land, over six acres large, adjoining the existing factory.

'That is where our cars will be manufactured,' he said, pointing to this vast tract of land. The need for a large, independent manufacturing unit for cars was proven right by several events that followed: the huge launch orders received for the Indica, the manufacture of other new cars such as the Indigo and Vista that were launched by the company in the following years and, of course, the rapid growth of the Indian car market.

'We thought of a unit for making Indica cars. He visualized a large, full-fledged car business that would transform the company. That was the difference,' says a senior manager, recalling this incident.

THE CAR-MANUFACTURING FACILITY

But what about the car-manufacturing facility itself? A new manufacturing unit can cost around US$2 billion, or even more—a huge amount that could have broken the company's back or even rendered the project a non-starter. Here, again, Ratan Tata and his core team at Tata Motors took a road less travelled, and it made all the difference.

Here is Ratan Tata's description of how it all transpired:

Very often, in developing a car abroad, the cost of development is about US$800 million [approximately Rs 3400 crore] and the cost of manufacturing facilities is around US$2 billion [approximately Rs 8500 crore]. In comparison, the Indica project cost us US$400 million.

Looking for an inexpensive manufacturing facility, we found a disused Nissan Plant in Australia. It was run for fifteen minutes every day only to keep the hydraulics and pneumatics in working order. It was offered for sale and we paid about Rs 100 crore for it—barely one-fifth to one-sixth of what we would have had to pay for a new plant. Our engineers dismantled the plant, all 14,800 tonnes of machinery, and shipped it to India in some 600-odd containers, facilitating the construction of the plant in Pune. This itself was a challenge, as it had never been done before. There were nagging doubts about whether we could dismantle an entire car plant and rebuild it. So, we tagged and identified the parts, then took them apart, and rebuilt the plant as we went ahead. Of course, we added considerable new equipment to make the plant self-contained.

You would need over two lakh adult human beings to reach a weight of 14,800 tonnes! In addition to shipping this huge weight across two distant continents, every part had to be carefully taken apart, so that it could be put back together. This Herculean task was accomplished within six months, and over just sixteen shipments. What could have been a nightmarish effort was made to look effortless because of the determination and rigorous effort of the entire team.

ROBOTS AND THE INDICA

Apart from the Nissan factory that was rebuilt in India, the manufacturing facilities for the Indica comprise five different areas: the engine shop, where engines for the car are made; the transmission shop, where the gearboxes and gear transmission systems are made; the press and welding shop, where some parts are pressed into shape and then welded together; the paint shop, where the parts are painted; and the final assembly shop, where the entire car is assembled.

These shop floors are a delight to visit because they are a picture of the latest technology at work. They are normally buzzing with a constant stream of systematic activity, with hundreds of parts being made, transported, stored and stitched together.

When I walked through these buildings, I was also struck by how large they were, stretching almost endlessly. The senior engineers nodded. 'Yes,' they said. 'The assembly shop alone is more than half a kilometre long. Walking was taking too much time. So we began using bicycles to move through the shop floors.' Thus was created the unusual sight of young men bicycling within shop floors where India's first car was being created. With such distances being covered every day on foot or bicycle, no wonder these engineers look so fit and healthy.

The welding shop is an impressive place that gives a view of the huge technology leap made by the Tata Group; it is a veritable 'hall of robots'. It resembles a scene from a science fiction movie or an Isaac Asimov novel, with giant robots effortlessly picking up large car parts such as doors or fenders, handing them over to other robots that weld the parts, and cars that are in various stages of completion moving along fully automated pathways. At some points, multiple robots work together on complex manufacturing operations. There are over 450 robots in this single hall, so you will find more than one whichever way you turn.

All across the hall, a million sparks fly as welding guns completely operated by robots and computers carve out shapes on the cars. The reddish-coloured robots are many times the size of a human being; their ability to lift such large pieces of heavy metal with ease is an accurate demonstration of their incredible strength. A layman like me felt at ease only because, being a science fiction buff, I believe in the first law of robotics (from Isaac Asimov). Every robot is designed to obey this law, which specifies that 'A robot may not injure a human being, or through inaction let a human being come to harm'!

The head of this welding shop and supreme commander of this army of robots is Abhijit Ghaisas, a soft-spoken engineer who walks with a certain sure-footedness and acknowledges greetings from several workers on the way.

'Robots are used here for welding because of their accuracy and repeatability. And, of course, because of ergonomic considerations, due to which human operators should not undertake some of these manually taxing tasks. We have three robotic lines here. And this is the first significant robotic line installed in India.'

THE INDICA ROLLS OUT

The final stage of manufacture is the assembly and testing of the cars. Today, the plant has the capacity to roll out 1000 shiny new Indicas per day, all ready to hit the road. But this was not the case when the voyage began.

Four shop floor operators who assembled the first Indica car found the going very challenging. Umesh Dhule, Sanjay Kurne, Kishore Jape and Uday Urankar were young lads in the Tata Motors factory back in 1998. Still on the right side of twenty, and hailing from the smaller towns of Maharashtra such as Kolhapur and Ahmednagar, they had just completed their apprenticeships. They had grown up in difficult economic circumstances, and spoke Hindi with the lilting Marathi accent that is common to this belt.

It took us eight full days to assemble the first Indica car. We did not even know the names of the parts, so how could we locate them properly? It took so long that we thought to ourselves, how are we ever going to meet consumer demand? We had heard that more than one lakh people had paid a lot of money and booked the Indica, and were now eagerly waiting for their car. Would we disappoint them?

We told our college friends back home that we were making India's first car. They laughed at us, and they said—'How can we ever make a new car in our country? Cars like this are only made in America and Europe, not in India.'

This was unfortunately the prevailing mindset about India's capabilities. However, it must be stated that this perception stood somewhat modified when the same college friends heard that the Tata Group was behind this venture.

Goaded by a sense of urgency and a desire to fulfil consumers' orders without delay, the rate of manufacture increased rapidly from one car per day to fifty to 100. Today, a new Indica car emerges from the factory every fifty-six seconds. From eight days to fifty-six seconds, now that's a remarkable journey! A few interesting stories from this journey provide some insight into the company and its people, and some reasons why India's first car was delivered so well.

Ratan Tata used to visit the Indica manufacturing facilities quite often. On one such early visit, he promptly noticed operators fixing the rear strut of the car manually. The operator would have to bend up and down 600 times to complete this operation on 300 cars each day. Ratan Tata called his managers immediately. 'How can we expect our men to do this throughout their lives? Surely it will damage their health. We must provide an automation solution, on priority.' The engineering department, amidst all its hectic schedules, rose to the occasion and developed a fixture to semi-automate the operation. This made life incredibly easier for the operators, who remember this fondly even today.

Two years later, the Indica was yet to deliver profits, and the company was staring at a massive loss because its commercial vehicles business was also facing a bad market. But, as the four operators recall, the company still gave them a very good wage increase that year. 'Frankly, we did not expect this. Neither were we in any position to demand such an increase in our salary, because we knew the poor financial situation. But the company was generous to us. That is why we love our company; that is why we give all our effort and energy to making these cars with all our heart.'

The operators also recall with pride that Ratan Tata has always been accessible to them, has routinely stopped by to exchange a few words whenever he visited, and has respected their ideas. In fact, many ideas from the shop floor were shared with the designers, and accepted. Worker empowerment and involvement also led to a very good implementation of the production process, contributing to the final smooth rollout.

An identical sentiment is expressed several years later by a young graduate engineer, Neil Kamal Gupta, who supervises many of these operators in the Indica assembly plant today. 'Our senior management respects us; they take our ideas on board. P.M. Telang and Girish Wagh [who headed the company and car business operations, respectively, in 2012] have full trust and faith in us, and that always makes me feel on top of the world! I want our latest Indicas to delight the customer completely, and I will do everything I can do to ensure that.'

With such splendid and committed effort, the first Indica rolled out from this assembly plant in the year 1999, just thirty-one months after development had commenced. Many people still vividly remember that it was a green Indica, a colour that is no longer manufactured today. Green was undoubtedly the right colour, given that the car was ready within three years, and it was now going full speed ahead. Everyone also remembers that Ratan Tata drove the first car, which was adorned with bright flowers. Many important dignitaries and the media were present for the celebrations.

After all, this was no ordinary vehicle. The name 'Indica' said it all: in ancient days, this was the name used by the mighty Greeks when they referred to India. Megasthenes, the Greek general and historian, wrote fascinating things about India in his famous book *Indica*. Now Indica was also the name by which the entire world would know India's equally exciting first car.

Here is a wishful piece of fictional modern history. If the Greek emperor Alexander the Great were alive and had visited India in these modern times, he would certainly have wanted to disembark from his famous horse, Bucephalus, and take a test drive of the Indica. He knew a thoroughbred steed when he saw one.

MORE CAR PER CAR

Tata Motors also focused a lot of attention on marketing the car to Indians in an unforgettable and compelling manner. Once again, this was a very different proposition from the company's existing business of selling trucks and commercial vehicles to fleet owners. To address the task, a separate strategic business unit and marketing organization was formed. It established new car dealerships and authorized service centres across the country.

Ratan Tata and his team thought that providing customers a new experience in car buying was an important part of giving them a new car. To establish these experiential standards, the company's own flagship dealership Concorde Motors was formed. Initially established as a joint venture with Jardine International Motors, it soon expanded to fourteen showrooms in key cities such as Bangalore, Mumbai and Delhi. It was kept lean but very responsive to consumer needs, offering virtually everything—sales, service and spares. Its objective was also to set the standards for dealerships across the country.

The big question now was: what should the central consumer proposition of Indica be? How should the car differentiate itself from other international brands? How best should this story be told to the common man, who had never before imagined an Indian car?

Rajiv Dube, the commercial head of this project, who later rose to become president of the passenger cars business of Tata Motors, embarked on this exciting journey with a newly created marketing team. An officer of the Tata Administrative Service, Rajiv had earlier worked in Ratan Tata's office, and therefore knew the chairman's mind well. He spearheaded his team to create one of the most memorable marketing campaigns ever in the history of the Indian cars industry.

Working closely with them in creating the winning advertisements for Indica was the reputed advertising agency DraftFCB+Ulka. Ambi Parameswaran, executive director and CEO of DraftFCB+Ulka, and also one of the country's foremost exponents in the discipline of marketing, recounts the story of how this was done:

> For us, Indica was not just a car. It was India's first ambition to take on the world. It was Tata Motors' passion on wheels. A conscious decision was made right from day one, to assume a confident, aggressive approach, to instil a sense of pride in owning a world-class Indian car.
>
> But first, we said, let us just show the car to consumers, and find out what they think, what they see as the most appealing features. So we parked the Indica at Worli (a prominent location in Mumbai), and we invited people to open the car and get in. There was tremendous response. Curiosity was so high; people just wanted to have a look at India's first car.

This was the same response that many managers of Tata Motors had experienced when they had taken the Indica for test drives on the roads of Pune. Ravindra Rajhans, the design engineer who had worked in Turin, narrates this story:

> I was driving an Indica late at night, around 10.30 p.m., a few months before it was launched. It was dark, and suddenly I saw a motorcyclist chasing my car. I was very apprehensive, having heard a few terrifying stories about highway robberies and dacoities. I drove faster, but so did the motorcyclist behind me. Eventually he overtook me, parked in front of my car, and stopped me from going further. I was now seriously worried, and prepared for the worst.
>
> The motorcyclist got down, along with a small boy who was on the pillion behind him. He said that his son wanted to see India's car—that was why he had been chasing me for so long. They saw the car and spent a few minutes appreciating it from all over. Then they thanked me and went away!

Apart from sheer curiosity, what did the hundreds of people who got into the Indica at Worli have to say? Listen to Parameswaran once again:

> People were pleasantly surprised that the Tata Group had made such a good-looking car. They asked us time and again, in Hindi—'Yeh gaadi Tata banata hai? Yeh toh badi garv ki baat hai. (Does the Tata Group make this car? This is truly a matter of pride.)'
>
> Everyone who opened the car was also delighted with the amount of space inside the vehicle. They kept saying there was far more space than they ever imagined.

These two insights—the hyper-curiosity it generated and the feedback that this was a great-looking car with lots of space inside it—were used to create the first advertisement campaign for the Indica.

Before the launch, a teaser advertisement further stoked curiosity, as it announced: 'India's most eagerly awaited car'. It created huge anticipation and lots of conversation around it. This tagline became so famous that it was picked up by the media and used extensively, even in unrelated areas. When India had a new prime minister soon after the launch of the Indica, this development was announced in newspapers as 'India's most eagerly awaited prime minister'!

However, even more famous and impactful than this teaser tagline was the next advertisement in the launch campaign. Building on the fact that the Indica offered more good looks, more space and more engine power, this advertisement described the vehicle as 'More car per car'.

This line was the result of inspired creative thinking, motivated by what consumers had said and several rounds of internal discussion with the Tata Motors team. Earlier lines such as 'The complete car' and the 'No compromise car' were discarded in favour of a line that exhibited attitude and total confidence. This was a perfect example of a resurgent India taking on the world. 'More car per car' became a phrase on everyone's lips soon after these advertisements appeared in newspapers and on hoardings across the country. In the final analysis, the line 'More car per car' was perhaps so successful because it was a perfect summation of Ratan Tata's clarion call, which had driven the entire Indica project from start to finish: 'A car with the internal volume of an Ambassador, the size of a Maruti Zen, the economy of diesel and pricing close to the Maruti 800.'

The Indica received a fabulous response, the best ever in India's automobile history till the time. The car garnered 1,15,000 'fully paid' bookings within eight days of its launch. This was many multiples more than the bookings obtained by other international cars launched during the same period. This also showed the tremendous enthusiasm with which Indians had welcomed the first car they could call their very own. Within a few months, the Indica had notched up a commendable market share of more than 14 per cent in its segment.

The unbeatable pull of the Indica was acknowledged by the competition in many other ways. Just a few hours before the Indica was formally launched by Tata Motors at the vast Turf Club grounds in Mahalaxmi, Mumbai, the market leader Maruti Suzuki announced a significant drop of Rs 25,000 in the price of its flagship car, the Maruti 800. This was perhaps on Ratan Tata's mind when he went on stage that evening to present the Indica to the crème de la-crème of the city. 'Thanks to Tata Motors,' he said, 'whichever car you choose to buy, you will now get more.'

THE AGONY AND THE ECSTASY

Many decades ago, the author Irving Stone titled his famous biography of Michaelangelo *The Agony and the Ecstasy*, in an attempt to capture the extreme emotional states that this genius experienced throughout his life. The same title best describes the first three years of the life of the Indica. Initially, there were several accolades, including record bookings that resulted in strong market shares. But dark clouds quickly gathered on this sunny horizon, and the company had to suddenly deal with a wave of unanticipated consumer complaints. Essentially, these revolved around several product quality issues that cropped up immediately after the launch.

Several consumers called in, complaining of high noise and vibration levels in the car. There were problems relating to winding the windows up and down. Performance of the engine came in for criticism. Word of mouth was quickly turning from highly positive to highly negative. Some Tata Motors veterans recall that this was not just a few isolated cases, but a flood of angry complaints. They wince, even today, when they speak about how customers turned violent at several locations. On the back of such negative feedback, sales of the Indica plummeted during the year 2000–01. Tata Motors announced its largest ever loss of Rs 500 crore during that year, and a few experts promptly blamed this loss on the failure of the Indica, and the company's decision to enter the passenger cars market.

The competition became hyperactive and began to write premature epitaphs for the Indica. A constant refrain heard in those days was that Tata Motors and Ratan Tata had made a big mistake in betting on an indigenously made car. And there is, of course, no dearth of condescending Western and Indian minds who never miss an opportunity to take potshots at India and other developing nations, which remain, in their minds, lands that are best suited to snake charmers, forests and elephants.

So was this the sad end of the Tata dream to make India's first car? Would it spell disaster for Tata Motors, which had made the back-breaking investment of Rs 1700 crore in the Indica project? Like the *Titanic*, had the Indica hit a fatal iceberg? Would it now drag down with it one of the most venerable companies of the Tata Group?

These were the heavy thoughts playing on everyone's mind when Ratan Tata called an emergency internal meeting at the Taj President Hotel in Mumbai, to take stock of the unfortunate situation and chart the way forward. Memories of that session are still vivid in the minds of many. Senior team members were encouraged by the chairman to vent their feelings of what had gone wrong, for as long as they wished. Many of them were sharply self-critical. It was clear that the huge financial loss had touched their souls, and the mounting customer complaints had hurt their pride. But, deep within, there was great resilience, undying hope, a commitment to make the venture a success.

Ratan Tata then steered the meeting in the direction of the improvements that were required. The conversation quickly converged on to what the team should address immediately. There was acknowledgement that some specific design flaws had to be rectified, even if this meant alterations in the basic design.

In the meanwhile, 'retrofit camps' were organized, where over 45,000 Indica cars were repaired, with forty-two parts being replaced entirely at the company's cost. Customer meets were held in every nook and cranny of the country, with a patient ear being given to every angry customer, and solutions being offered wherever possible. Senior managers from the marketing, design and manufacturing teams participated in these meets.

The Tata Motors team knew that pride and survival were simultaneously at stake. Of course, the company had stumbled, and had to pull itself up very quickly. The chairman was leading this effort from the front, and all product changes necessary had to be implemented on a war-footing. There was some writing on the wall already, and there was little time left to erase it.

If courage is required to launch a breakthrough exploration of unknown lands, guts of steel are required to sustain the voyage when it runs into such rough seas. The team at Tata Motors proved itself equal to this daunting task. Working with Formula 1-like speed, they developed and implemented the required design changes. Vendors produced these altered parts. A new, robust Indica was ready by 2001, with key quality problems having been completely eliminated. It was launched in the market as Indica V2.

The word 'V2' announced the change loud and clear. This was also a technical-sounding suffix, therefore appropriate for a car. If Indica had been 'More car per car', the new Indica V2 was 'Even more car per car'. A fantastic television advertisement, which highlighted the product features of the new car, even as it re-emphasized the many positives of the original Indica, also helped build consumer conviction.

An interesting sidebar is worth mentioning here. This advertisement ended with a scene of several oriental-looking people, including the Indian actor Kelly Dorjee, bowing to the new Indica V2, in a tribute to its features. The thought was perhaps to depict the Indica V2 as being so good that even the Japanese, who are the masters of car making, pay salute to it. Such exaggeration is, of course, the lifeblood of good advertising. However, the Korean car company Hyundai used this scene as a basis to launch a complaint against this ad film with the Advertising Standards' Association of India (ASCI). While this complaint was eventually not upheld, it highlights the impact the new Indica V2 and its advertisement campaign had on its competitors.

Indeed, the impact of the Indica V2 was extraordinary and immediate. It marked not merely the revival of the Indica but its brilliant success. It became the fastest-selling automobile in Indian history when it completed sales of 100,000 cars in less than eighteen months. Despite an overall economic slowdown in 2001, it recorded a growth of over 46 per cent in that year, whereas most international competitor brands clocked only single-digit growth during the same period. The market share zoomed to over 20 per cent during the year 2001–02.

The commercial success was accompanied by other accolades too. Ratings of the Indica V2 by the J.D. Power study, a fiercely independent and widely respected review of cars, jumped dramatically. The 2003 J.D. Power India customer satisfaction study ranked the Indica diesel car as the best in the operating costs category, even ahead of the market leader, Maruti 800. The reputed television programme *BBC Wheels* declared the Indica the 'best car in the Rs 3 lakh to Rs 5 lakh price category'.

The confidence was back, there were big smiles all around. There had been a rather large hiccup, but the team at Tata Motors had proven itself more than equal to it. India's first indigenously designed car had conclusively proven that it was an indisputable success.

MORE THAN THE INDICA

The Indica transformed Tata Motors from a successful truck maker to a modern automobile company, very sensitive to the pulse of consumers. A series of successful cars and SUVs have been launched by the company in the wake of the Indica, including the Indigo, the Vista, the Manza and the Aria. And, of course, the Nano, which has received universal acclaim as one of the most significant innovations in cars after the Ford Model T. Today, Tata Motors consistently occupies either the second or the third rank in the large Indian cars market, and the day is not far when (and here we borrow a phrase from Turin) it will aim to be Numero Uno.

The Indica also served as the perfect catalyst for transforming the car industry in India, ushering in the modern era, in the wake of economic liberalization in the country. It established the supply chain for the indigenous manufacture of cars by developing a range of competent vendors, and collaborating with the best names in the world. This has served as a natural platform for many other global brands of cars to make their entry into India. It re-established Indian pride in engineering and manufacturing. By making India one of the few countries in the world to produce its own indigenously designed car, it emphasized that the engineering sector in the country was alive, vibrant and kicking.

It became a symbol of Indian prowess in developing world-class consumer products. The Indica was yet another pioneering venture by the Tata Group, going where no Indian company had gone before.

THE HEART OF COURAGE

I often wonder: where does such great courage come from? Does it come from deep within outstanding individuals and teams, as they pursue their passions and dreams? Does it emerge from a very strong sense of duty to the country, to society or, in a more limited sense, even to one's family? Or does it simply come from fearlessness, which often lends itself generously to a noble purpose?

Here is what Ratan Tata has to say about the Indica, the spirit and the heart of courage. 'I think we were more brave than foolish actually. Over the years, Telco had introduced a series of products that took to the Indian roads, competed with Japanese products when those were introduced, and found their rightful place in the country.' He was referring here to commercial vehicles made by the company, such as the successful 407 and 709 series, as well as crossover vehicles such as the Tata Estate, Sierra, Sumo and Safari.

'In addition, I had faith in Telco's engineers.' His belief in the company's engineers, particularly the 300-odd young engineers who were raring to go, was an important starting point for embarking on the voyage of the Indica.

'Can we do something that has never been done before? I would like to believe that it can be done. We can make it happen; we just need to make sure that we do it.

'It is important, particularly for the younger people in India, to believe in what we are doing and that we can do much more. I hope the younger generation will take India to new heights, which I am sure they can. They need to believe in and recognize the potential of their own capabilities.'

THE ROAD AHEAD

Fourteen years after the Indica was launched, there are still many big challenges ahead of the Tata Motors cars business. Competition from large international brands with deep pockets and global resources has only got tougher. Achieving larger scale is even more critical today to keep costs low. Consumers have become more demanding, and ensuring world-class quality of products and services is essential. However, for a company that successfully created India's first car, taking a path that was so different, refreshing and challenging, this will only create multiple springboards for many more acts of courage.

WALCHAND HIRACHAND

Excerpts from *Business Legends* by Gita Piramal

is rags-to-riches story is enough to make Walchand stand out from the crowd, but it's what he achieved for Indian shipping that makes the Maratha Jain a legend. When Walchand bought his first steamer—a passenger liner—he innocently expected his entry into this business to be as plain sailing as everything had been for him in the past. But he had set himself up in competition with the British India Steamship Company (BI), the world's largest shipping company. One, moreover, that didn't believe in allowing a little friendly rivalry. As Mahatma Gandhi once said, 'Indian shipping had to perish so that British shipping might flourish.'

When Walchand entered shipping in 1919, India's mercantile marine consisted of a few small tramps serving tiny unknown ports along India's coastline. By the time he died in 1953, he had wrested a 21 per cent share of Indian coastal traffic from British shipping interests. Walchand was forbidden to carry passengers overseas, and 21 per cent isn't much. It meant that BI and the others still controlled 79 per cent of Indian traffic in Indian waters. But it was a start. As Sardar Vallabhbhai Patel once said, 'The triumph of Walchand's life lay in persistence over adversity, faith over scepticism and hope over despair.'

Apart from his achievements in shipping, Walchand built several of India's enduring monuments. His construction firm built the Bhor Ghats tunnels through which trains shuttle between Mumbai and Pune. He laid the huge pipes which bring water to Mumbai from Tansa lake, and built numerous bridges, dams and railway tracks all over the country.

Walchand also built India's first shipyard, first aircraft factory and first car plant. Later the first two were nationalized and the Birlas' Hindustan Motors overtook Walchand's Premier Automobiles—but Walchand will be remembered as the man who pioneered these businesses. Even more remarkable, Walchand founded these businesses often without a silver rupee in his pocket.

Like G.D. Birla, Walchand was born into a family that was, by rural standards, relatively prosperous. Birla's father had two very good camels. Walchand's father had a tonga. Neither listened to the advice of the elders and branched out from the family business. Birla became a jute broker circa 1910 at the age of fifteen. Five years earlier, Walchand, at age twenty, had become a building contractor.

The young Walchand's first job—laying a seven-kilometre railway line—was worth Rs 80,000. By 1939 Scindia was India's seventeenth-largest business house with assets of Rs 3.66 crore. Of the Indian groups, only Tata, Dalmia, Birla and Wadia were bigger than him. According to Ravi K. Hazari, author of the industrial policy resolution of 1976, Walchand's scorching pace established the Doshi group as one of India's top ten business houses by the time India became independent. Group assets in 1953—the year Walchand died—were probably in the region of Rs 70 crore with a net worth of Rs 37.13 crore.

Gandhi once wrote in *Young India*: 'Scindia was conceived as much through patriotism as through ambition.' From its inception, Walchand claimed that Scindia was a national enterprise concerned not only with its own interests but with those of Indian shipping as a whole. Rajat K. Ray, a business historian, agrees. 'The growth of the Indian shipping and shipbuilding enterprise practically meant the growth of Scindia Steam,[1] for even smaller Indian companies survived because of its help,' says Ray.

Mansukhlal Master, chief executive officer of Scindia, emphasizes this point as well. According to him, Walchand saw to it that British interests did not force the exit of small Indian shipping companies. And where possible, he did his best to help them. For example, a steamer of a small Indian shipping firm was impounded by the Bombay Port Trust for non-payment of dock dues. 'Its chairman

---

[1] Scindia Steam Navigation Company was started by Walchand Hirachand and Narottam Morarjee and Company.

needed Rs 5000 immediately to get the ship released; Walchand paid that amount and the company survived and continued to run its ferry service.'

According to Master, when the British wanted to use freight rates as a weapon to drive smaller companies out of the coastal trade, Walchand not only declined to be a party to the move, but actually persuaded the BI director in London to accept arbitration by the government. The opportunities he created helped to keep the smaller shipping companies alive even though Scindia lost a few lakhs every year in the process.

Every time Scindia's flag—a blood-red swastika in a white circle on a blue background—was going to be hoisted on a new ship, Walchand would invite nationalist leaders to do the honours. 'It was the fashion—and the safe course—then for any new concern to seek the patronage of British rulers and high officials,' says N.G. Jog, a Scindia historian. But Scindia ships were launched by leaders such as Vithalbhai and Vallabhbhai Patel, Motilal and Jawaharlal Nehru. 'This association with national leaders may seem a great asset today, but it called for courage in the first thirty years of Scindia's existence.'

Walchand's experience as a military contractor and his later rivalry with Lord Inchcape convinced him that Indian businessmen could never obtain from the Raj the kind of favours British businessmen routinely received. Railing against this discrimination, Walchand energetically provoked the media into highlighting the issue. The stream of articles, editorials and features generated by Walchand's efficient public relations may not always have achieved tangible victories—an example being the failure of Tata Construction to get a portion of the Back Bay Reclamation scheme despite his efforts in this regard—but the emotional appeals to economic nationalism had more than a symbolic value.

The British reacted to Walchand's needling with fury. Among his fiercest critics was Geoffrey Tyson, editor of *Capital*, a Calcutta-based financial magazine. Referring to Walchand's campaigns as 'clever propaganda', Tyson deprecated the 'hundreds of newspaper articles on the subject [of his plans to build cars and aircraft in India], the scores of speeches made by politicians and industrialists and petitions [which] have flowed into Government offices in a steady and swelling stream during the past few years'. Ticking off Walchand for wanting to run before he could walk, Tyson argued that 'the controversy has got far removed from realities. The fact is that until India can design, make and mass-produce her own petrol engine, we will not have a truly indigenous motor industry. And the same thing goes for an indigenous aeroplane industry.'

Tyson had a point. The ventures Walchand was interested in called for sophisticated technology, were capital hungry and required long gestation periods. Walchand wasn't short of daring, but he didn't possess three key requirements: technology, money or patience.

Some felt Walchand was plain foolhardy; certainly, he was often on the brink of going bust. His long-suffering partner, Narottam Morarjee, dubbed Walchand Mr Rightaway Now. 'Some of Walchand's actions were so unexpected that it left his associates bewildered. No time would be given them for reflection,' complained one. And as Walchand flitted from idea to idea, semi-implemented proposals piled up like old newspapers.

A visit to Hollywood enthused him so much that he wanted to set up a film studio. He invited V. Shantaram to join him but the idea never took off. He bought a mining lease which brought him little more than bills. He acquired a foundry which he couldn't manage profitably. He built a sawmill which had to be closed down. Changes in the government sugar policy made him diversify into this field even though his construction and shipping business badly needed funds. This lack of focus perhaps explains why he didn't leave the kind of legacy expected from a man of his genius.

Walchand's entry into shipping was as whimsical as his entry into construction. When a broker sold him the SS *Loyalty*, Walchand really wasn't thinking long-term. He was then an ordinary railway contractor trying to establish himself as a building magnate in Bombay. His mindset was that of a contractor and he had yet to acquire an industrialist's long-term perspective. In his mind, the SS *Loyalty* was a quick-in, quick-out deal to be completed within a twelve-month time frame. None knew—least of all Walchand—that the reckless purchase would turn him into a legend.

As with the Kirkee contract, the shipping idea originated accidentally. Walchand was returning to Bombay from a trip in north India in January 1919 when he bumped into a senior Crompton executive, Mr Watson, on the train. He'd met Watson before, and over lunch the executive casually mentioned that a steamer which had been purchased by the maharaja of Scindia during the war was up for sale. Walchand was so fascinated by the idea of a shipping venture that on reaching Bombay he drove straight to the docks to inspect the ship. Before the day was out he had roped in some friends to pitch in and help him buy it.

At first glance, the shipping venture looked to be an attractive proposal. There was an acute shortage of steamers to England. Civilian traffic, both passenger and cargo, had built up during the four and a half years of war, and Walchand guessed that he could charge any fare he wanted. According to Watson, the *Loyalty* was licensed for another year and new permits would not be required. In gratitude to the maharaja of Gwalior for buying the steamer and converting it into a hospital ship as his contribution to the war effort, the government was ready to help him sell it by making a few concessions. And at Rs 25 lakh, the maharaja's asking price wasn't steep.

Walchand's firm had fattened on army contracts, but not enough to enable him to buy the ship on his own. This didn't pose too much of a problem. Bombay's mill owners had minted money during the war (profits had jumped by 120 per cent to 365 per cent) and were looking for investment outlets. Nor would the money be tied up for too long. Watson estimated that they could easily get their investment back within a year or two. The clinching factor, in Walchand's mind, was that with the end of hostilities, his construction business was likely to see a downturn. He would need extra work and the shipping proposal sounded as good as anything else he'd heard. Perhaps Walchand could be forgiven his naivety: he was barely twenty-seven at the time.

When the train pulled into Bombay's Victoria Terminus, Walchand sent his wife home and went with Watson to the docks to see the *Loyalty*. It was love at first sight. Walchand found her trim construction, the comforts provided for passengers, the coloured glass of her cabin portholes to be 'in princely taste' and very attractive. 'Then and there I resolved to leave no stone unturned in order to buy the SS *Loyalty*,' he would later recall.

Touring the steamer with its captain, Walchand tried to get an idea about the ship's tonnage, the number of passengers she could accommodate, the maximum estimated rates per ton of freight and per man, the cost of a voyage from Bombay to London and the maximum profit to be expected from fares. His rough calculations based on this information tallied with Watson's promise that money invested here could be recouped in a year or two. In his construction business, Walchand normally went into enormous detail, which is why he could so often and so successfully undercut his competitors. Inexplicably, he plunged into shipping on the word of two strangers—one of whom, at least, and possibly both—hoped to earn a large commission on the sale.

The moment he stepped off the ship, instead of going home, Walchand went straight to the office of Narottam Morarjee, the mill owner who had financed the Deolali barracks project. Walchand's prompt and profitable execution of the Deolali contract had given Morarjee a very good impression of Walchand. When the builder arrived unannounced, Morarjee listened carefully to the young man. As Walchand had suspected, Bombay mill owners had made so much money during the First World War that they didn't know what to do with it and where to park it. It didn't take Walchand long to convince Morarjee.

This was on 17 February 1919. The next day, Walchand went to meet two other men of 'influence and substance': Lallubhai (later Sir) Samaldas and Kilachand Devchand. A lawyer from Baroda and one of Bombay bigger financiers, Samaldas (1863–1936) was a professional director on the board of over a dozen blue-chip companies. Active in city politics, Samaldas was on the Governor's Executive Council, had been president of the Indian Merchants' Chamber (1917–18), joined the Council of State in 1920 and became revenue member of the Governor's Council in 1923.

Kilachand Devchand (1855–1929), better known as Bombay's 'Rice King', was a leading Gujarati trader. Kilachand had chartered steamers to export goods during the war and so knew something about shipping rates, but neither he nor Samaldas were at first convinced about the profitability of Walchand's proposal. 'However, in view of Narottam Morarjee's very high standing in the mercantile community and his financial strength together with Walchand's energy and ability, they supported the ship-purchase plan,' said one record.

Working overtime, in just under six weeks, the four partners paid the maharaja, took possession of the ship, floated Scindia Steam Navigation Company, appointed bankers and auditors, rented an office in Ismail Building on Hornby Road, and formed a new managing agency firm. Scindia's managing agency firm was the newly formed Narottam Morarjee and Company. Half its profits (and losses) were Morarjee's, while Walchand's share was four annas to the rupee (25 per cent). Samaldas and Kilachand's stakes were two annas each. Morarjee was chairman.

It had an eight-member high-profile board: apart from Morarjee, Walchand, Kilachand and Samaldas, the other directors were Ratansi D. Morarjee (Narottam's nephew), F.E. Dinshaw (solicitor, financier and Tata director), C.E. Randle (Bank of Baroda) and A.J. Raymond (E.D. Sassoon). Its secretary was Mansukhlal A. Master, seconded from Morarjee's office. Scindia was listed on the Bombay Stock Exchange on 27 March 1919 with an authorized capital of Rs 4.5 crore, of which the promoters wanted to raise Rs 1.5 crore.

The Scindia offer was one of the largest public issues of the time. In 1907 Sir Dorab Tata and his brother Sir Ratan had floated a record-breaking Rs 2.32 crore for Tata Steel. During the Tata issue, the Swadeshi movement had encouraged hundreds of small investors to put their money in steel, but the bulk of the issue was subscribed by a handful of well-heeled professional investors. The same was probably the case in Scindia's offer.

The Tata issue—Morarjee, incidentally, was a founder-director of Tisco—was just about subscribed. Scindia's promoters collected a little over Rs 1.87 crore. It was an overwhelming response. But it's not easy to understand the enthusiasm when the sad story of Indian shipping was so well known.

In the past sixty years several Indian entrepreneurs had tried to establish shipping companies, but not one had survived the ruthless competition from British firms such as the British India Steam Navigation Company (BI) and P&O Company. In 1870 a group of traders from Surat had tried to establish a service between Chittagong and Rangoon for the Burmese rice trade but were forced into liquidation. According to the BI, they 'retired on a more thoughtful consideration of the strength of the British India Company and its up-to-date vessels'.

In 1892 Jamsetji Nusserwanji Tata, the legendary founder of the biggest Indian business house, started a steamer service between India, China and Japan. In retaliation, three British companies operating these routes cut their rates from Rs 19 per ton to Rs 1.5 and Tata withdrew licking his wounds. The next casualty was a Madras-based company which went bust in 1904. A couple of years later, Chidambaram Pillai, a Keralite trader, promoted the Swadeshi Steamship Company.

Plying between Tuticorin and Ceylon, Chidambaram managed to stay afloat for almost five years. As usual, BI cut its rates, but Pillai received 'feverish patriotic support', says Rajat K. Ray, a historian of the commercial Raj. 'Finally, BI and British officials, including port authorities, deliberately sabotaged the Swadeshi line. Several "accidents" were engineered in which its ships were rammed both in port and at sea. Official influence was used to deter customers and the Swadeshi line's office was harassed by minute checking and rechecking of its accounts.' Not only that, Pillai was arrested for his political activities and, in his absence, the shipping company folded up. BI's sanitized version is that the Swadeshi line 'failed largely through lack of experience in ship-management'.

An Indian contemporary account noted that most of the 102 Indian shipping companies registered between 1860 and 1925 with a total capital of Rs 46 crore went into liquidation one after another. BI considered the early 'story of the Indian effort in the field of shipping and of the little freight and rate wars that inevitably ensued, as long and really rather tedious'.

But public memory is short; it was boom-time in Bombay, and in 1919 people flocked to invest in Scindia. One possible explanation for the mad scramble for Scindia shares could lie in the name Walchand had chosen for the new enterprise.

Apparently many people assumed—wrongly—that the Gwalior durbar had a stake in Scindia Steamship. In fact, neither the maharaja nor the state of Gwalior had anything to do with its financing or running. 'Possibly, Walchand intended, by naming his shipping company after a leading royal house, that the various Indian maharajas, princes, sardars, zamindars and so on should look on it as their own and give it their protection,' suggests one account. 'Rightly or wrongly, Walchand was attracted to big names,' says an old family friend, 'and this frequently had an adverse effect on his reputation but it didn't make a difference to him. He still went ahead. It was all quite deliberate.'

Earlier, Walchand had been disappointed with Morarjee's refusal to name Scindia's managing agency as 'Morarjee Goculdas and Company' after the mill Narottam's father had promoted in 1871. Walchand wanted to cash in on its blue-chip status.

Having collected the money, the partners paid the maharaja and took possession of the *Loyalty*. The next step was to reconvert her from a hospital ship back to a passenger liner. Inquiries with one ship-repairing firm disclosed that the work would take six months and cost Rs 10 lakh. The ship's transport licence was for only one year. If they couldn't earn any revenue for six months and the remaining six months' earnings were consumed by the cost of repairs it would be impossible to recover their money 'in a year or two'. Walchand's lack of homework was beginning to show.

On further investigation, Walchand heard that if the repairs were executed in England, they could be done in six weeks for Rs 1 lakh or 1.5 lakh. Without confirming these details with an English company and booking a shipyard, Walchand decided to get essential makeshift repairs done in Bombay, fill the ship with passengers, sail to London and complete the repairs in England. His bubbling enthusiasm convinced even the cynics on the board.

When Scindia announced her maiden Bombay–London service via Marseilles, it received an overwhelming number of bookings. Yet, on the day of sailing many applicants failed to appear, including some 'rajas, maharajas, sardars, nawabs and so on.' Many berths were left empty and since Walchand had rather naively not taken advances, the anticipated revenue was short by nearly Rs 1 lakh. Also, assuming berths to have been fully reserved, Walchand had disappointed some of his own friends. 'It was a distressing situation but beyond remedy,' he told Narottam and the others. 'A definite sailing date had been fixed and it wouldn't be proper to extend it.'

The *Loyalty* left for London on the afternoon of 5 April 1919. That morning, Mahatma Gandhi had called on Morarjee to bless the new venture and wish it all success. After Independence this date would be celebrated as National Maritime Day. 'Apart from those who had come to see off their friends and relatives, there were hundreds of people who had thronged the wharf simply to wish bon voyage to the first Indian passenger ship sailing to Europe. An emotional upsurge overtook the passengers and onlookers alike as the SS *Loyalty* sounded the last siren and pulled up her anchor,' reported a journalist covering the scene.

As the shore faded, Walchand's distress was allayed by the joy of going to Europe on his own ship. It was his first trip abroad. Many people had failed to turn up but there were still several celebrities on board. Maharaja Hari Singh of Kashmir was there along with the maharaja of Kapurthala and his Spanish wife, the thakur saheb of Limbdi with his three sons, Prince Dilipsingh with his cousin Ramsingh, the thakur saheb of Bhavnagar, Sir Chunilal V. Mehta, the chief justice of the Bombay High Court and his wife, M.C. Chagla, the famous lawyer and, of course, Narottam Morarjee, accompanied by his seventeen-year-old son Shantikumar, who was to be enrolled in Harrow.

The *Loyalty* berthed in Marseilles eighteen days later, where most passengers disembarked since the ship needed urgent repairs. It had been smooth sailing so far but, ominously, Walchand and Morarjee found it difficult to hire agents for the end-of-voyage cleaning up, of unloading cargo and reloading with fresh cargo and all the connected operations. It didn't take them long to figure out why. Wherever they went, the story was the same: nobody wanted to upset BI and its chairman, Sir James Mackay.

JAMES MACKAY

Walchand's adversary was a man of similar qualities and character as himself, who grew up in a harsher school of life. Born in a middle-class Scottish family, James Lyle Mackay (1852–1932), later Earl Inchcape, dropped out of school when he was orphaned at the age of twelve. Since he had a neat handwriting, he managed to get a job copying documents at a solicitor's firm. Bored with the job, he became a clerk in a rope factory. Four years later he was in London, clerking at Gellatly, Hankey, Sewell and Company, shipping, insurance and forwarding agents. This was in 1872, when Mackay was twenty years old. The Suez Canal had opened barely three years earlier and British shipping was expanding. Mackay was in the right place, at the right time and in the right business.

One day his boss asked him if he was willing to go to India and join Mackinnon Mackenzie in Calcutta. Three others were asked as well, but Mackay was the only one to agree on the spot. He got the job. Mackinnon Mackenzie ran BI, which by the late 1880s had a virtual monopoly over mail, cargo and passenger traffic in the Indian Ocean and the Arabian Sea. The company's founder, William Mackinnon, was now an ageing senior director who had made his money and wanted to retire. He was looking for fresh talent to take over the running of the company. Mackay was quick to assess the situation.

Once he knew the business, Mackay was sent to Bombay, where he spent four years increasing the firm's profits. When he returned to Calcutta in 1880, it was to take charge of Mackinnon Mackenzie. He stayed there for twelve years and shuttled between England and India for the next eight. His influence expanded beyond business while he was in India through his appointment to various posts, among them membership of the viceroy's legislative council. He returned to England in 1901, where, as BI chairman, he engineered its merger with the P&O in 1914. Under Mackay's leadership BI became the world's biggest shipping company.

During the First World War, Mackay helped the government not only by buying war bonds but also with ships and commercial advice. As a reward he was first made a viscount and later became Earl Inchcape of Strathnaver in 1929. By the time Walchand entered shipping, Mackay was already one of Britain's ten richest men and nicknamed 'the Napoleon of Shipping'. John Morley, as secretary of state to India, recommended Mackay for the viceroyalty, but Prime Minister Asquith turned down the suggestion. Such was the man Walchand thought to challenge.

Living in Bombay and still on the periphery of the business elite, Walchand didn't know much about Mackay and cared less. He was much more worried about getting a seaworthiness certificate from Lloyd's for his steamer. By the time the *Loyalty* docked in London, it needed repairs badly. Of equal importance was to find and appoint a capable clearing agent. Once again, Walchand's lack of homework and rash management was evident. Inquiries and appointments could have been made in Bombay. Had he done so before setting sail, he would have been better prepared for the reception he got in London. After the Marseilles experience, he knew that the BI and Mackay would create difficulties, but he 'never thought that they would be so savage and murderous'.

As Walchand and Narottam started their rounds of shipping agents and shipyards, the rejections mounted. Even after a dozen rebuffs, they refused to give up. There was little choice. They had raised money in India, they had tied up their own money in the venture, how could they cut losses if they gave up? And what about their reputation and the loss of face? Narottam had been abroad earlier, in 1912–13, but it was Walchand's first trip abroad and neither wanted to go back defeated. There had to be a shipyard which would undertake the *Loyalty*'s repairs. The lad from Sholapur in his poorly cut worsted-wool suit kept up the hunt. His relentless effort finally bore fruit. One day he met someone who had little love for James Mackay, a man named Kennedy.

Kennedy was a partner of Gellatly, Hankey and Company, where Mackay had once been a clerk. In the old days, Mackay and Kennedy used to sit at adjoining desks. The head of BI had forgotten his old colleague, but Kennedy hadn't forgotten Mackay. When Walchand heard that Kennedy knew Mackay, he asked him to try and set up a meeting. Mackay refused to meet Walchand but Kennedy succeeded in wrangling an appointment for Walchand with Sir William Crawford Currie. Currie was a senior BI director who would become BI's sixth chairman in 1938.

Walchand sent a complete account of the meeting to Scindia's board of directors in Bombay. Currie had told him that BI looked upon Scindia's intrusion into their field as 'downright piracy', wrote Walchand. He had been warned against using 'shameless bluster and a fat purse'. BI had built their business 'through years and years of infinite toil and devotion', Currie had said, 'and the sooner you remedy your mistake the better. Otherwise you will go the way of your predecessors.' Walchand ended his report by adding, 'The night is dark; but keep watch, and be ready to greet the dawn. From now on, difficulties are likely to come one after the other.'

The poetry failed to inspire at least two of his partners. One exclaimed that they had been trapped. This was a clear warning not to succumb to Walchand's blandishments, said another. The necessity of allaying the board's uneasiness added to Walchand's problems. Had it not been for Kennedy's attitude, Scindia might have gone under. Far more supportive than Samaldas or Kilachand, Kennedy accepted Scindia's work though his firm normally handled cargo ships and not passenger liners. And he made arrangements for the *Loyalty*'s repairs. His desire to bring down Mackay a peg or two might have influenced Kennedy's decision, but that didn't concern Walchand and Morarjee.

What did keep Walchand awake at nights was that his original estimate of the *Loyalty*'s repairs was way off the mark. Once again Walchand was paying the price of his impetuousness. In Bombay he had been quoted Rs 1 lakh to Rs 1.5 lakh. In the event it was

Rs 7 lakh. And 'six weeks' became over five months. There was no way that Scindia's first profit and loss account would be in the black. Walchand consoled himself with the reflection that at least his ship was being repaired.

A PALACE COUP

Forced to kick his heels in London, Walchand hired a Miss Sweet as his secretary and began studying BI's profitability and that of shipping in general. He made a short trip to Holland to see the shipbuilding yards there. As information poured in, he became convinced that this was the business to be in. Now every difficulty and obstacle Walchand encountered, instead of frightening him off, made the stocky Maratha dig in his heels. Clearly, he couldn't fight Mackay or run a shipping company with just one steamer. He had to buy more ships.

As he looked around he heard that the Palace Shipping Company in Liverpool was trying to hawk its entire fleet of six medium-sized cargo steamers for a million pounds. At current prices, it was an attractive offer, particularly as some steamers were already on fixed charters and thus brought in a steady income. Walchand calculated that the remaining ships could be very profitably deployed along India's coastline. Sitting in Bombay, Scindia's board wasn't even mildly tempted. After their experiences with the SS *Loyalty*, they were in no mood to expand. In London, Walchand couldn't understand his partners' nervousness and refused to give up the idea. 'Walchand knew precisely when and how to bait his hook for any man and thus in one way and another he won over his partners and eventually secured their consent,' a director later recalled wryly.

Curiously, soon after Walchand had placed a deposit on the ships, an article appeared in *Fair Play*, a London shipping magazine. The feature roundly criticized 'Indian merchants who had entered the field . . . were incapable of maintaining shipping standards . . . and [whose] hopes were doomed to final frustration'. Walchand went to meet the editor to present Scindia's side of the picture and win him over.

Walchand came out of *Fair Play*'s office having made a friend but also extremely worried. Apparently ship sales were governed by a Defence of the Realm Act (DORA) which stipulated that anyone outside Britain wishing to buy a steamer had to first obtain the shipping controller's sanction. Davidson, the broker negotiating the Palace Shipping deal, had not once mentioned DORA. Walchand had already paid £100,000 as earnest money. Could he lose the money and the ships?

When he asked Davidson this question, the broker brushed it aside. 'That old Act? Why, the war's over. It can't apply today. In any case, it's part of the seller's responsibility, not the buyer's.' The answer didn't satisfy Walchand and he set up a meeting with *Fair Play*'s editor. 'What business had you,' Davidson chided the editor, 'to put the wind up for nothing by bringing up an imaginary section of DORA? A man like you should have known better.' The editor heard him out in silence, then extracted a copy from the cupboard behind him. The section was there in black and white. For the first time, Walchand was shaken.

Pulling a fistful of strings, Walchand managed to get appointments with Sir Prabhashankar Pattani and Sir Bhupendranath Basu, both councillors of state, begging them to suggest a way out of his difficulty. Unable to help directly, they nonetheless arranged a meeting for him with Lord Montagu, then secretary of state for India. Rebuffed by Montagu, Walchand called on the shipping controller, a Mackay crony. 'You must pay the penalty of your mistake,' he was told coldly. 'This transaction has to be cancelled. There's no help for it.'

Characteristically, Walchand refused to give up. With his back to the wall, Walchand bombarded the India Office with questions. Don't we Indians count as British subjects? How can you apply this section of DORA to the British empire? India had supplied more men and money to the war effort than all other colonies. If it were applied, wouldn't it have an undesirable effect on India? The new political reforms have already raised suspicion about your intentions. This incident could intensify these suspicions. It might even provoke a conflagration, he warned.

Walchand's threats hit home. India was a powder keg after the Jallianwala massacre of April 1919 and Mahatma Gandhi's agitation against the Rowlatt Acts. To keep Walchand quiet, a face-saving device for everyone was quickly discovered. Scindia could buy the Palace Shipping Company and not just the ships. Walchand duly applied for approval, and the shipping controller duly attached his approval to the sale. He also added the rider that Scindia couldn't buy more ships, that the Palace ships had to remain on the British registers for the next six months and that British taxes were paid.

BACK TO BOMBAY

There was now nothing more to keep Walchand in England but the SS *Loyalty*. The Palace Shipping Company's takeover formalities had been wrapped up. The shipyard finally informed Walchand that the *Loyalty* was ready to sail. All that remained was to get fares for the homeward voyage.

No sooner did this news flash round shipping circles than the phone rang at Scindia's newly appointed clearing agents, Gellatly, Hankey and Company. 'If I hear that the SS *Loyalty* has got even one passenger through you, understand that from that moment you lose the BI's support,' threatened the voice at the other end. This was not a warning that Kennedy, who'd already put himself out on a limb to help Walchand, could ignore.

Remembering the hoary adage, self-help is the best help, Walchand advertised 'Passengers Wanted' in the local newspapers, hired an extra room in the hotel he was staying in, and became his own clerk. Within days he had all 352 passengers he needed. This time Walchand presumably took advances on the fares. Getting 1500 tons of cargo to fill the *Loyalty*'s holds and provide ballast was a more difficult task. Walchand wrote to several firms exporting machinery to Bombay, but none of them were prepared to send their goods on a Scindia ship.

'Even Tata Steel lacked courage,' recalled Walchand, 'and where a strong firm like Tatas refused, what could the smaller units do?' Richardson and Cruddas, a large engineering firm, at first placed an order for the ship's entire capacity but later withdrew its offer. Even with every berth filled with passengers, without ballast the steamer could not sail. Sir James Mackay's plan had succeeded. Unwilling to be thwarted, Walchand, with Morarjee's backing, bought 1000 tons of cement and 500 tons of pig iron to fill the holds. They would sell this cargo in Bombay and recover what they could.

Walchand sailed back to Bombay on the *Loyalty* towards the tail end of 1919. Pacing the deck, Walchand counted the days he had been away. It would be good to be back.

SUBROTO BAGCHI

Excerpts from *Go Kiss the World* by Subroto Bagchi

ADVENTURES IN DCM

By spring of the next year, time had begun to drag its feet. All my friends were pursuing the more proven path while I had jumped off from the train at an unknown junction, not knowing where I was going or when the next train would arrive. It created a sense of loneliness. I couldn't shake the feeling I was on the cusp of change. Studying law was just marking time. In Bhubaneswar, anyone could enrol for a law degree irrespective of educational competence. Working in the secretariat for two long years before I could sit for the civil services examination seemed like an endless tunnel. I needed a proper job. I needed a career, which was not the civil services because that meant waiting, being a burden on someone. And in any case, the civil services did not mean much to me. I kept applying for any job for which I could remotely justify my eligibility. So, when I saw an advertisement from the DCM group for management trainees, half unsure that they would even consider me with a political science degree, I applied. A few days later, I received a call. After a round of aptitude tests, group discussions and interviews at the regional level, I made it to the finals. I think what paved the path for me was the fact that the head of DCM's management training programme, Colonel Kucchal, probably liked the 'best NCC cadet' bit in my resumé.[1] Maybe it was something else. After the final round of interviews at the regional level, I was told I needed to go to Delhi for the national-level selection.

---

[1] In 1975 (a few years before the interview), Bagchi was chosen as the best NCC cadet of the country.

My friend Anup Mohapatra lent me his jacket and a good shirt and a tie. DCM paid first-class train fare from Bhubaneswar to Delhi for me to attend the interview. I boarded the Utkal Express to Delhi with great expectations. It took two long days. From my first-class berth, I watched the world go past me as the train wound its way through the lush green forests of Madhya Pradesh and the ravines of the Chambal valley, past the vast fertile fields of Uttar Pradesh, past the historic city of Agra, to finally pull into Hazrat Nizamuddin Railway Station in posh south Delhi. Throughout the journey, I couldn't escape the feeling that I was being taken to where I would finally belong.

The final interview was conducted in an imposing boardroom at DCM's corporate office by the entire top management. Eighteen men, including Dr Bharat Ram and Dr Charat Ram, the two managing directors and heirs of the founder Lala Shriram, peered down at the candidates. The panel included Dr Bansi Dhar, deputy managing director, and the legendary Mr Dharma Vira, whose claim to fame as the erstwhile governor of West Bengal was that he had sacked a chief minister named Siddhartha Shankar Ray. My interview began with a conversation on the power of conflict. Soon it moved to a discussion on the theory of karma in the Bhagavad Gita and then to Hegelian dialectics. I felt it was my day; I was cruising.

I returned to Bhubaneswar; the offer to join the DCM group as a management trainee arrived in the post. Being selected was seen as a great achievement. The DCM group ran one of the most coveted management trainee schemes in the country and paid rather well. The starting salary was more than three times what I was earning as a lower division clerk. Armed with the trunk my father had given me when I was a schoolboy, a few hundred rupees arranged by Amitav,[2] a basic set of clothes and old bedding, I took a train to New Delhi to report for work. I had been assigned to Delhi Cloth Mills—the oldest textile mill in the group. Located in the shabby area of Bara Hindu Rao, it sat between what is New Delhi and Old Delhi. The road in front of the mill started from Bara Hindu Rao on one end and went towards

---

[2] Amitav is Bagchi's brother.

Kishen Gunj, where many of the millhands lived in dilapidated, low-cost housing. People on the road jostled with horse-drawn carriages, pushcarts, makeshift tea stalls and squatters. During the change of shift, thousands of workers would pour in and out, many dressed in no more than striped long underwear and a fatua, a compromise between an undershirt and a shirt with a pocket in the front to keep the attendance card, small change and some chewing tobacco. The air was thick with vehicle exhaust, the smell of horse and cow dung, beedi smoke and communism. One look at the place was enough to make a true-blue, pedigreed MBA run away. But I wasn't true blue and pedigreed and the secretariat in Bhubaneswar had prepared me well to feel quite at home in a non-glamorous setting. Delhi Cloth Mills, my workplace for the next five years, was a far cry from the opulent boardroom where I had been interviewed but relevant to the discussion on Hegelian dialectics in a somewhat convoluted manner.

I started my training in the time office. At the gate of the mill, at the blast of the siren, thousands of workmen, some barefoot, some semi-clad, would march in with their attendance cards in hand. They had the smell of beedi and sweat from the previous day's work and their struggle for food and sleep in the ghetto-like worker's colony. They handed over the attendance cards to clerks with thick glasses sliding down their noses. The clerks sat under whirring fans black with accumulated soot. They marked the workers' struggle for yet another day, payable as wages, in a large register.

After learning how the time office worked, I shifted to the pay office where the wages were calculated, then I went to train on the shop floor where the bales of cotton became spun yarn, learnt how they were woven into warps and wefts before being dyed and printed and then cut into metres of cloth that would be packed in bales to be transported to hundreds of destinations, before finding their place in retail showrooms that flaunted neon DCM signs, to eventually drape a nation. For an entire year, I worked in various departments of the factory. I also learnt the demand side from a more sophisticated marketing department that generated the indents, housed outside the factory in air-conditioned offices. I went to see how actual trade took place in the bylanes or sarais of Chandni Chowk in Delhi where wholesalers and retailers haggled, cheated each other, worked and laughed together. In between, they ate hot samosas and *matthi*, and drank *banta*, a soda drink in a bottle with a marble ball in its neck that made a mini explosion when opened.

After just a few months on the job, management trainee salaries were further revised. I was now earning one thousand eight hundred rupees a month—six times what I had made in the government. My friends were still in college and here I was remitting money home dutifully every month. I used to address the money-order form to my mother and each time the receipt came back signed by her, I marvelled at the steady signature that masked the fact that she was actually a woman whose eyesight had been permanently robbed by destiny.

What similarities exist between the days that I spent at the secretariat and those that I live at MindTree[3] today? How does the work there resemble my work here? Or for that matter, does the world in which I live and work at this stage of my career even remotely resemble the sights, sounds and smells of Kishen Gunj, off Bara Hindu Rao, Delhi, 1977?

Our lives are like rivers—the source seldom reveals the confluence. Does a river fret over the long journey and about its end just as it is about to spurt? It simply does not do that, caring instead to flow, to begin its journey, and on its way builds a beneficial relationship with anyone who comes in contact with her.

After a year of on-the-job training, a management trainee was designated as an officer on special duty. This involved becoming an understudy to a senior manager and some real work. I was asked to report to Mahesh Chand Bahree who was the works secretary of Delhi Cloth Mills.

On my arrival in his office, I was greeted with a mixture of warmth and apprehension.

---

[3] Bagchi is one of the co-founders of MindTree, a global technology services company.

'Sonny boy,' said Mahesh Chand Bahree, adjusting his trademark dark glasses and thrusting his big chest forward, 'my principle in life is: Killer, get killed.'

Bahree was a powerful man who had come up in life the hard way. Starting life as a textile engineer, he had lost one eye when a spindle had gone right through it on the shop floor. After that accident, he was given administrative work and he now looked after a wide range of commercial functions. The man was extremely knowledgeable and competent. But at some level, he was also insecure. Someone had told him that I had been made his understudy to eventually replace him. The principle about elimination of a potential adversary which he greeted me with was in that context.

But I liked the man. He had a certain aura, an earthy charm and undeniable competence. Above all, he treated 'small people'—drivers, peons, loaders—with respect and camaraderie. He spoke to illiterate workmen in their language, cracked jokes with them, but pulled them up when required. He knew each and every worker's family background. His knowledge of government regulations made even government officials treat him with respect. He did not have children and I missed my father. So, when he used to call me 'sonny boy', I loved it. After a few weeks of working with each other, he became comfortable enough to lower his guard and I ignored the veiled threat he had held out on the first day. We became a great team.

Every morning, even before the siren would signal the start of the general shift at 9 a.m., I would pull into the parking lot on my brand new Yezdi motorcycle, pretending it was a MiG-21 fighter aircraft, to see Mahesh Bahree already waiting there. He always arrived before me. A big man, he dressed carefully to appear casual and irreverent. Towards that end, he wore a bush shirt and never tucked it in. His overall demeanour would have qualified him to be a general in any army.

Mahesh Bahree was never alone. Even at that early hour, there would be a couple of people around him. It could be a worker who was on his way to the spinning department, an excise inspector, a colleague from marketing or a security guard. What fascinated me was how they were all attracted to his presence, and as they stood casually chatting with him for two, five or ten minutes, he was actually debriefing them. Mahesh Bahree knew everything that was going on in the mill, all the time.

After I had safely manoeuvred the make-believe MiG-21 into a parking position and taken my flight helmet off, the big man and the boy-man would make a round of the factory. He had two alternative starting points for the walking tour. Either we would begin at the cotton godown or at the coal yard—they were at two ends of the vast smoke-stack factory, separated by a few kilometres. Between the two points was the unending shop floor that converted cotton into yarn, yarn into woven cloth, dyed the woven cloth in different colours, printed it, sized and packed the bales before stacking them in the warehouse. This warehouse was Mahesh Bahree's territory. So was the coal yard. The factory could not depend on the irregular supply of electricity from the Delhi Electric Supply Undertaking, a government undertaking. Coal was required to generate power and steam that the plant needed for certain operations. The supply of coal had three government agencies involved—Coal India that mined the coal, the Railway Board that allocated the wagons for transporting the coal and the zonal railway departments that brought the coal from the mines to the plant. It was a difficult combination to manage and the plant always remained hand to mouth in the supply of coal. If the coal did not arrive on time, the cotton was useless. It was Mahesh Bahree's job to ensure that the coal yard was always full. The godown where the cotton was stored did not come directly under his purview, but its load level told him how much coal was required. At any point of time, he knew what the marketing forecast was and what the cotton stock actually looked like, and then he did the math in his head on how much coal his men needed to arrange for. He could have read the MIS report on his table; his job did not require him to walk to the coal yard and cotton godown every day. But he preferred getting his information hands-on.

During the one-hour walking tour every morning, Mahesh Bahree would acknowledge a steady stream of greetings. With some he would exchange a few words, with others he would share a joke, and some he would acknowledge with merely a grunt. If any of the recipients was a character of significance, he would tell me all about the person and what to expect of him. He was like a big burly bear teaching his younger one the ways of the jungle.

Like many great men, Mahesh Bahree too had an Achilles' heel. He had a soft corner for one of his section heads who took undue advantage of his proximity to the boss. The man had a group of assistants under him, who themselves were very undisciplined and unionized. Bahree, inexplicably, tolerated them right under his nose. Instead of working, Bahree's favourite section head used to loiter, run errands for Bahree and sometimes just sit in front of him doing nothing. As fate would have it, the group was asked to report to me. The section head was used to working directly under Bahree and thought I was a notional boss who would simply humour him. He had no idea that I disliked my subordinate hanging out with my boss as his primary activity, day in and day out. I did not play ball and tension began to brew. Things came to a head one day when he made disparaging remarks about the company's management in front of a visitor in my presence. He was the boss's man and much older than me, but I was not going to take this lying down. I demanded that he be transferred from the department to the shop floor for his inappropriate remarks unless he apologized to me. Mahesh Bahree was in an awkward situation. He referred the matter to his boss. Having taken a stand, I had to see things through to their logical end. I informed my bosses that they had twenty-four hours within which to transfer the man out or else I would be putting in my papers. When the deadline expired, I submitted my resignation.

The prospect of unemployment loomed large. I spoke to Amitav and told him what had happened. Still struggling to get his own professional toehold and barely able to make both ends meet, he simply said, 'Come singing back.'

Life sometimes deals you a blank cheque. However, it pays to defer its encashment. Rather than return to Bhubaneswar, I decided to wait for the system to respond. Next morning, the phone on my desk rang. I was being called to the new executive director's room.

The DCM group had diversified into chemicals, rayon, foundry, computers, automotive and many other businesses. In addition, there were a whole bunch of businesses like electrical equipment and refrigeration under the Shriram name. The DCM group had originated with the pioneering efforts of an industrialist, Lala Shriram, who was no more. His two sons, Dr Bharat Ram and Dr Charat Ram, owned the various businesses with clear demarcation between them. Both were very different people, with vastly different leadership styles. Dr Bharat Ram's businesses included textiles and within that, among several mills, was Delhi Cloth Mills. It was the mother unit set up by Lala Shriram. However, it was also in a state of decay that no one seemed to be able to stem. When I joined in 1977, there was a young and dynamic general manager named H.N. Chaturvedi. Despite all his efforts, things only got worse. Into my second year, the owners decided to bring in Brihaspati Dev Pathak to replace Chaturvedi. Pathak, who was in charge of the rayon business, had been with the company since the days of Lala Shriram, had shown great calibre and was trusted by all the family members. He had the reputation of having successfully run Delhi Cloth Mills at one time and it was felt that he could turn things around.

Brihaspati Dev Pathak had arrived amidst much hope and fear—hope for a turnaround, fear for what may happen if it didn't. As a sign of respect, he was addressed as 'Pathakji' by everyone. Cynics, however, called him 'paon choo Pathak', alluding to his love for people to bow down and touch his feet as a mark of sycophancy when he moved around the factory. He was also known to listen to a group of cronies, had a flaming temper, a pronounced hatred for smoking and alcohol and, some said, Punjabi managers. Mahesh Chand Bahree was a smoker, enjoyed his drinks in the privacy of his own home, made no bones about it and was a Punjabi.

Pathak was a freckled, small, old man, but had the energy of a bull. Once, on a trip with him to see the rayon plant at Kota, Rajasthan, he invited me to stay in his house. He ran his business like a spiritual dictator. While driving to Kota, his driver suddenly braked because a cat crossed the car's path. That is considered a bad omen in any part of India. If a cat crosses the road, most drivers stop, back up a few yards and then start again to neutralize any evil. When his driver did this, Pathak admonished the driver, dramatically adding, 'Don't stop the car. Let the cat wonder whose path she was trying to cross today.'

Having made up my mind to leave DCM rather than cower in front of my boss's sidekick, I was now sitting across Brihaspati Dev Pathak, a man more than three times my age and in the ultimate position of power. After listening to my explanation, all he asked was, 'Have you ever seen a seed sprouting from under a big boulder?'

'Yes, sir.'

'When the seed is under the huge rock, who has the upper hand, the greater power?'

'The rock, sir.'

'Precisely. The relative balance of power is in favour of the rock. The rock can crush the sapling. The sapling, however, does not assert itself, does not fight the rock; it gently circumvents the rock and keeps growing along its side. And one day, that same sapling has become a huge tree. At that time, where do you think the rock sits?'

I kept quiet.

'It remains at the feet of the tree forever.'

The message was clear. As a sapling, I was choosing to fight the rock. Pathak wanted me to circumvent it. I took back my resignation, walked to the errant man's desk and gave him a hug.

Pathak's taking over the plant resulted in no magical turnaround. Workers, staff and managers became more political; gossip and backbiting multiplied like lice. Then the textile unions in Delhi gave a call for a strike, demanding a total relook at the prevailing wages. The management of the already bleeding Delhi Cloth Mills decided to take the issue head-on and all negotiations failed. Six thousand factory workers went on strike. It was an unusual experience for me to see a lockout declared in a factory. With spying and counter-spying, there was a deadlock between management and workers. The workers took turns to sit in front of the main gate as a sign of protest. Days turned into weeks and soon it was clear that the strike may even last six months. The company was running out of cash, there were prior sales obligations and unmet export commitments while thousands of bales of cloth lay inside the mill. A court order allowed the company to move out all the finished goods but the question was how to take them out while the unions blocked the main gate?

Mahesh Bahree suggested moving trucks to the coal yard behind the plant and moving the bales of cloth out through a back gate at night. No union worker would bother to go there. I was assigned to supervise the movement of goods under cover of darkness. It would have been quite possible but for the long distance between the finished goods warehouse and the coal yard and the only way of moving the cloth bales was to use manual labour. The effort was so huge that after one night we were able to move out only a couple of small truckloads. We gave up the idea. More than twenty truckloads of finished goods were waiting inside to be evacuated.

The only option that now remained was to storm the front gate, take the picketing workers by total surprise and clear the goods from the warehouse before the workers realized what was going on. The workers' colony was some distance from the mill. The predicted response when the picketing workers discovered what was happening would be to run to the colony to bring other workmen, their spouses and children and create a human blockade that would not allow the trucks to leave. That could lead to violence. The police were willing to cooperate with us on one condition. They would give us protection, for just one hour, but if anything went wrong, they would not use force against the striking workers.

Mahesh Bahree was willing to take the gamble but it required a reconnaissance trip inside the plant to plan the minute-by-minute manoeuvre. It had to be foolproof. We only had this one chance for success. Bahree could not be seen anywhere near the factory as every picketing worker would recognize him. I volunteered to go in there dressed as a security officer. The law guaranteed full protection to the plant's security personnel. It was at once a daring and a juvenile plan. If the trick failed, I could get lynched. Anything could happen thereafter. Mahesh Bahree thought for a while and gave me the go-ahead.

The very next day an official-looking car pulled up in front of the main gate with me dressed in khaki uniform, sunglasses and a peaked cap pulled over my face. The strikers gave contemptuous looks and went about their game of cards. I was inside.

On the designated day, twenty trucks escorted by the Delhi Police moved in. There was one hitch though. The police had guaranteed us protection for one hour only inside the premises. Once the loaded convoy was out of the gate, they could not give protection; it was a risk the management would have to bear. The story went that in another mill striking workers had run after the last vehicle of a convoy and set it on fire. That was a real possibility, of people jumping on to the last truck and resorting to arson. It was too late to worry about that risk now, but I sensed that it created fear in the minds of the truckers. Who would be willing to be the tail of the convoy? I looked them in the eye and said I would be on the last truck—not with the driver in his cabin. I would ride in the back. A cheer went up, the truckers jostled to be the last so they could have Bagchi saab as their *khalasi*, the driver's sidekick who sometimes rides the load.

The operation was completed, not giving enough time for the strikers to react in numbers. The convoy rolled out. It was the first and last time I had the privilege of sitting on the back of a loaded truck riding the roads of Delhi.

Mahesh Bahree's greatness was in trusting a twenty-two-year-old management trainee with an operation whose success was less than certain. He taught me to take risks, to allow people the freedom to try things out without the fear of consequences.

LAUNCHING MINDTREE

With hindsight my decision to join Lucent Technologies was a bad one and the blame is largely mine. It is interesting how high achievers bent upon making a wrong decision produce convincing arguments and these then begin to take on a life of their own. I had spent ten years in Wipro and in that time had learnt many things. One of the high points during those years was the time I spent in the corporate office during which I learnt about Total Quality Management. Now I wanted to learn all about Innovation, because it was the next frontier. What better place, I argued, than Bell Labs which filed nearly 3.5 patents a day? Bell Labs, after the split from AT&T, was now owned by Lucent and one division was setting up a software development centre in Bangalore. The people who 'sold' me the job did suggest that it was the Bell Lab Development Center. In reality, it had nothing to do with the legendary Bell Labs and all the assignment required was a middle-level manager to assist the head of the centre, an expatriate manager from the US. It took me exactly a week to realize that it was yet another multinational company's software development centre with the additional twist of being an extremely political organization. Each day at work became increasingly difficult for me. But hadn't I been responsible for choosing this company, the change in my career and an environment that wasn't right for me? Why had I not done due diligence before taking the bait?

In the Panchatantra, there is a story of a poor Brahmin who sees an old tiger in a forest. The tiger has a golden bangle in his paws and offers it to the man. The man is frightened and doesn't want to go near the tiger. The tiger moans that he is too old to hunt and kill and is now at the end of his life. He is toothless and his claws have all but fallen. The tiger wants to make penance by offering the bangle to a good man so that he can atone for a life of violence. He requests the Brahmin to take a dip in the pond nearby and receive the bangle from him so that he can breathe his last. The animal sounds so genuine, the poor Brahmin pities the tiger; he believes the story. He enters the pond, only to get stuck in the mud. The tiger promptly devours the Brahmin. The question is: Who killed the man? Is it the tiger or the man's greed?

What were the real factors that pushed me to change my job? I can add more reasons to the list, apart from the ones given earlier. In reality, high achievers are also their worst enemies and sometimes make near-fatal mistakes. I was going through a mid-life transition whose impact neither I nor the organization I worked for understood. Some of the issues that bothered me could have been raised by me candidly; some would have sorted themselves out in time. The solution did not lie in accepting an assignment in an organization I was temperamentally not suited for. It was too large a risk at forty.

As the ghost of Innovation started to take on a life of its own within me, I went a step further. I told people that I would work for just five more years, focussing on Innovation as a theme, and then move on to doing four things for the rest of my life: read, write, travel and teach. I was romanticizing the idea. But look at the inherent stupidity of the idea: given today's life expectancy, people work well past their sixties! And here I was, saying that I would hang up my boots at forty-five. On top of that, do reading, writing, travelling and teaching really require a job change? Doesn't any senior-level corporate job allow you enough time to do these things without the need to quit altogether? But who can argue with one's own self?

I sold three hundred vested Wipro shares for three hundred rupees each and walked out of another two thousand shares that were unvested. In the following three years, the value of that holding, after several splits, would have been worth a few million dollars, thanks to how Wipro's stock fared. When I joined Lucent, its shares were trading at around hundred dollars apiece. In the same period, their price went down to one dollar a share. While my salary at Wipro was half of what Lucent paid me, the stock gain would have covered the salary differential a few hundred times over. But all this is realization with hindsight. At that moment, when I changed jobs, I wanted to learn about Innovation.

Saying goodbye to senior colleagues at Wipro was not difficult. It was devastating saying goodbye to the thousands of junior colleagues who looked up to me. Many thought of me as a role model. In a telling moment, one colleague, Tanaz Kadwa, barged into my room. She was in anger and pain and about to cry. She looked me sternly in the eye and said, 'So, even god has feet of clay,' and without waiting for my response, left, banging the door behind her. I was speechless; I was guilty and judgement had been delivered.

There is nothing more painful in life than to see your gods fail. The teacher you once loved and respected and considered the last post of integrity turns out to be an ordinary, vulnerable, favour-seeking man. The honest-to-the-core role model in the family turns out to be nothing more than a self-serving individual putting on a façade, whose sense of morality is specific to a given time and space. It is the inevitability of growing up without which we cannot become complete human beings. Yet, I feel the convulsion each time my gods fail. And many years after Tanaz stormed out of my room, I remember how I failed Tanaz.

Azim Premji had warned me that I would have a tough time dealing with internal politics in a large multinational company and he turned out to be prophetically accurate. On the one hand, India was opening up to many great opportunities and, on the other, internal power play among Lucent's many business units made it difficult for the company to scale new heights in India. It was clear to me that I was wasting my time. Though joining Lucent turned out to be a poor decision, the time I spent there was useful in two ways: it gave me the opportunity to reflect on the emerging service economy and the role Indian software companies would play in it. It also caused enough pain for me to pursue the idea of starting out on my own. Nothing works better than the promise of a great future and the simultaneous sensation of standing on a burning bridge.

On 17 June 1998 I reached out to Krishna Kumar (KK), an erstwhile colleague at Wipro, who was chief executive of their newly formed electronic commerce division. I had great admiration for KK. I had watched him work from a distance and felt that the two of us would make a great team. Following a phone conversation, we met in Karavali restaurant in Bangalore for lunch. There we agreed that we were destined for something larger than what we were both doing and decided to create an aspirational organization that would be higher up the value chain; an organization that would be value-centric, socially connected and based on the principle of shared wealth creation. The idea of MindTree germinated that day. As MindTree was born and grew over the course of the next decade, it seems to us that it is indeed the purpose for which life was preparing us, one experience at a time. For me, MindTree became the bridge between who I was and who I was meant to be, from making it big in life to making it good.

At first, it was just a dream. Between June and August of 1998, KK and I met almost every night. On weekends, he and I would take our bikes and go cycling into the wilderness behind the development where we lived. We would sit under huge rain trees, talking about how to set up a great company. We decided to expand the group of co-founders and I spoke to Namakkal Parthasarathy whom I had left behind at Wipro's global R&D division. We also reached out to a couple of venture capitalists who showed preliminary interest in our ideas. In August that year, my work took me to New Jersey where Lucent had its headquarters. A chance meeting there with Anjan Lahiri, an ex-colleague who had migrated to the US, led to the expansion of the seed team. Through Anjan, we added Kamran Ozair and Scott Staples to the team. They were working with Anjan at Cambridge Technology Partners. On my return to India, I spoke to my colleague Rostow Ravanan at Lucent and he readily agreed to join as the finance expert. An ex-KPMG hand, he brought strategy and finance knowledge that the team would need in the days to come.

We decided to get together as a team to flesh out the mission, vision and values of the company of our dreams. We took time off from our respective jobs and drove down to Visakhapatnam on the Bay of Bengal coast, a little more than a thousand kilometres by road from Bangalore. For over a decade, I had been fascinated with the beach there—my first visit was on behalf of PSI to present a plan to the Indian Railways for computerizing locomotive maintenance. I had fallen in love with the beauty and seclusion of the rocks along the coastline. There was something special about the place; for some reason, I liked to think of it as a sacred space. Come Christmas Eve 1998, we drove down in two cars all the way from Bangalore; Anjan flew down from the US. We holed up at The Park hotel for a whole week—it was where I had stayed on my first visit. We took breaks only to eat and sleep; the conversations were intense. We plastered conference room walls with ideas on flip-charts. We took turns at facilitating discussions on how to match our individual needs, our personal goals, our strengths and limitations. We talked about the unfolding opportunities around us and what it would take to create value out of them and then spoke about the mission, vision, values and differentiation for the yet-to-be-born corporation. At the end, we thrashed out a preliminary business plan. Armed with a PowerPoint presentation, we returned to start scouting for venture capital.

By February 1999, the list of venture capitalists we were talking to had grown. It was some coincidence that two old friends, Som Das and Sudhir Sethi, had in the meantime joined Walden International, a Silicon Valley venture firm. Som and Sudhir started showing interest and encouraged us to fine-tune the business plan. In March, I was again sent to the US and met Som and Sudhir to close the deal but what Som told me sent me for a spin—Ashok Soota had decided to leave Wipro to begin something on his own. Ashok and Som's acquaintance went back to the latter's days at VLSI and Ashok had asked if Walden would be interested in funding him. Som had agreed in principle but had also told Ashok that someone he knew well had progressed significantly on a similar plan with Walden. Ashok being Ashok, had guessed that it was me. Som suggested Ashok combine forces with us to build one company. Ashok thought that Som should speak with me first. It was a miracle. No one in his senses would ever have imagined Ashok leaving Wipro! Here was one of the most respected people in the industry willing to join hands with us! It took no time for KK, Rostow, Partha, Anjan and I to confabulate on this new possibility. Scott and Kamran did not know Ashok and had very little understanding of the dynamic, leaving their part of the thinking to Anjan. We all agreed that Ashok would be the perfect leader for us and we intimated Walden that we would merge our ambitions and, all things being equal, would like them to be the lead venture capitalist. We got our second venture partner, V.G. Siddhartha of Global Technology Partners, with Ashok's coming on board. (Siddhartha went on to found the Café Coffee Day chain.) We settled the valuation of the company and raised 9.5 million dollars by giving away 44 per cent of the company. We kept aside 16.67 per cent of the ownership for future employees; the rest was to be held by the founders.

When word broke in July that Ashok was quitting Wipro and that we were coming together to form a new company, the story hit the headlines. For weeks together Bangalore was agog with excitement. Prior to Ashok coming on board, I had reached out to Kalyan Banerjee, another ex-colleague at Wipro, who had promptly agreed to join. After Ashok's decision to leave Wipro, Srinivasan Janakiraman, known as Jani, who was at the time chief executive of Wipro's global R&D, was desolate. When I had moved out of there to join Premji's office, I had handed over the mantle of chief executive of global R&D to Jani. He told Ashok that with my departure from Wipro, he had lost one wing and now with Ashok going away, the other one had been clipped. He just didn't want to stay behind at Wipro. Ashok asked me to meet him to talk him out of the idea or get him in as the tenth co-founder. Consequently, Jani and I met at Cubbon Park in Bangalore and after a short conversation it was clear that our paths were destined to be the same. With Jani, the founding team was complete.

Years later, it has become clear to me that professional respect for each other, a shared value system and middle-class upbringing is the glue that has held this team together. We all come from very modest backgrounds. And all of us are first-generation entrepreneurs.

Ashok's father was a colonel in the Indian Army. KK's father was a doctor in the railways. Jani's father was a village postmaster. Partha's father was a travelling ticket collector on trains. Rostow's father was an accountant in a brewery. Kalyan's father became a geologist and spent all his life in the coal mines. Scott's father was an air force pilot who eventually changed careers to become an accountant and his mother was an elementary school teacher. Anjan's father served in the army and Kamran's father was a civil engineer in Pakistan. Looking back, our past gave us an unspoken code of conduct, a certain inbuilt capacity to work hard and a shared understanding of why we had decided to be in this together.

After Ashok came on board, we revisited the business plan several times: it was now time to find a name for the company. We decided to go about it in a professional manner, engaging a company in California called Name It that went through our mission, vision, values and business plan and then engaged their contributors all over the world—they came up with 729 possible names. From these, we whittled down a shortlist of ten and voted for MindTree. Later, a friend of Ashok told us to our delight that MindTree is *manovriksha* in the Upanishads—the eternal provider of intellectual solutions! With the name chosen, we now had to think of a visual identity. We decided to ask a group of children with cerebral palsy at the Spastic Society of Karnataka to come up with the visual.

My personal association with the cause of cerebral palsy started when I returned from the US in 1993. While working in the Valley, I was amazed to see the extent of corporate involvement in local communities. Many corporations took active interest in local affairs, in issues ranging from education to health to affirmative action. The idea went well beyond charity; it was about creating inclusion, learning from each other and harnessing the power of the organization to channel volunteerism. On my return I requested Dr Mitta to give me a cause to work on, in addition to my job at Wipro. He introduced me to the Spastic Society of Karnataka. I had no idea about cerebral palsy, autism or other such neuro-muscular conditions.

During my very first visit to the Spastic Society school in Bangalore, I met Sheena Watson, a visiting art teacher from Ireland. She was painstakingly trying to teach young children with cerebral palsy to hold a paintbrush. For her, it was not just an effort to make the children creative; it was therapy for a more fundamental problem—muscular control. For each of these children, holding the brush was an effort to teach the hand, eyes and face to obey the brain. I stood transfixed as each child held the brush, dipped it in paint and laboured to produce brilliant pieces of art. Probably because many of these children cannot speak or express themselves without severe effort, their paintings have extraordinary vibrancy. The colours are spectacular and spontaneous—as if compensating for the gaps of an unseen god. It was also a moment of great self-realization for me. These children were, as they were painting, not focussed on their disability but on their dreams.

While thinking through the formation of the company, we had not only thought through our mission, vision and values, we had also decided that our DNA would be imagination, action and joy. Weeks before the launch of MindTree, when we had decided to speak to the Spastic Society of Karnataka, we asked them to allow us to interact with the children for a week so that we could explain to them the idea of MindTree and then work with them to create the visual identity of the company based on the DNA of imagination, action and joy.

After a few days of running a workshop on what is a company, why a company has a logo and, above all, what kind of company MindTree intended to become, the children got down to designing. Initial designs were disappointing. The children had understood the word MindTree quite literally. But we did not give up. Another workshop was conducted to give the children an appreciation of many famous logos and they were encouraged to discover subliminal meaning in them: they were required to interpret values in the visual identity of a brand. Then the magic happened. Something clicked, as if a combination lock had suddenly snapped open in their minds. From labour on their faces, we could now see the delight of discovery. From among the ten designs we received, it wasn't difficult to pick up the astounding work of seventeen-year-old Chetan, who said in support of his work that the upward blue stroke in his creation stood for limitless imagination, the red background denoted action and the yellows were 'bubbles of joy'.

As a token of our appreciation, we gifted five thousand shares of MindTree to the Spastic Society of Karnataka. Another student, Latha, who had captivated us with her smile, became our first receptionist. When Bill Clinton visited India as President of the United States of America and met with CEOs of IT companies, we took Chetan along to meet him. President Clinton autographed

Chetan's logo. Every MindTree facility we have subsequently designed is a museum of art produced by the children of the Spastic Society of Karnataka.

Having tied up the founding team, the venture capital, the name and the logo, MindTree opened for business on 18 August 1999. Ashok Soota was chairman, I was chief operating officer, KK took on the role of president of IT services and Jani as president of the R&D services business.

DHIRUBHAI AMBANI

Excerpts from *Business Maharajas* by Gita Piramal

Ambani's opportunity to break into PFY manufacturing came when the Indira Gandhi administration threw open the doors of this business to the private sector in early 1980. This was the moment Dhirubhai had been waiting for and Reliance applied immediately for a licence. So did forty-three others. Ambani knew he could build a great plant but pitched against him were the heavyweights of Indian industry: the Tatas, the Birlas, the Bangurs, the Garwares, the Mafatlals and the Thapars. It was then believed that amongst those whose opinion counted in the selection process were Veerendra Patil, the then petroleum minister, and Pranab Mukherjee, who headed finance. According to the grapevine, four business houses had been shortlisted during the first round, but Ambani's name was not on it.

However, when the selection process was finally over, the winner was Reliance. The surprising decision left the Mehras of Orkay, the Jindals, the Singhanias and the Mafatlals out in the cold. On the cocktail circuit, gossip linked the government's decision with Dhirubhai's formidable political contacts, symbolized by a lavish party which he hosted in a New Delhi five-star hotel for Mrs Gandhi immediately after the January 1980 Lok Sabha elections. This was a crucial election which saw the end of the Janata Party rule (1977–80) and Mrs Gandhi's triumphant comeback despite the excesses of the Emergency (1975–77). Dhirubhai's party was almost Mrs Gandhi's first public engagement after becoming prime minister.

Kapal Mehra's name apparently had been on the shortlist. According to Perez Chandra of *Business India*, 'The Mehras of Orkay had to make a representation to Mrs Gandhi to get a licence. They were eventually granted one in 1985 but even then the licence of 10,000 tpa that Reliance got was more than 40 per cent above that of Orkay. In addition, Pranab Mukherjee's parting gift to Dhirubhai included a licence to expand capacity to 15,000 tpa.'

Dhirubhai disputes the suggestion that his political links played a role in Reliance getting the licence. 'My proposal was financially better structured,' he claimed. 'I told the government that I was putting my company's own resources, and that the others would have to borrow from the financial institutions. My main edge was that we could mobilize our own resources.' But what about Pranab Mukherjee's role? Didn't he help to get this and four other projects cleared? 'People who wanted to criticize Pranab Mukherjee used me as gunpowder. Pranab was in the finance ministry, which does not issue licences. Also, how many people have got licences in India, and how many have implemented these licences? The country should salute people who implement projects quickly.'

Dhirubhai had already built up a reputation for quick project implementation. Earlier, he had set up a worsted spinning plant within eight months of getting a licence. At Patalganga, where Reliance acquired an area twenty times larger than necessary for the polyester filament yarn project, the villagers didn't know what hit them. The PFY plant came up in eighteen months. Perhaps the best accolade came from Richard Chinman, the then director of Du Pont International: 'In the US it would take us not less than twenty-six months to erect and commission such a project.' Later, when building its huge petrochemical plants at the Patalganga and Hazira (Gujarat) complexes, Reliance would be driven by a sense of urgency because it couldn't afford cost overruns. Ambani, like Aditya Birla, knew that delays in project implementation could tip profits into losses. And once plants were up and running, they had to work at full capacity, round the clock.

To help him build the PFY plant, Dhirubhai pulled his eldest son Mukesh out of Stanford where he was studying for his MBA and dropped the untried, untested twenty-four-year-old chemical engineer from Bombay University into the deep end.

'My father told me: "You will take this over and I will only give you one person from Reliance. Everybody else has to be new,"' recalls Mukesh. 'So a team had to be established, we had to select the right technology. The first thing that happened was that I came to the office and found there was only one person with whom I would work for ten or fifteen years. Gradually we got the other people. We are a very professional set-up.

'When we started the plant, everybody was recruited on merit. We advertised and we were very proud. The credit for this decision should go to my father. I told him that it's a Rs 100-crore project and shouldn't he hire a guy who has worked twenty-five years in the polyester industry and maybe pay him Rs 20,000 per month. He said: "No, you do it. If you think you're going wrong you come back to me but go ahead and do it." That's the kind of encouragement that is required today. Initially everybody was pessimistic, everybody I talked to said it's difficult. But we went in with an open mind and tried our very best. We were on stream in forty-eight hours.' On November 1, 1982, bare months after the bear raid which made a legend out of his father, another Ambani won his spurs.

In selecting technology for the plant, father and son honed in on USA's Du Pont de Nemours. Explaining their choice, Mukesh said: 'We already had a good working relationship with them, so it's not that Du Pont did not know Reliance. We used to buy fibres from them. We made a presentation to them about what we wanted to do and also told them this could be an opportunity we were losing. If we didn't do it, somebody else would. They kind of stuck to the idea. After setting up our plant, their business with India has grown— they've sold technology to five joint sector projects. It was the right decision for them.'

To get Du Pont to sell him their technology, Dhirubhai promised everything but equity. 'Technology is available for the asking in the international bazaar,' pointed out Dhirubhai.

'So why do I need to make a foreign company my partner and give them 51 per cent?'

Some Indian businessmen seek tie-ups with global giants for technology, a few to share risk and others for funds. Ambani's need for the latter lessened as the government reduced restrictions on local companies. As he said, 'Now I get my rupee funds from my investors. For my foreign exchange requirements, I can access the international markets. But we are open to consider joint ventures where we have an active role to play.' By 1994, Dhirubhai had negotiated over fifteen collaborations with the world's best companies but he refused to take on any of them as a partner.

Like Rahul Bajaj, Ambani hasn't taken partners because he could never play second fiddle. And Dhirubhai likes to move fast. He could never accept the conditions under which B.K. Birla worked in Century Enka, a synthetic yarn maker and a joint venture between the Birlas and Holland's Enka International. 'At Century Enka, everything needs Enka's approval,' said S.P. Sapra.[1] 'Enka is used to the slow growth European environment. So they are incrementalist and cautious. They slow down the Birlas . . . If Dhirubhai had created an alliance with Du Pont everyone in India would have said, "Great, he has got Du Pont in India." But it would have slowed everything down.' And passivity is anathema to Dhirubhai. D.N. Chaturvedi, a long-time financial consultant, understates the case when he says, 'Once a decision has been taken, Dhirubhai becomes an impatient man until the project is implemented.'

As a Burmah Shell clerk, Dhirubhai recognized that 'whatever information must come, must come'. As an exporter, he had had to overcome the reluctance of foreign buyers worried about Indian companies and their unpredictable delivery schedules. Perhaps that's why Dhirubhai named his company Reliance. He met every commitment on time, regardless of cost. Narayan, president of the textile division, provided an example. 'In 1973, the rotary machine at Naroda broke down on a Friday evening. The import of the component to be replaced would have normally taken two or three months. So I went abroad the same night, bought the component and got it back on Sunday night and the plant was in production from Monday afternoon.'

To meet Dhirubhai's deadlines, Mukesh's young project team discarded several established business practices in favour of unconventional methods which have now become part of Reliance's

---

[1] S.P. Sapra—President of Reliance's polyester staple fibre division.

corporate culture. One of these was letter writing and paper shuffling, which Mukesh sought to abolish totally. 'Problems were discussed at face-to-face meetings with contractors and decisions were communicated directly. If each contractor were to write to the other and then to us, we would have wasted valuable time,' said Mukesh. Another tenet dispensed with was that of choosing the lowest bid in a tender. 'Sometimes we accepted tenders which were two and a half times higher than the lowest bid,' he recalled. Reliance's criterion was whether the contractor could deliver on time.

In his climb to the top of the corporate ladder, Dhirubhai had already absorbed and adopted the two key strategies of self-reliance and speed. In implementing the PFY project, Ambani adopted two other co-related strategies: size and sales. He would use this set of four values over and over to drive Reliance's spectacular growth.

At a time when the size of the PFY market was 6000 tpa, Ambani built a 10,000-tpa plant with a built-in provision for a further 15,000-tpa expansion. According to H.T. Parekh, who as head of ICICI sanctioned Reliance's first institutional loan, 'Dhirubhai always spoke of international standards and sizes. Initially I admit that I had some doubts whether he would really be able to carry it through. But he has disproved me by his resourcefulness.'

Most businessmen, uncertain of demand, played safe by building small plants. Ambani turned the concept on its head. According to Sapra: 'Dhirubhai would systematically remove the barriers that were constraining demand.' In the case of PYF, Ambani felt that there was tremendous latent demand, but that it was curbed because at the time the government reserved PYF for small-scale weavers in the 'art-silk' industry. The big mills had to use cotton. This was the key barrier to consumption and a limited market.

To get round this problem and stimulate demand, Ambani launched a 'buy-back' scheme where Reliance sold its 'Recron' brand of yarn to small powerlooms who then sold the grey cloth back to the company for finishing and eventual sale under the Vimal brand name. In a sense this was a repeat of the Naroda experience where Dhirubhai had used powerlooms to get round government limitations on production. He would also repeat the careful nurturing of suppliers just as fabric vendors had been nurtured during the hectic days of 1977–80 which saw a new Reliance outlet opening virtually every day.

Huge capacities in a relatively underdeveloped market put intense pressure on Reliance's sales and marketing teams. 'We gave a fantastic amount of financial support to the little weavers,' said Sapra. 'We gave them ninety days credit to create demand.' Once the positive loop of supply-led demand creation became fully operational, the company would revert to its tight-fisted operating policies. 'Today, 90 per cent of our sales is on cash basis. Whatever we ship today, payment is received by 2 p.m. tomorrow.'

By 1983, PFY had replaced textiles as the major revenue earner in Reliance's portfolio. Ambani kept adding to capacity, upgrading technology and modernizing. 'This continuing growth allowed Reliance to emerge as the lowest-cost polyester producer in the world,' says Ghoshal.[2] 'In 1994, its conversion cost was 18 cents per pound as against the costs of 34, 29 and 23 cents per pound for West European, North American and Far Eastern producers.'

Before this happened, there was a major hiccup. On the night of July 24, 1989, a vigorous monsoon downpour filled to overflowing the nearby 'apology of a river' and Reliance's Patalganga complex was damaged by flash floods. Technical experts from Du Pont flown in at considerable cost estimated a minimum period of ninety to a hundred days before the complex could be operational again. Local newspaper reports, based on the opinion of India's best experts, were even less optimistic. Reliance had the entire complex fully functional in twenty-one days.

K.K. Malhotra, head of manufacturing operations, explained how they did it: 'Understand the havoc. After the water receded, we had to remove 50,000 tonnes of garbage—silt, dead animals, floating junk—before we could get to the actual recovery work. All our sophisticated electronic and electrical equipment had been under water for hours . . . We set up a control room to connect the

---

[2] Sumantra Ghoshal—Head of strategic planning at London Business School.

site with the outside world. Then we took time to carefully look at
the damage and quantify the work. Based on that quantification, we
set up objectives for each plant, when it would be on track. Each
day at 11 a.m., I would have a meeting for an hour to review the
work. On the third day, I asked the Du Pont people, "What do you
think?" We had planned to get our two huge compressors ready in
fourteen days. They said, "Out of two, if you can get one ready in a
month, you will be lucky." I phoned Mukesh that evening and said,
"I want those guys out of here. If they say this, it will percolate . . .
it will break the will." We had the compressors one day ahead of
schedule, and the whole plant going a week ahead of plan.'

The real secret to speed, according to Malhotra, lay in two things:
careful planning to quantify tasks and then saturating the tasks with
resources. 'Most companies do not quantify the tasks, do not quantify
the resources required . . . Anyone who says we will do this in twenty-
four months has not done a proper estimation, for only by accident
can the real requirement match such a nice round number . . . We
assess the requirement precisely.'

He continues: 'And then, once the plans are done, we saturate
resources. We put in the largest amount of resource that the task can
absorb, without people tripping over each other . . . If I had all the time
in the world, I would optimise. But given my opportunity cost of lost
production, it almost does not matter how much it costs because, if I
can get the production going earlier, I always come out ahead . . .Only
when you put the value of time in the equation do you get sound
economics and then saturation almost always makes sense.'

'And, finally, we follow the dictum: coordinate [operations]
horizontally, when in trouble go vertical. That dictum—both parts of
it—are also vital for speed.'

While Mukesh was proving his mettle at Patalganga, Anil (a
chemical engineer from Bombay's KC College) was studying for an
MBA in marketing at Wharton. On his return to India in April 1983,
Dhirubhai sent him to Naroda to cut his eye-teeth. 'I left America
in four hours flat after writing my last examination paper,' recalled
Anil. 'When I came home I said, "Dad, I've graduated." He said, "No

big deal. Come on, let's go to office." I asked, "There's no rest, no holiday?" My dad said, "Nothing doing, no holiday."'

Events in Delhi, however, were spinning at Mach 1 velocity. Hardly had Anil established a regular routine for shuttling between Bombay and Naroda than the government finished processing Dhirubhai's applications for the manufacture of four new products calling for fresh capital investment of almost Rs 8bn. Once again Patalganga was humming with activity as the brothers began implementing two of the approvals.

JAMSETJI TATA

Excerpts from *The Creation of Wealth* by R.M. Lala

At the age of forty-three in 1882, Jamsetji read a report by a German geologist, Ritter von Schwartz, that the best situated deposits of iron ore were in Chanda district in the Central Provinces, not far from Nagpur where he worked. The area named was Lohara, after the iron ore deposits nearby. In the vicinity, Warora had deposits of coal. Jamsetji is believed to have visited Lohara himself and obtained specimens of Warora coal for testing. He took a consignment of coal with him and had it tested in Germany. The coal was found unsuitable. The mining terms offered by the government were too restrictive and Jamsetji gave up the project. But the idea of giving India a steel plant abided with him.

For the next seventeen years Jamsetji maintained a book of cuttings on minerals available in India. A steady flame burnt in his heart before blast furnaces were to be lit in Jamshedpur. In 1899 the Viceroy, Lord Curzon, liberalized the mineral concession policy. The same year, Major R.H. Mahon published a report on the manufacture of iron and steel in India. Mahon said that the time had come to establish an iron and steel works on a considerable scale. He suggested that the Jharia coalfields in eastern India would provide the necessary fuel. For iron ore he suggested Salem district in the South, Chanda district in the Central Provinces, and Bengal.

The next year, Jamsetji was in England seeing the Secretary of State for India, Lord George Hamilton. Hamilton had respect for him. The idea of the steel plant which Jamsetji unfolded sparked the imagination of the British statesman. Jamsetji said he had first thought of the idea as a young man. Now he was sixty and blessed with more than enough for his needs. If he undertook this project it would be for the sake of India. Could he expect the support of the government, Jamsetji enquired. Hamilton assured him and wrote accordingly to Lord Curzon.

Speedily Jamsetji instructed his office in Bombay to obtain prospecting licences, and proceeded to the U.S. himself. He wanted the best technical advice. He studied coking processes at Birmingham, Alabama, visited the world's largest ore market at Cleveland, and in Pittsburgh met the foremost metallurgical consultant, Julian Kennedy. Kennedy warned the enthusiastic though ageing Indian that even preliminary investigations would cost a fortune and there was no guarantee of returns. If, said Kennedy, a thorough scientific survey was made of raw materials and conditions, he would build the plant. He suggested the name of Charles Page Perin as the best man to undertake the survey. To Perin, Jamsetji went.

Perin later described his encounter:

I was poring over some accounts in the office when the door opened and a stranger in a strange garb entered. He walked in, leaned over my desk and looked at me fully a minute in silence. Finally, he said in a deep voice, 'Are you Charles Page Perin?' I said, 'Yes'. He stared at me again silently for a long time. Then slowly he said, 'I believe I have found the man I have been looking for. Julian Kennedy has written to you that I am going to build a steel plant in India. I want you to come to India with me, to find suitable iron ore and coking coal and the necessary fluxes. I want you to take charge as my consulting engineer. Mr Kennedy will build the steel plant wherever you advise and I will foot the bill. Will you come to India with me?'

I was dumbfounded, naturally. But you don't know what character and force radiated from Tata's face. And kindliness, too. 'Well,' I said, 'yes, I'd go.' And I did.

Before Perin arrived, he sent his partner Weld to prospect for the raw materials.

Geologist C.M. Weld arrived in April 1903 and set out for exploration with Dorab Tata and a cousin Shapurji Saklatvala, who was elected to the British House of Commons. Chanda district was one of the finest for shikar. The trouble was they were not hunting for tigers but for iron ore. They travelled by bullock-cart. Clean water and food were difficult to obtain, they were often compelled to brew their tea with soda water. As days went by, the immensity of the task they had taken on began to dawn on the prospectors.

Weld was meticulous in his observations. Initially, iron ore and limestone were found but Chanda district was short of the right type of coal. Even the iron ore was in pockets and not in continuous areas. So, sadly, the Chanda scheme was abandoned.

Weld was all set to go home and any businessman other than Jamsetji would have tried to cut his losses on an expensive consultant. But Jamsetji invited him to stay on, and explore for iron ore, coal and fluxes irrespective of location. Weld said that he then realized that Jamsetji was inspired by something far greater than the desire to merely amass a fortune.

The next signal came from an unexpected quarter at the very moment Dorab Tata went to tell the chief commissioner of Chanda district that Tatas had abandoned the prospecting at Chanda. As the commissioner was out, Dorab Tata aimlessly drifted into the museum opposite the Nagpur Secretariat, to await his return. There he perceived a geological map (in colour) of the Central Provinces. On the map, at Durg district, 140 miles from Nagpur, dark colours indicated heavy deposits of iron ore. To Durg did they repair.

As they climbed on the hills of Dhalli and Rajhara, their footsteps rang with the sound of metal. They were walking on a hill of the finest ore in the world—67 per cent iron. Coking coal and limestone were needed, and, above all, a steady supply of water. But water there was none. So they had to look elsewhere. Their labours were not wasted. Fifty years later those very hills were to furnish the ore needed for the steel plant at Bhilai.

Again the hand of fortune intervened. A letter arrived from an Indian geologist, P.N. Bose, who had originally marked the Durg area for ore. Now working for the Maharaja of Mayurbhanj, he had discovered rich iron ore in the state. It was within range of the Bengal coalfields and the ruler was keen to develop his state. In the wooded hills where elephants roamed and tribal Santhals eked out a precarious existence, the lofty Gorumahisani Hill rose to 3000 feet. It was a superb storehouse of iron ore later estimated at thirty-five million tonnes, with an iron content of over 60 per cent. Other neighbouring hills were also rich. All the prospects were pleasing, but where was the water? A reservoir proposed had proved impracticable. The search went on. Early one morning Weld and his assistant, Srinivas Rao, plodded down a dry stream on their horses. It was heavy going through the sand. 'At length we came upon a sight which filled us with joy; a black trap-dike, crossing the river diagonally, and making an almost perfect pick-up weir. It seemed too good to be true.'

Weld and Srinivas Rao clambered up the river bank shouting with excitement. They found themselves close by the village of Sakchi near the meeting point of the two rivers, Kharkai and Subarnareka ('gold-streaked'), which, together never run dry. A couple of miles away was the railway station of Kalimati. They had come to the end of their search. Three years earlier Jamsetji had passed away at Bad Nauheim in Germany, but his dream was to outlive him.

Tatas had braved the jungle; now they had to brave the financial world. It was initially suggested that capital for such a large and pioneering project would have to come from the London money market. In 1907, the London market was passing through a bad patch and financiers in London also wanted to exert control if they were to invest.

Some faint-hearted souls said India would not be able to raise the considerable capital. Tatas decided to take the plunge into the Indian market, and issued their prospectus to raise Rs 1.5 crore in ordinary shares, Rs 75 lakh in preference shares, and Rs 7,00,000 in deferred, a total of Rs 2.32 crore. From early morning till late at night people besieged Tatas' offices in Bombay and within three weeks 8000 investors had subscribed. The hidden wealth of India surfaced for her first great industrial adventure. From this amount of Rs 2.32 crore a steel plant of 1,00,000 tonnes capacity plus the township was set up.[1]

Jamsetji's company had obtained concessions for iron ore, rail freight, and had taken the risk and the burden of the exploration. All the concessions were turned over to the new Tata Iron and Steel Company for an allotment of Rs 15 lakh worth of shares in the new company and Rs 5,25,000 out-of pocket expenses to be reimbursed in cash which Tata Sons put in equity, adding Rs 4,75,000 of their own money. The total Tata stake was Rs 25 lakh—about 11 per cent of the total capital subscribed.

Between the two rivers, a city had to be planned. As the jungles were cleared, in place of towering trees, steel chimneys arose. At the same time, in another part a township grew.

Though the Maharaja of Mayurbhanj had given highly favourable terms to Tatas, the local 'kings' of the jungle were less hospitable. Tigers killed two tribal labourers. An elephant driven frantic by the din of dam construction stampeded over a number of huts and flattened them. One night a bear crawled into the hut of the railway superintendent and delivered a cub under his table!

Erecting a plant of this nature in the wilderness was called by contemporaries 'a titanic enterprise'. Communications were slow; machinery was hauled over vast distances from home or abroad; labour had to be trained. There was then no pool of technicians or scientists at home to draw upon.

In the early stages, coal was not of uniform quality; designs of furnaces were found unsatisfactory. Even the German crew for the blast furnace was not up to the mark. Charles Page Perin was summoned again from America.

The chief commissioner for the Indian Railways, Sir Frederick Upcott, had earlier told Perin: 'Do you mean to say that Tatas propose

---

[1] In the 1980s, modernization of the Tata Steel plant of 2.1 million tonnes cost Rs 1000 crore, and an additional capacity of 6,00,000 tonnes will cost Rs 1500 crore in the 1990s. This is not only a measure of the new technology but also indicative of the fall in the value of money.

to make steel rails to British specifications? Why, I will undertake to eat every pound of steel rail they succeed in making.'

On 16 February 1912, the first ingot of steel rolled on the lines of the Sakchi plant amidst much rejoicing. During World War I Tatas exported 1500 miles of steel rails to Mesopotamia. Dorab Tata commented dryly that if Sir Frederick had carried out his undertaking, he would have had 'some slight indigestion'.

In December 1916, a confident chairman of the company was to speak to shareholders of: 'Bumper earnings; production 30 per cent above original design . . . ready and willing markets . . . order book full to bursting.' The success was intoxicating. An ambitious programme was taken in hand to expand the steel capacity by five times. The expansion programme ran into stormy weather. Spiralling post-war prices, transport and labour difficulties completely upset price calculations. It seemed the stars were conspiring to crush the fledgling enterprise. Japan was the largest customer of pig iron. An earthquake struck Japan and prices fell. The faint-hearted reeled under the misfortunes. One director suggested that the government be asked to take over the company. Thereupon R.D. Tata,[2] a cousin and colleague of Jamsetji, sprang to his feet, pounded the table and declared that the day would never come as long as he lived.

One day a telegram came from Jamshedpur that there was not enough money for wages. R.D. Tata and Sir Dorab Tata (who was knighted in 1910) struggled to raise funds. In November 1924, the steel company was on the verge of closing down. Sir Dorab pledged his entire personal fortune of Rs 1 crore, including his wife's jewellery, to obtain a loan of Rs 1 crore from the Imperial Bank of India for a public limited company. It was touch-and-go whether the firm would survive.

---

[2] There were two Ratan Tatas—one was Ratan Dadabhai Tata, the father of J.R.D. Tata, who was related to Jamsetji. The other was Jamsetji's second son, Sir Ratan. When Tata & Sons was founded in 1887, the three original partners were Jamsetji, Dorab and R.D. Tata. Jamsetji's son Ratan, quite young at the time, was made a partner later.

Sir Dorab's readiness to sacrifice was honoured by providence. Soon, the first returns from expanded production came in and gave the company a breather. Meanwhile, a new threat had arisen from the dumping of foreign steel. Thanks to Motilal Nehru and the Congress Legislative Party, the British government finally consented to impose protective duties on imported steel and paid a bounty on steel rails for three years from 1924.

Throughout this struggle for survival not one worker was retrenched. The shareholders went without a dividend for twelve out of thirteen years. There was a certain vision and spaciousness about the men and the times they lived in.

Just before the first ingot of steel rolled in Tisco in February 1912, R.D. Tata had told the shareholders: 'Like all infants this company will have its infantile ailments, its period of convulsions and teething as well as hours of smiles and caresses. It will be then that your courage and ours will be tested.'

His prophecy was to come true.

In October 1923, also speaking to the shareholders at the time of the great struggle and crippling shortage of money, R.D. Tata told them: 'We are constantly accused by people of wasting money in the town of Jamshedpur. We are asked why it should be necessary to spend so much on housing, sanitation, roads, hospitals and on welfare. . . . Gentlemen, people who ask these questions are sadly lacking in imagination. We are not putting up a row of workmen's huts in Jamshedpur—we are building a city.'

And in his last address to the shareholders in June 1925, a year before he died, he said, 'We are like men building a wall against the sea. It would be the height of folly on our part to give away any part of the cement that is required to make the wall secure for all time. That is why we and you have to use this money which we have made firstly to build up this great industry which we are making for India and we should not think of dividends until we have done that. Now let me come from the general to the particular—to this sum of Rs 64 lakh net profit which we have made this year and which we propose to use chiefly to strengthen our wall . . .'

R.D. Tata said about the profit they had made that year (after a couple of difficult years): 'We hold this money in trust for you—but you yourself hold it in trust for the Indian nation which has at great sacrifice given you in the shape of protection more than the whole net profit we have made.'

The upward swing came with World War II in 1939. The value of Tata Steel appreciated. Armoured cars were fitted with bullet-proof plates and rivets made by Tata Steel. They were called 'Tatanagars'. There was such pride when a report came from the Eighth Army in the western desert, that even when a 75 mm shell burst on one side of a 'Tatanagar', the metal plates buckled but were nowhere pierced, and the occupants were all safe.

After World War II, in association with Kaiser engineers of the USA—the plant which before the war expanded to a million tonnes—was further expanded to two million tonnes.

The mother of heavy industry in India, Tata Steel has spawned many children around herself in Jamshedpur—The Indian Tube Company (now the Tubes Division of Tata Steel), The Indian Cable Company, The Tinplate Company of India, Indian Steel and Wire Products (started by Sir Indra Singh), Tata-Yodogawa, Tata-Robins-Fraser, Tata Refractories and the biggest of all, Tata Engineering and Locomotive Company (Telco).

To get the plant moving in those early years took some doing. The general superintendent, T.W. Tutwiler, an American, was a terror. Beneath a ferocious exterior resided a soft heart. He fired people at the slightest provocation but hired them again gladly. He liked no frills. Every Christmas the directors journeyed to Jamshedpur ostensibly for the board meeting, but, it was said, really to please Tutwiler and play with him his favourite game of American poker. Till his last days in Jamshedpur, Tutwiler could never understand how Indians could beat an American at his own card game.

A chemical engineering graduate called Jehangir Ghandy went to Tutwiler for a job. When asked, Ghandy replied he would prefer to work in the laboratory. Tutwiler bawled out that he wanted no 'goddam booklearning' and asked him to report at the coke ovens at 6 a.m. the next day. Years later when Ghandy took over as the first Indian general manager, there were not many things he did not know. Not only steel but men were forged at Jamshedpur.

Tutwiler was succeeded by a genial Irishman, John Keenan. Keenan relates the story of a serious accident in the works when a ladle with 75 tonnes of molten metal crashed on the ground with a deafening sound emitting sparks and burning metal. The confused and frenzied shouts of men were heard above the inimical hiss of steam as red-hot metal hit puddles of water.

Keenan could take only three of the injured men in his small car to hospital. He chose one who seemed to have a better chance than the others to survive and told his helpers to bring him.

The man shook his head in negation. 'Do not take me away,' he said. Turning his head feebly, the Hindu nodded towards the body of a half-burnt Muslim and spoke. *'Hamara bhai ko le jao'* (take my brother), he said clearly. The Hindu who was in pain and in danger of death remembered, not that the Muslim was of a different faith, but that he was his brother.

The company in its own captive mines and collieries, has a task force of 23,000 people, in addition to nearly 55,000 in the works and the township of Jamshedpur, at the Adityapur complex, the bearings plant at Kharagpur, and in the sales offices and stockyards of the marketing division around the country. In 1971, when the coal industry was nationalized the then minister, Mohan Kumaramangalam, left the mines of the company untouched because he wanted nationalized units to 'sharpen' themselves against the more efficiently run Tata collieries.[3]

A memorable day in the life of Tata Steel was the Golden Jubilee when Prime Minister Jawaharlal Nehru came to open the public gardens bequeathed to the city by the steel company. The prime minister was at his best. He gave perspective to the younger people, 'It is very easy for those of us who think in terms of today to belittle what has been done by those who preceded us, not realizing the conditions under which they lived . . . when you have to give the lead in action, in ideas—a lead that does not fit in with the very climate of opinion, that is true

[3] *Economic Times*, 17 January 1979.

courage, physical or mental or spiritual, call it what you like—and it is this type of courage and vision that Jamsetji Tata showed and it is right that we should honour his memory and remember him as one of the big founders of modern India . . . We have our planning commissions but Jamsetji Tata formed himself into some kind of a planning commission and began his own—not a five-year but a much bigger plan.'

In 1978, two ministers of the Cabinet proposed nationalization of the steel company. The Tata Workers' Union first sent a cable of protest to the prime minister. They who worked in the plant, the mines, the collieries and in sales, all resolved on 7 January 1979, that nationalization would be detrimental to the interests of the nation and to all employees of the company. The government did not touch Tata Steel. In October 1979, the company celebrated fifty years of industrial harmony.

Until 1979, a good part of Tata Steel machinery was either twenty-five or fifty years of age. The government controlled the steel prices so tightly that government steel plants ran at huge losses to the public exchequer and Tatas barely avoided losses and gave a modest dividend purely by managing to work this old plant at over 100 per cent efficiency. There was no money for modernization, leave alone expansion. By 1980, the government realized its folly and partially decontrolled steel prices. Tata Steel went in for modernization with a modest programme of Rs 225 crore in Phase I. With further government relaxation of prices they went into Phase II of modernization of Rs 850 crore. Thus, over Rs 1000 crore was spent to update the equipment. Expansion was to come later with a Rs 1500-crore plan to increase the capacity from 2.1 million tonnes to 2.7 million tonnes of steel. Along with expansion it was decided to produce improved and special qualities of steel. Tata Steel is the first company in the private sector to touch Rs 2000-crore turnover per annum.

Tata Steel has either started or revived a number of companies. Some of them are Tata Pigments Limited, Special Steels Limited, Tata Metals and Strips Limited, Ipitata Sponge Iron Limited and the Indian Steel Rolling Mills Limited. Others include Kalimati Investments Company Limited, Tata Korf Engineering Services Limited, Tata Timken Limited, Tata Davy Limited, Tata Man. Ghh. Limited, Tata Korf Metals West

Bengal Limited, Kumardhubi Metal Casting and Engineering Limited, Tata Aquatic Farms Orissa Limited, and Nicco Corporation Limited (Steel Division). Such is the management reputation of Tata Steel that when a plant gets 'sick' in, say, West Bengal, its government appeals to Tata Steel to set it right. Today Tata Steel operations are no longer limited to eastern India but extend to western and southern India.

In 1984, J.R.D. Tata stepped down after forty-six years as chairman. Russi Mody, who for fifty years made an outstanding contribution to the company, especially in terms of human relations, succeeded him as chairman.

A former vice-chairman of Tata Steel, J.D. Choksi, summed up the unique position of the company in the Indian context. 'There are,' he wrote, 'certain corporations the world around, which stand out from their fellows. They need not be the largest or the most prosperous in their country or even in their given field but their achievements and traditions are epochal and in peoples' minds identify the trade or industry to which they belong with themselves. They may be in trade or commerce opening up new frontiers and new territories, such as, for instance, the East Asiatic Corporation of Denmark, or they may be established in one place in a basic or key industry. The Tata Iron and Steel Company is such a corporation. It is part of the geography and landscape of India— as much a part of her as her great mountain ranges and rivers.'

For generations to come such a company is to be held in trust for the nation.

IMPULSE TO LEARNING

The Presidency Universities of Bombay, Madras and Calcutta had given India its first graduates with a background of western education.

In 1889, Lord Reay, Bombay's popular Governor, said in a convocation address that education could no longer develop if universities remained purely examining bodies. He called for 'real universities which will give fresh impulse to learning, to research, to criticism, which will inspire reverence and impart strength and self-reliance to future generations.'

Such advanced learning was not available in India, so in 1892 Jamsetji endowed a fund for the higher education abroad of deserving students. Some of India's early engineers, surgeons, physicians, educationists, barristers and ICS officials benefited from the endowment. Once the Indian Civil Sevice was thrown open to Indians, Jamsetji was especially keen that deserving Indian students should take advantage of it. (Some years later, in 1924, it was calculated that one out of every five Indian ICS officials had been a J.N. Tata Scholar.) But the progress of the early years was too slow for Jamsetji's liking.

Writing to Lord Reay on 17 November 1896, he told the Governor of Bombay that 'no more . . . fruitful results, can be provided than (by) a national system of education.' He continued: 'The efficiency of general education must depend, in the last resort, on the efficiency of the highest university education.' In September 1898, Jamsetji announced an offer that was to astonish men of his day. He decided to set aside fourteen of his buildings and four landed properties in Bombay for an endowment to establish a university of science. His donation was worth Rs 30 lakh in those days, equal to over Rs 10 crore of today. It was half his wealth. The other half he left to his two sons.

His offer fetching an interest then of Rs 1.25 lakh a year was hailed in many quarters, but some of his fellow Parsis regretted that the wealth of the community was being diverted to a scheme from which few Parsis would benefit, when such wealth of the community could be used to give clothes, food, medical facilities and housing to Parsis in need. In reply to them, Jamsetji, in an interview, spelt out his views on philanthropy:

> There is one kind of charity common enough among us, and which is certainly a good thing, though I do not think it the best thing we can have. It is that patchwork philanthropy

which clothes the ragged, feeds the poor, and heals the sick and halts. I am far from decrying the noble spirit which seeks to help a poor or suffering fellow-being. But charities of the hospital and poor asylum kind are comparatively more common and fashionable among us Parsis. What advances a nation or community is not so much to prop up its weakest and most helpless members as to lift up the best and most gifted so as to make them of the greatest service to the country. I prefer this constructive philanthropy which seeks to educate and develop the faculties of the best of our young men.

The proposal of Jamsetji was presented to the new viceroy, Lord Curzon, in 1898, the day after his arrival in India. The proposal was put to him by a deputation led by the vice-chancellor of the Bombay University. Typical of Jamsetji, he did not say much on the occasion himself but let the vice-chancellor, Mr Justice Candy, and others do the talking. Curzon was lukewarm, and had two major doubts about the scheme. The first was whether qualified Indians would be forthcoming for such advanced scientific training. Secondly, whether there would be employment opportunities for them in a country that had no industries worth the name.

To report on Jamsetji's scheme, the Secretary of State for India requested the Royal Society of England to send out an eminent scientist. The Royal Society selected Professor William Ramsay, the discoverer of rare gases (including helium and neon), who was later to be awarded the Nobel Prize. After a quick tour of the country in ten weeks Ramsay reported that Bangalore was a suitable site for such an institution. On Curzon's doubt whether the qualified students would come to the institute to be trained in scientific methods, Ramsay recommended liberal scholarships. Ramsay also indicated certain industries that could be developed in India. Later Curzon appointed a committee, consisting of the principal of the Roorkee Engineering College, Colonel J. Clibborn, and Professor David Orme Masson of Melbourne University to draw up 'a less ambitious plan' susceptible to expansion according to circumstances. The Clibborn–Masson Committee recommended Roorkee as a suitable area.

Meanwhile, Curzon was writing to the Secretary of State for India, Lord Hamilton, on 26 June 1901:

> We are endeavouring to save Tata's scheme from the shipwreck which his ambitions and Ramsay's exaggerated ideas threatened it, and are asking the Committee (Clibborn–Masson's) to consider and submit a scheme under which the annual expenditure will be limited to £10,000; £2000 of which will be provided annually by the Government of India for ten years.

It may be mentioned that Jamsetji's endowment alone provided £8000 (Rs 1,25,000) a year. Curzon also wrote to Hamilton that his government would propose to create the institution on a more modest scale and then if Jamsetji declined it, the responsibility for destroying the scheme would be upon Jamsetji Tata and 'we shall escape the odium which would have been fully bestowed upon us.'

Jamsetji had hoped 'that corporations, the native chiefs, sardars' will gradually see their way to bountifully help such an institution. For this reason he insisted that his own name should not be attached to the institute. The Maharaja of Mysore did come forward with a generous offer of 371 acres of land in Bangalore for the institute, a gift of Rs 5 lakh for construction and a recurring grant of Rs 50,000 a year. But no other source of revenue came forward. The Curzon government was taking its own time and was concentrating on cutting down and controlling the scheme. Did Curzon comprehend fully that what Jamsetji was after was not just a university of science but a new 'national system of education'? According to the original plan proposed by Jamsetji, the university was 'destined to promote original investigations in all branches of learning and to utilize them for the benefit of India.'[4]

The original plan of Jamsetji included: scientific and technological education; medical and sanitary education, including research in bacteriology; and studies in philosophy and education (including

[4] Resolution of the Government of India, Home Department, No. 434–448, Simla, 27 May 1909.

methods of education), ethics and psychology, Indian history and archaeology, statistics and economics and comparative philology.

The canvas that Jamsetji was working on was too vast for his contemporaries to fathom, far less to accept. The largesse he had given for the institute was from his private account. To increase the regular income of the institute, he wished to levy and lay aside a certain commission from his business. His colleagues in business opposed him. Jamsetji must have felt hurt. Though he could have pushed through his idea, he graciously bowed to the desire of his colleagues and restricted his endowment to his personal wealth. Attacked by some co-religionists, denied co-operation from those he had inducted into his business, confronted with an arrogant Viceroy who could not understand the greatness of the giver or of his gift, any other man than Jamsetji would have withdrawn the offer. In fact the British reckoned that he would. Lord Hamilton, who had sympathy for Jamsetji, wrote to Lord Curzon in 1903: 'My impression is that Tata will drop his scheme and devote a certain proportion of his endowment to practical purposes in connection with electricity or the development of the iron industry.' But Jamsetji was not easily deflected from the accomplishment of his purpose. In 1904, Jamsetji added a codicil to his will urging his two sons not to use this money set aside for the university. If need be, he requested they may add to the university from the wealth he was leaving them. While the scheme was still being considered and a provisional committee was looking into it, Jamsetji died on 19 May 1904. Perhaps the *Times of India* was thinking of him and Lord Curzon when it wrote the following day that Jamsetji's 'sturdy strength of character prevented him from fawning on any man however great, for he was great in his own way, greater than most men realized.'

In the year, 1905, when Lord Curzon was on leave in Bexhill, he finally gave the green light to Dorab Tata, by agreeing that the government would meet half the cost. Dorab, who was educated at Caius College, Cambridge, and knew quite a bit about the West, wrote to a friend in India that year: 'One thing is certain. India is not ripe for the institute and I doubt very much that Britain is ripe.' In prophetic tones he continued:

If we make the effort to give India what she might have we shall have achieved something, even if the institute, when established, fails to answer our expectations. It is thus, I think, that the beginnings of all great reforms take place. The man who sows never gathers the fruit. It is left to somebody else at some remote date to make the tree bear fruit. All that the man who sows ought to be content with is that the tree should remain alive so that at some future date another might give it the right treatment and make it bear fruit.

'To give India what she might have' became the lodestar of the House.

A director was speedily appointed in 1906. When the vesting order came from the Government of India in May 1909, it was generously worded. The order which vested in trust the properties endowed by Jamsetji Tata, spoke positively of the enlightened promoter and donor. The order stated that 'the Governor-General in Council has no desire to associate himself intimately with the actual administration of the institute, or to claim a determining voice in the settlement of the lines of research to be followed and the methods of instructions to be employed.' The powers were vested in a Senate, a Court and a Council of the institute. To the credit of the British government and its successor governments of independent India, this autonomy of the institute and its academic freedom have been honoured. From its inception the institute is a tripartite venture of Tatas, the Government of India and the Government of Mysore (now Karnataka). In view of its national importance the Government of India bears the expenses.

The institute opened in 1911 with three major departments of General and Applied Chemistry, Electro-technology Chemistry and Organic Chemistry. Chemistry, which now is divided into several disciplines, in those days covered a very vast field. In the 1940s and 1950s aeronautical engineering, high voltage engineering, internal combustion engineering and several others were added. Today the institute has over thirty departments.

The Indian Institute of Science, Bangalore, has occupied a preeminent position in national life. The Council of Scientific and Industrial Research was established in New Delhi only in 1942 and India then set on the path of opening national research laboratories in the late 1940s and 1950s. The first Indian Institute of Technology opened at Kharagpur in 1950. Bombay, Madras, Kanpur and Delhi IITs came up by 1961. In the early years the institute at Bangalore focused on utilizing indigenous materials to benefit industry. The Mysore Soap Factory and Sandalwood Oil Factory were among the early beneficiaries. The origin of the hydrogenation industry can be traced to the work done by the department of organic chemistry.

Like Tata Steel in Jamshedpur, the Indian Institute of Science in Bangalore has spawned many children. The Central Food and Technological Research Institute in Mysore, the Lac Research Institute of Ranchi and the National Aeronautical Laboratory in Bangalore are the direct offshoots of the Institute of Science. The institute also provided the nuclei for the National Chemical Laboratory and the National Metallurgical Laboratory. The alumni of the institute provided the backbone for our national laboratories and the CSIR.

Distinguished names in science and industry have been closely associated with the institute. The industrial genius Sir M. Visvesvaraya was closely associated with the management of the institute for three decades. Nobel Prize winner Dr C.V. Raman was director of the institute for four years and did his important work on crystals and spectroscopy at the institute where he was the head of the department of physics for many years. Professor Max Born specially came to see the work being done by Dr Raman at the institute. Dr Homi Bhabha did his pioneering work on cosmic rays during the years of World War II and Lord Wavell visited the institute as Viceroy mainly to see Dr Bhabha's work. Also at the institute was Dr Vikram Sarabhai, who succeeded Dr Bhabha as the head of India's atomic energy programme. Dr Satish Dhawan, who became director of the institute in 1961, was later selected to concurrently head the Indian Space Research Organization.

When asked what are the distinguishing characteristics of the institute, its director, Dr C.N.R. Rao,[5] says, 'For success in intellectual endeavour the first requisite is freedom. We are the most free in India; truly autonomous. Once a member joins a faculty nobody bothers him, be he a lecturer or professor. Rank does not come in the way of a person's work. People are able to devote themselves to their research. Any staff member can get seed money for his research.'

Professor M.N. Srinivasan of the Faculty of Mechanical Engineering observes, 'The three distinguishing characteristics of the institute are: it has created an environment for research, it promotes creativity and witnesses intense activity. At all hours of the night several students—including ladies—can be walking to their laboratory through the campus to carry out their research and get computer time. All courses are taught in the framework of research and even for a Master's degree about half the time is given for laboratory research.'

The total student strength of the institute is 1400 inclusive of students doing research work and course work. The faculty strength of the institute is 440.[6] In numbers, its pool of research workers is the largest in any educational research institution and next only to the Bhabha Atomic Research Centre (BARC). Staff and students of the Indian Institute of Science produce a thousand research papers a year. About one of every ten members of the Indian Academy of Sciences is a member of the institute. India's top scientific award is the Bhatnagar Prize and the Indian Institute of Science has by far the largest number of awardees. Its research projects and funding is the largest of any academic institute in India—Rs 15 crore recurring grant and another Rs 6 to Rs 8 crore for identified research projects.[7] Most

---

[5] He was succeeded by Dr G. Padmanaban, an eminent scientist in the department of biochemistry. The present director of the institute is Professor Goverdhan Mehta, a distinguished scientist in the department of organic chemistry and former vice chancellor of the Hyderabad University.

[6] In 2003 the student strength was 1700, with a faculty of 450. Two thousand research papers are produced annually.

[7] Recurring grant was Rs 80 crore from the central government and another Rs 68 crore in identified research projects and about Rs 15 crore towards plan grants in 2002–2003.

of the research is in the frontier fields and in the practical application of science to industry, to rural development, to low-cost housing. For example, the institute has invented a wood-burning stove made of mud with an efficiency in the range of 35–45 per cent which is being used in the whole state of Karnataka leading to a 65 per cent saving in firewood. The entire poly-silicon technology of the country has sprung from the institute. The institute has contributed to the progress of India's aeronautical and space programme and assists private industry with consultancy.

The institute has a wind tunnel and a water tunnel. The wind tunnel, for example, tested the ability of the second Howrah Bridge to withstand pressures.

The institute's Continuing Education Programme upgrades the knowledge of 3000 scientists and technologists annually.

The reason why Jamsetji Tata did not want to give his name to the institute was spelt out by him in a letter proposing his scheme to Lord Reay in 1896. Jamsetji said:

> It is my firm belief that corporations, native chiefs, sardars and native gentry will gradually see their way to bountifully help such an institution. . . . I want no title for myself, nor do I wish my name attached to anything. The national movement ought to bear a national name and every separate benefactor might be at ease as far as I am concerned that his endowment won't bear a name subsidiary to any.

That is why he did not want his name to be lent to the institute.

In the Platinum Jubilee year, the institute decided to build a modern auditorium with a seminar complex and name it the J.N. Tata Auditorium.

Tatas continue to be represented on the Court, the Council and the Finance Committee which are the decision-making bodies. According to its former registrar S.S. Prabhu, 'Tatas have provided, at crucial times, the healing touch.'

When Jamsetji Tata dreamt of the institute, he wrote:

The objects of the institute shall be to provide for advance instruction and to conduct original investigations into all branches of knowledge . . . likely to promote the material and industrial welfare of India.

His dream has been fulfilled.

M.S. OBEROI

Excerpts from *Dare to Dream* by Bachi J. Karkaria

Mohan Singh Oberoi came to Simla exactly a hundred years after the first European set foot in the place. In 1822, Captain Charles Pratt Kennedy had been despatched, to establish a rudimentary order on the hill states, and proved to be a trailblazer in other ways as well. Monsieur Victor Jacquemont, adventurous member of the Natural History Museum of Paris, who had stayed in Pratt's rough-hewn house amidst the deodars, had written home that the artillery captain was as hospitable as the surrounding terrain was not. He served elegant breakfasts and magnificent dinners, the latter stretching over a full four hours. The French naturalist, who pre-empted Emily Eden by roughly a decade, added his own comment on the incongruity. In a letter to his father in Paris, he wrote:

> Isn't it strange to dine in silk stockings in such a place, to drink a bottle of hock and another of champagne each evening, to have delicious Moccha coffee and receive the Calcutta papers every morning?

It might be recalled that the Hon. Miss Eden arrived in Simla sixty years before the mountain railway did. Not that its lack deterred the well-heeled gentry who made the annual trip every summer. Today, you can fly into the hill station, but there is no guarantee that the experience of travelling in a Vayudoot Dornier in a high wind will not be akin to a ride in a 'dhoolie' (*doli*) which was described as 'sitting in a half-reefed top-sail in a storm'. This canvas and bamboo litter was the main mode of travel for those who could not do it astride a stomping chestnut mare.

Once up, however, it was little short of paradise for the 'heaven born service', and minor functionaries. Lord Curzon may have bought the Retreat in nearby Mashobra to escape the 'despotism of the despatch boxes', but, by all accounts, an officer had difficulty remaining a gentleman in that rarefied atmosphere.

It was very early in its imperial existence that Simla acquired the reputation of being the haunt of flirt, philanderer and fortune-hunter, of match-maker and maiden-chaser, and, by Gad! the cad. It was only a killjoy like Honoria Lawrence who primly pursed her lips and dismissed Simla society as 'a bundle of tinsel, rags and dirt', its conversation the 'contents of a dustpan, a many-sided buzz of scandal, and vanity, hasty censure, mutilated praise and insincere profession'.

While the Punjab Government also moved up to Simla and the Indian Army was headquartered there, it was the annual migration of the Government of India that gave Simla its airs. There is, of course, sufficient record of affairs of the State and serious decision-making, not all of it as florid as George Abereigh-Mackay's in *Twenty-one Days in India*:

> How mysterious and delicious are the cool penetralia of the Viceregal office. It is the sensorium of the Empire, it is the seat of thought; it is the abode of moral responsibility! What famines, what battles, what excursions of pleasure, what banquets and pageants, what concepts of change have sprung into life here? Every pigeon-hole contains a potential revolution, every office box cradles the embryo of a war or death. What shocks and vibrations, what deadly thrills does this little thunder-cloud office transmit to far away provinces lying beyond rising and setting suns.

Simla had indeed come a long way since the time it had been merely a sanatorium for English men, women and children, pallid and plagued by an assortment of unknown tropical fevers, who had sought permission from the joint owners of the 'pergannah', the Maharaja of Patiala and the Rana of Keonthal, to build their houses there. Permission had been given and rent not demanded, only the stipulation that 'they should refrain from the slaughter of kine or the felling of trees, unless with the previous permission of the owners of the land' (Colonel E.G. Wace's Settlement Report on Simla District).

Young Oberoi quite forgot his failed test as he gazed upon the purposeful stride of power, the glide of furred and ostrich-feathered creatures from a world very far from Bhaun, or even Lahore. The Mall had lost none of its impeccable turnout, even if the empire had lost some of its innocence since the Prince of Prussia's physician, Doctor Hoffmeister, noted during a visit a dozen years before the Revolt of 1857:

> No-one ventures to make his appearance there who is not mounted on a handsome horse, or who cannot sport the whitest linen, the most stylish cut of coat or showy uniform and white kid gloves, for one must make special toilette here in order to enjoy the open air.

Mohan Singh saw the flamboyant princes of the Punjab in their crested rickshaws drawn by liveried coolies, but didn't dream that he would be supervising their passage in a short while. Even less, as he stared in wonder at the baronial proportions of the Viceregal Lodge, did he imagine that, decades later, his line of destiny would meet it at a tangent. Mohan Singh walked as if in a daze and found himself outside a grand doorway that seemed to attract the most beautiful and the best. 'Faletti's Cecil Hotel', said the wrought-iron tracery on its awning.

Like Charles Forte before the sleek file of restaurants in London town, like the callow Lee Iacocca outside the Ford Motor Car Company in Detroit, the twenty-two-year-old Mohan Singh Oberoi stood dreaming before the soaring nine-storeyed facade of Simla's Cecil Hotel. With a hundred rooms, it was the glittering station's most scintillating hostelry. The only other that could be mentioned in the same breath was Simla's Grand Hotel, housed in what had once been Bentinck Castle, summer home of the Governor-General who had banished sati and *thuggee* from the land. While the Cecil was owned by John Faletti, its competitor belonged to his Italian compatriot, Signor Peliti, whose delectations in butter and sugar had so entranced Lord Lytton that he had brought him to Delhi as Viceregal confectioner.

Faletti and Peliti, their similarly lilting syllables were not the only coincidence. Cecil's rival bore the same name as the Calcutta hotel where, a quarter century later, Oberoi would hurtle into the big league. But the young man could not have grasped the irony that crisp summer morning high up in the hills. He could not have known the game plan that fate had begun charting out for him as it turned him away from the secretariat, and drew his footsteps towards the Cecil, and his destiny towards a future far removed from clerkdom.

Mohan Singh stood riveted to the kaleidoscope of power and style moving before his eyes and made his decision. He was not leaving Simla till he had got a job at the Cecil. Flicking away an invisible piece of fluff from his best worsted trousers, he pulled himself up to his full height, ordered his pounding heart to calm down, and, taking courage in both hands, strode confidently through the front door. The hall porter threw him out.

'No vacancies,' he said. Famous first words. Words that spur some, deter some. The young man did some game-planning of his own. The Manager was sure to go home for lunch and the customary afternoon lie-down. He befriended a nearby shopkeeper, persuading him to point out the quarry. As soon as Mr Grove, for that was his name, strode into sight, Mohan Singh walked smartly up to him and said, 'I am looking for job, sir. Do you have a vacancy at the Cecil?'

D.W. Grove's eye took in the youth. The perfect knot of his tie did not escape his notice, nor did the shine on his shoes. The suit was not expensive, but it was well pressed. The Manager did have an opening, but did not think it would measure up to the expectations of this smartly turned out chap. He said so. Trying to keep the excitement out of his voice, Mohan Singh said, 'I'll be glad to take any job you offer, sir.'

'See me at three this afternoon,' said the Manager, and walked away. It was some time later that Mohan Singh Oberoi realized, to his consternation, that he had not told Grove his name.

The error of omission was indeed a hurdle. One as big as the snooty hall porter. 'How can you have an appointment with the Manager if you say your name won't mean anything to him?' he demanded. But Mohan Singh's charm had got him out of tricky situations in the past and would do so often enough in the future. The porter let him through.

Mohan Singh Oberoi, host to the world, began his career as a clerk at the Cecil at fifty rupees a month, staying in a one-room tenement called Band Quarter 4, ten feet by nine feet, at the bottom of the hill.

FORMIDABLE GERTIE

Mohan Singh Oberoi's main duties seemed to be confined to keeping track of the hotel's coal supplies. But he displayed his celebrated initiative virtually from day one. Ramchand's shop in the lower bazaar supplied fuel to Cecil Hotel, and the new clerk conscientiously insisted on every consignment being weighed again on delivery. This practice was maintained with all supplies as he rose through the ranks and became his own master.

One day, he figured out that he could effect a considerable saving for his employers by ordering the infinitely cheaper coal-dust balls. He could light the boilers with them at night, they would burn slowly while the hotel slept, and the next morning, all it would take would be a scuttle or so of rock coal to get the fire crackling and the water on the gallop. Cheaper coal, but hotter water; happier guests, higher profits. The pattern had begun to take shape.

It was not long before D.W. Grove decided that the talents of the man from the Mall should not remain hidden under a bushel. He summoned him to his office, and said, 'Mr Oberoi, didn't you type out your application letter? So may I presume that you are familiar with the machine?' 'Yes, sir,' said young Mohan Singh eagerly, and promptly volunteered the information that he knew shorthand as well. Grove said, 'In that case, would you please take a letter.' He dictated,

> Dear Mr Johnson,
> We are in receipt of your letter of the 8th. We have reserved a room for you from September 19 to September 25, 1922. The reservation consists of a room facing the valley. A bathroom is attached. The charges are Rs 15 per day, inclusive of meals.
> Assuring you of our best services, I remain,
> Yours truly,
> Sd. D.W. Grove.

Young Oberoi took it down in shorthand, typed out the letter without an error and handed it to his boss. He was elevated to Guest Clerk and his salary upped. After some months, D.W. Grove acquired Simla's fashionable Davico's Tea Rooms, and left Cecil Hotel. The Manager and his 'find' would meet again, in a considerably altered equation, at the Grand in distant Calcutta.

Ernest Clarke took D.W. Grove's place as Manager of the Cecil Hotel, and an enduring relationship began to cement between the middle-aged Englishman and the young shaven Sikh, one impressed by the lad's diligence, enthusiasm and initiative, the other by the Briton's meticulousness, decency and sense of fair play. Clarke and his clerk worked together to keep up the hotel's formidable reputation. With not a little help from Gertie.

Gertrude Clarke was the terror of the bearers, and the sound of her sensible shoes clacking across the linoleum had the immediate effect of accelerating the speed of sweeping, dusting, polishing. She could spot a speck at twenty paces. Indeed, Ernest Clarke was in the habit of getting work accomplished by using the magic words, 'Memsahib wants it done.'

Hotel-keeping in Simla had progressed not a little since the time the Prince of Prussia's physician had, in addition to his observations about the Mall during his 1845 tour, commented on the fact that a hotel had recently been 'set up for the accommodation of strangers, a thing utterly unheard of in the plains of Hindustan. A Frenchman is at the head of the establishment and we find ourselves very well off in his house'. The good doctor was thus spared the inconvenience of 'sleeping on moist ground', the all-too-uncomfortable hazard of travelling in such godless parts.

Incidentally, the same missive revealed that he had even unearthed a couple of old pianofortes. 'I have,' wrote Dr Hoffmeister with ill-disguised anticipation, 'selected the best of the two, and tuned it for the sake of playing some old favourite now and then in the evening, or accompanying a duet.'

Its shorter-lived rival may have had the grand antecedents of a castle but the Cecil had started life in 1868 as the modest, one-storeyed Tendril Cottage. It changed several hands, sometimes ignominiously by public auction. It was rebuilt, and then had to be torn down almost immediately because of poor construction and raised again. Tendril Cottage became a hotel only after it was bought by the hill station's well-known Hotz family, some of them photographers, others crack electricians who had brought light to the Maharaja of Patiala's palace at Chail and his house in Simla as well as to several PWD buildings.

Mrs Hotz nurtured Cecil Hotel to glory, and then sold it to John Faletti, some say in a fit of pique against the constant needling of the Simla Municipal Corporation. She went off to look after Wildflower Hall in neighbouring Mahasu.

INNS AND OUTS

Mrs Hotz's huff was Mr Faletti's fortune. The suave Italian had not only turned around Simla's United Services Club, he was little short of a royal favourite. John Faletti had won a place in the heart of the Prince of Wales through the traditional route of his stomach. His Royal Highness was well pleased with the catering arrangements made during the vastly successful tour of 1905–06, so when King George arrived to survey the brightest jewel in his crown, it was naturally Faletti who, by command, laid the splendid table of the royal shooting camp in Nepal.

By the time Edward, as Prince of Wales, came out in 1921–22, the Italian was entrusted with the catering for the entire tour, both in India and Burma (now Myanmar), picking up honours for his services to the Crown.

With testimonials from no less than His Imperial Majesty, it was not difficult for John Faletti to enter hoteliering, and, like Oberoi, he did it through the Cecil, albeit at a more exalted level. Even before he laid his soft, stubby and sure hands on it, Mrs Hotz's enterprise was established enough to command a buying price of Rs 2,50,000 way back in the first decade of the twentieth century. Faletti, realizing its even greater potential, spent almost another Rs 6,00,000 on renovating the main building.

John Faletti ran the Cecil and the hotel in Lahore that bore his own name as private enterprises till 1916, when he decided to go public, floating the Associated Hotels of India (AHI) Company with a capital of six million rupees. It was India's largest—and first—chain, and comprised, apart from these two hotels, Maidens in Delhi, Flashmans in Rawalpindi, Deans in Peshawar, Corstophons and Longwood also in Simla, as well as another Cecil, this one at Murree, the other balmy hill station on the western side of the still-undivided Punjab.

By the time Ernest Clarke and Mohan Singh began polishing its plaque, a chronicler, in 1925, had unequivocally labelled Simla's Cecil the hotel of the East 'par excellence'. The Cecil did its bit to give the twenties their roaring adjective, laying out the red carpet every Saturday when the Viceroy himself might grace the occasion and place the crown on the voguish 'bobbed' hair of the Miss Cecil Queen. Flapper fashions from Europe had taken only the length of a P&O voyage to arrive at this trendy centre of empire, and the wild gyrations of the Charleston, in a flourish of patent leather pumps, kicked the staider dances off the varnished ballroom floor.

Mohan Singh closely observed the panoply and pageantry that passed by his desk all day. He was a quick learner, grasping the social nuances as well as the nitty-gritty of hotel management and he could not have found better role models than the privileged guests of the Cecil: British officers, Indian royalty, black knights, upholders of justice, the sterling company boxwallahs. Not restricting his efforts to the job description of Desk Clerk, he took on several responsibilities, including those of cashier. For the princes, he became a sort of strong room and the occasion often arose when he would discreetly suggest a better way of putting to use the sums of money entrusted to his safe keeping. Always very subtly, never overstepping the limits of decorum, but usually with success. Mohan Singh quite clearly had inherited his mother's unfailing instinct for handling finance. It won him many friends and future patrons.

One night, after stormy parleys with the still obdurate upholders of the Raj, Motilal Nehru came to Mohan Singh, manning the reception desk, and asked if there was someone who could type out a document. The young man volunteered to do it himself, retyping to ensure a completely clean copy. He then delivered the six, neat, long pages to the formidable barrister. Motilal read it through, and handed him a hundred rupee note in quiet appreciation. Mohan Singh's salary then was sixty rupees a month. He used the unexpected windfall to buy himself and his wife their first watches. There was enough left over for a blanket to replace their threadbare one, as well as new clothes for the children.

Mohan Singh was busy and happy, synonyms in his lexicon. By five in the morning, he would have made the steep, nearly vertical, climb up the hill from his cramped Band Quarter 4 to ensure that the boilers were ready to hiss and the room-bearers were sufficiently awake to answer the bells for morning tea. He made the difficult climb again to and from lunch at home. His young wife would wait to hear the crunch of his shoes coming down the incline before she started rolling out the chapatis for lunch. He took a little time off for the simple Punjabi fare in preference to the stews and roasts.

Besides, he wanted those few minutes with the family that gave him the reserves to take up his second shift and work late into the night. In the evenings, he would take his wife and children for a stroll on the Mall, proud of the fact that, despite his lowly station, they were all well turned out enough to walk the smart avenue which still demanded the standards of *toilette* that had so impressed Dr Hoffmeister some eighty years ago.

Perhaps Ishran and he would laugh together in remembrance of the first night of her arrival in Simla from Murree. 'I had subjected Band Quarter 4 to a thorough cleaning in excited anticipation, but an army of bedbugs marched out of the mattress and up the wall.' Or they would recall how he had ordered several pairs of satin slippers as a surprise for his little bride: 'They were in all the colours of the rainbow, but they were all a size too small.' Perhaps Ishran would tell him of their daughter Rajrani's latest prattle or, more likely, complain about little Tikki. 'He took perverse pleasure in throwing all her kitchen paraphernalia into the *khud*. Our first son had arrived in 1924, and we'd named him Tilak Raj, the anointed one.'

Tikki, as everyone soon began to call the little terror, had a mind of his own, often in conflict with his mother's notions of a child's behaviour. But the father only smiled indulgently. In his eyes, his 'little rajah' could do no wrong. And surely the boy had the makings of a businessman. Whenever someone gave him a gift of cash, he would run out into the garden and bury it: 'I'm planting a money tree,' he would say.

Their second son, Prithvi Raj Singh, was born in 1929; like his Rajput namesake, he would stamp the Oberoi dynasty with his own distinctive imprimatur. Since Tilak Raj was Tikki, Prithvi Raj soon became Biki. Next came another daughter whom they named Swaraj in anticipation of a still distant independence, and, finally, the baby of the family, chubby little Prem.

Rajrani grew up with Bhagwanti in quiet Bhaun, being the only girl in the boys' school which she attended specially for the

English classes. As far as her grandmother was concerned, the value of knowing the language elbowed out any dangers that might lurk in co-educational corners. She had taken Tikki as well, but the boy proved a handful even for her.

For many years, during the long winter vacations and the shorter summer breaks of their hill schools, Rajrani, Tikki, Swaraj, Biki and little Prem, ran wild and free amidst the wheat-fields of Bhaun, or in their grand-uncle's orchard, a few miles away where they gorged themselves on bunches of juicy pink *lokart* and the magenta, caterpillar-like Indian mulberry, known locally as *shatut*.

In many ways, the Gibraltar-like Bhagwanti never faltered in her support to her son and his family.

HOTEL NUMBER ONE

One morning in 1927, while Mohan Singh sat filling up the guest ledger, Ernest Clarke entered the office and asked, 'I've been given a year's contract to run the Delhi Club. Would you care to come down and join me there?' The young assistant hesitated only for a fraction. Then he said, 'With pleasure.' He did not forget to add the 'sir'. It was a reckless decision, leaving an established chain for an uncertain future. The decisive factor was faith. No salaries, terms or designations were discussed. Mohan Singh questioned very little about his boss, least of all his sense of fair play. At the end of the month, Clarke gave him an envelope containing seventy-five rupees.

Ernest Clarke made quite a killing on that contract. Enough, in fact, to think of taking on a hotel of his own. Where else, but back in his old haunt. Mohan Singh followed him to the Carlton, a small hotel at the other end of the Simla Mall. Clarke leased it from the Bank of Upper India Limited in 1929, which, in turn, had taken it over in 1925 from its original owner, P.W. Fitzholmes of nearby Kasauli, for Rs 1,50,000. Ernest Clarke renamed the hotel after himself, though one can still see 'Carlton' spelt out in mosaic under the carpet of the reception area.

Clarkes Hotel came nowhere near the style of the Cecil. With fifty rooms, it was only half its size. The Cecil, being a close neighbour of the Viceregal Lodge, had basked in its glory, and had many of the same amenities built into it. Clarkes had a less well-heeled clientele and worse plumbing.

Messrs Hotz & Brandon, Associated Chartered Architects, Delhi and Simla, who had been asked by Clarke to evaluate the property, had pronounced in their letter of 29 January 1929:

> . . . the Main Building has sunk considerably towards the south west corner and the floors of all the rooms need to be jacked up and levelled. Almost all the bathrooms are abnormally dark and therefore insanitary. The access to the bathrooms for the servants is scarcely short of scandalous as the staircases are narrow, steep and there is insufficient headroom provided . . . Taking into account the above features, and the fact that there is no modern sanitation in the building, I would not recommend you to acquire it for a sum exceeding Rs 1,75,000.

In short, it provided just the sort of challenge to someone determined to learn everything about hotel-keeping, brick by brick. Clarke took it on lease from the bank at Rs 9000 a year. The hotel started as a one-man show. Within a year, it became a two-man show. Under an indenture dated 17 March 1930, Mohan Singh Oberoi was made partner. Now, with a stake in its future, he convinced Clarke that they should buy it over mortgaging the property against the loan; they would have to pay just marginally more than the rent as interest and repayment.

Clarke certainly did not have access to the kind of money needed to make the down payment, so Mohan Singh decided to tap the wealthy associates of his mother. The first name that sprang to mind was that of the distinguished Rai Bahadur Kahnchand Kapur who had so impressed him years ago. Mohan Singh went to see him in Sirmoor state, where he was Dewan. The young, shrewd hotelier's negotiations had helped beat down the figure to Rs 40,000 lower than the valuers' estimate but Kahnchand could not muster the Rs 1,35,000 that was still needed. However, he got in touch with the affluent Delhi contractor, Sardar Bahadur Narain Singh, who agreed to loan the money, provided the property was mortgaged in the name of his son, Jagjit. Once again the irony. Narain Singh had built, among other capital landmarks, the Imperial Hotel, which his other son, Ranjit, would inherit, and which later would figure decisively in the life of our principal protagonist.

Ernest Clarke and, more than him, his wife, the domineering Gertie, yearned to see the home country. Young Oberoi could be relied upon to look after the hotel. They went on a long-deserved vacation. When they returned after six months, they could not believe the difference Mohan Singh had made to the property. For the first time in its history, he had advertised, proclaiming 'under European Management', which was not technically untrue. He had persuaded the army to patronize his hotel; and having livened up the Clarkes' bar, he drew the younger government set as well. Occupancy doubled to 80 per cent. Ishran Devi had worked shoulder to shoulder with her husband to achieve the miracle, going herself to the bazaar to ensure the right quality, measure and price. Yet, at the end of her long day's journey into night, Ishran Devi sat and caringly removed the wrinkles in her husband's suit the old-fashioned way, with a heated brass pot, a *garhvi*: a proper iron was beyond their budget.

Ernest Clarke was impressed. And his faith in his own abilities was not a little shaken. He would soon have greater reason for self-doubt. Simla's distance was some protection against the effects of the Depression that had sunk the globe into a similar state of mind, but the financial situation was not reassuring. Apart from the loan, the duo had paid Rs 7000 on registration and other fees and Rs 34,000 on repairs, mainly to introduce some light and air into the dingy bathrooms at which the valuer had turned up his nose. They had even replaced the old thunder-boxes with more sanitary conveniences.

The Delhi Club contract had brought in a lot of money, but not enough. Expenses, interest and insurance on the Simla hotel had mounted. There were also heavy liabilities for the Grand Hotel on Delhi's Underhill Road that had been leased along with the Carlton, and also renamed Clarkes Hotel. Ernest and Gertie usually spent the winter in Delhi, going up to the hill hotel once during those months to see the snow. Oberoi and his cousin, Partap Singh Dhall, were left entirely in charge of the Simla Clarkes. From Delhi, on 24 November 1933, Ernest wrote a panicked letter to his young partner.

For the first time, and certainly not the last, Mohan Singh was confronted by a severe financial problem. For the first time, and certainly not the last, the clear-headed approach came into play. Within four days of the date on his partner's letter, in fact, just one day after he received it, he sent a reply and a solution.

He wrote, 'Personally I do not think the solving of our difficulties lies in disposing of the property. (It) will not be in any way advantageous to us, but on the other hand it will be disastrous to the business and to us all.' He explained how Jagjit Singh would never give them a worthwhile option, 'considering the time the country is passing through'. There was no hope of his charging them a reasonable rent, and they might end up 'paying Rs 3600 over and above the Rs 11,400 we pay as interest/rent, taxes and insurance and ultimately lose the property as well'.

But he found a loophole. Instead of paying Rs 20,000 a year towards capital that they were committed to, they should pay only half that amount, since under the agreement, 'We are hurt only if two instalments of Rs 10,000 are not paid one after another.' He also pointed out that, should they be unable to meet even the one instalment, they should try to persuade Jagjit Singh to settle only for interest and no return of capital till their financial situation eased. His plan was to pay just as much as was necessary to keep the creditors happy and just as little as was needed to keep their own heads above water. More important, he explained to Clarke, on account of a short-term setback, they should not act impulsively to destroy what they had built up. 'It is more than possible that with the New Delhi hotel things may turn better and then we will be sorry to have lost a property which we have set up with great pains to our taste and requirements.'

The gambit paid off, the hotel was saved, a month-long conference of ICS officers at Metcalfe House as well as the horse shows of the season filled all the rooms of the Delhi Clarkes and the money began to flow in again. However, a situation soon arose that was analogous to the warrior chieftain Shivaji's lament on hearing that his militia had wrested the Simhagarh Fort but that his General had been killed, '*Garh ala, par simh gela*', the play on the citadel's name translating as, 'we've won the fort, but lost the lion'. Clarkes Hotels, from the year after, would be without its namesake. Not that the other lion, Mohan Singh, really minded.

Gertie Clarke was keeping indifferent health and prevailed upon her husband to return home for good. Mohan Singh was only too ready to take over the whole show, goodwill as well as liabilities. Ernest Clarke's shares were worth Rs 20,000, at today's prices, a modest sum, but near unaffordable in those difficult days.

Ishran Devi saw her husband's inner struggle as he stood so near his ambition, and yet so distanced from it. Quietly she took out the modest store of jewellery she had received at the time of her marriage, and placed it before him, keeping only the ring he had given her from his own earnings. Mohan Singh refused. She held her ground. This was no time to allow macho notions to come in the way of their future, she said. With finality. Mohan Singh fought the lump in his throat, and went to the jeweller on the lower Mall. At the fifteen rupees a *tola* price of those days, it simply was not enough. The jeweller gave him only five hundred rupees for his wife's entire trove.

Husband and wife did not sleep that night, but by morning they had worked out another option. They would ask Rai Bahadur Kahnchand Kapur to help out. Mohan Singh again took the first bus to Nahan, the capital of Sirmoor. The elderly gentleman was, again, pleased to see how well Bhagwanti's boy was shaping. Touching his mentor's feet, Mohan Singh made some small talk, and then came to the point. Kahnchand knew how much hinged on this figure. He made a quick calculation. This time it was a request modest enough for him to manage.

The cash was bundled up in a cloth bag and put into the family Model T Ford. Mrs Kapur said she would go too, and Kahnchand's son, Hari, also decided to join the expedition. Mohan Singh took the wheel, and they set off for Simla via Kalka. With trepidation they drove through the forests and the sparsely inhabited countryside.

Mrs Kapur saw a dacoit behind every bush. Hari was caught in the vortex of adventure, but Oberoi kept his mind only on the road ahead of him. They were afraid of getting waylaid and robbed at blunderbuss point, instead they ended up stuck in the shallows of the Narkanda which they thought the Ford could ford. Finally, they extricated themselves and got to Simla. Years later, Mohan Singh would tease his 'aunt', 'Bhaboji, remember how you sat tight on top of the bundle of notes in the middle of the river?'

Under the deed of dissolution dated 14 August 1934, Mohan Singh Oberoi became the 'sole, absolute and exclusive owner of the business known as Clarkes Hotel, Simla and Delhi'. It came a day in advance, but Oberoi could not have hoped for a better—or more portentous—thirty-fourth birthday present. As his first-born child, Rajrani, gave him a birthday kiss that nippy autumn morning, he whispered softly, 'Just wait, *bitti*; when you grow up, wherever you go, there'll be an Oberoi hotel.'

ADITYA VIKRAM BIRLA

Excerpts from *Aditya Vikram Birla: A Biography* by Minhaz Merchant

THE EARLY BUSINESS YEARS

By 1969, the three generations of the most successful branch of the Birla family—G.D., B.K. and Aditya—were all running flourishing but independent enterprises. G.D. Birla, now seventy-five, had lost none of his enthusiasm for business or for life. He travelled the globe incessantly, forging international alliances, expanding Gwalior Rayon and Hindalco[1] and playing the role of senior corporate statesman. He was appointed to countless government committees and represented the government as a delegate on several foreign tours.

G.D. had long made clear that money did not interest him any more. He publicly declared the lofty ideals of his companies and family: 'It has been the policy of the House of Birla not to build up business with a view to the accumulation of capital but to develop unexplored lines, harness the undeveloped resources of the country, promote knowhow, create skilled labour and managerial talent, spread education and, above all, add to the efforts of the leaders of the country who have been struggling to build a new, independent India, free from want, the curse of unemployment, ignorance and disease.'

Shyam Sunder Kanoria, a former president of FICCI (which G.D. had helped found), once accompanied G.D. Birla on an industrial delegation to the US and Europe. After observing the Birla patriarch for a few days, he remarked: 'I was struck by the difference in nature, outlook and lifestyle between G.D. and the European and

---

[1] The two flagship companies of Birla Empire were textile manufacturer Gwalior Rayon (Grasim) and aluminum producer Hindalco.

American tycoons we met. It was not a difference in business acumen, for when it came to driving a bargain G.D. could be as hard-headed as any of them and usually got the better terms. But what they could never understand was that one who ranked as India's top industrialist should lead a life of such spartan simplicity and be so indifferent to the pursuit of pleasure.'

By the end of the 1960s, a decade during which the Birlas celebrated the centenary of the group's founding by G.D.'s grandfather Shiv Narayan in 1862, the family had a presence in an extraordinary range of industries: cars, cement, newspapers, shipping, textiles, synthetic fibres, cables, tea, chemicals, power and aluminium. There were 150 Birla companies involved in manufacturing or trading and the group was a close second to the House of Tata as India's pre eminent industrial family.

Though his companies did not match G.D.'s in size, profits or fame, B.K. Birla's Century twins—Century Textile and Century Enka—were rapidly becoming significant profit and growth centres. Century Textiles initially belonged to Sir Chunilal Mehta, a prominent Bombay businessman. Rameshwardas (R.D.) Birla, G.D.'s brother, had bought a large block of shares in the company from the stock market in 1945. Further market purchases followed. Soon the Birlas owned 50 per cent of Century's stock. The family asked Sir Chunilal to take two Birla nominees on the board. This was summarily refused. Simultaneously, the company's fortunes plunged and losses mounted.

This was an unacceptable state of affairs for the Birlas who controlled a majority of the company's equity but had no say whatsoever in its management. The Birla family elders offered to help financially and managerially but Sir Chunilal stood firm. He would not relinquish control or even cede partial authority. With few options left, the Birlas forced their nominees on to the board at the next annual general meeting. Shortly, full mangement control of Century passed to the Birla family. It was a bloodless coup.

Basant Kumar, then thirty-one, though not yet a director of Century, was asked by his uncle, Rameshwardas, to start a viscose rayon division in the company with a capacity of 6 metric tonnes per day. The cost: Rs. 5 crore, a huge sum in 1952. The order for machinery was placed with an American firm, Kohorn, in 1954 and the plant commenced production in September 1956. By the late 1960s, Century Textiles and its sibling, Century Enka, were the crown jewels of B.K.'s personal corporate empire just as Gwalior Rayon and Hindalco were of G.D.'s.

Having already decided not to join his grandfather's Gwalior Rayon-led empire, Aditya in 1969 'continued expanding his own small group of companies, principally comprising Eastern Spinning, Hindustan Gas and Indian Rayon, none of which were yet major money-spinners. The Rs 10-crore caustic soda plant was still on the drawing board. Aditya now turned his attention to Thailand. When he was at MIT, Aditya had been fascinated by the way capitalistic America did business: no licences, permissions, quotas, limits, shortages or penal rates of tax. If he could not expand quickly enough in India to satisfy his soaring ambitions in business, he decided there was only one way ahead: go global.

In retrospect, it was an extraordinary decision. India was in the grip of a socialist government; draconian foreign exchange regulations were in force; industrial expansion was ruthlessly controlled by New Delhi. There were virtually no Indian business houses with a significant presence abroad. The Tatas had representative offices but no major joint ventures overseas. The Birlas had their Ethiopian textile mill but virtually no other enterprises outside India despite G.D.'s own sweeping global outlook and contacts. The Indian capital market was undeveloped and raising money abroad was unheard of.

In this daunting environment, Aditya Birla decided to defy conventional wisdom and staked his future on setting up a joint venture abroad. Despite the apparent odds, he was convinced that one day in the future the Indian economy would be liberalized and by setting up parallel business enterprises overseas his group would then straddle the best of both worlds. His Indian companies would benefit from the experience the group would gain from competing in open markets overseas. And the foreign companies of his group would grow unfettered by the suffocating blanket of Indian government control even while benefiting from captive sales to—and purchases from—the group's companies in India. It is a testament to Aditya's vision that this is exactly what happened. From 1969, when Aditya's first overseas venture was set up in Thailand, to October 1995, when he passed away, the AVB group's revenues from its foreign operations rose to nearly equal those from all its Indian operations, including G.D.'s flagships which passed on to Aditya in 1983. But back in 1969, for a young man not yet twenty-six, the decision to go global displayed both exceptional prescience and self-belief.

While Aditya wrestled with the practical problems of starting a foreign-based company—how, for instance, would he fund the venture in hard currency when the Indian government refused to grant foreign exchange for even travel or medical emergencies?—there were other pressing personal matters on hand. He and his bride Rajashree had settled down to a quiet but contented life in idyllic Basant Vihar. The couple socialized frequently with a close circle of friends. Aditya kept himself busy with his growing clutch of companies and regular games of badminton in the family's private court.

Rajashree continued her studies at Loreto College and the couple soon decided it was time to start a family. Their first child, Kumar Mangalam, was born on June 14, 1967, at Woodlands Nursing Home. Kumar was a healthy and happy baby and gave his young parents few problems. Calcutta in 1967 was not a pleasant city to live in, with frequent communist-inspired labour strikes and Naxalite attacks. The Birlas had just recovered from the trauma of the fire in their Indian Rayon plant in April 1967 and were now, two months later, confronted with a strike in their office building. As a result, when Kumar Mangalam was born, both B.K. and Aditya were working from home. 'Whenever my husband had a chance,' says Rajashree, 'he used to come up to our room and play with him.'

Kumar, like Aditya, was the apple of G.D. Birla's eye and though he was now spending far more time in Delhi, Bombay and overseas than in Calcutta, he phoned regularly to ask about his great-grandson's progress. Aditya meanwhile was a doting father.

'He would bathe Kumar, change his nappies and spend a lot of time with him,' recalls Rajashree.

In many ways, when he looked back, Aditya came to regard 1967 as the watershed year in his life: it was the year in which his son was born and the year in which the first seeds of his future international aspirations were sown. Between 1967 and 1969, Aditya despatched several key executives—Agarwal, Mundhra and finally Mahansaria—to Thailand to lay the groundwork for his first overseas venture, Indo–Thai Synthetics Ltd. Aditya himself made a whirlwind four-day visit to Bangkok in June 1969 to secure financial and government backing. Indo–Thai Synthetics commenced commercial production in September 1970. Unlike Eastern Spinning five years earlier, it was commissioned on schedule and within budget.

Aditya's overseas ventures were founded on two principles: Birla management and foreign money. The NRIs and local investors who typically held up to 75 per cent of the joint-venture companies' equity were delighted to cede managerial control in return for high dividends. Vijay Mehta, the Antwerp-based diamond merchant, and Amarnath Sachdev, the Bangkok-based textile trader, were typical large investors in Aditya's foreign companies. The Birlas' equity was contributed through the supply of ancillary machinery and fabrication materials to circumvent India's foreign exchange laws, an arrangement that worked with remarkable felicity and would power the group to multinational status in less than two decades. Meanwhile, the large new caustic soda plant in Nagda was taking shape and would go into commercial production in October 1972, marking Aditya's entry into speciality chemicals.

While he shuttled between Calcutta and Bangkok, Aditya also tried to spend time with his young family. It wasn't easy. Business pressures took their toll and Rajashree, who had completed her graduation at Loreto College, was often left in the gregarious company of Aditya's two younger sisters and mother. Toddler Kumar kept her busy. She had supportive parents-in-law in Basant Kumar and Saraladevi and the atmosphere at Basant Vihar was congenial.

By 1970, however, when Kumar was three, Calcutta had become difficult to live in. The Naxalite insurgency was threatening law and order; business families felt particularly vulnerable. The Birlas decided to increase their business activities in other states as a strategic ploy. Gwalior Rayon and Hindustan Aluminium kept G.D. Birla out of Calcutta for long spells. With Aditya too deciding to expand abroad and the Indian Rayon plant located at Veraval, the family began to seriously consider moving base from Calcutta.

In December 1969, Jayashree, nearly twenty, had married businessman Prakash Mohta and settled down to a quiet, domesticated life. Manjushree[2] was still finishing school. In 1971 it was decided to send her to college in Delhi, partly to take her away from a Calcutta increasingly riven by political violence. Saraladevi spent a large part of the next three years in Delhi with Manjushree while Basant Kumar shuttled between Calcutta and Delhi.

Basant Kumar and Saraladevi were now growing increasingly disenchanted with the political turbulence in Calcutta. They again examined the possibility of Aditya and his family shifting permanently to Bombay. It was a critical decision and one that would change the course of Aditya's and Rajashree's lives. The move to Bombay would serve two purposes apart from eliminating the threat of Naxalite violence. 'First,' explains B.K., 'we felt that Aditya and Rajashree with their young child, Kumar, could blossom in Bombay in an independent atmosphere, not restricted under our umbrella. Second, I felt Aditya would expand his business horizons more while based in a cosmopolitan and commercial city like Bombay rather than Calcutta. Of course, he and Rajashree would come here often and we would go to Bombay and spend time with them. But I thought he would grow both as an individual and as a businessman after moving to Bombay.'

Aditya and Rajashree were enthusiastic. They had friends and roots in Calcutta but they were also young and Bombay appeared an exciting place to live in. Decision made, the couple prepared to shift to the city in early 1971. For Aditya and Rajashree, Bombay promised to be a novel experience. It was more liberal and cosmopolitan than Calcutta and far less insular. The couple arrived at their new home

---

[2]   Manjushree is Aditya Vikram Birla's sister.

in Bombay on February 5, 1971, four months before Kumar's fourth birthday. In retrospect it was to prove the wisest decision the Birla family had made after investing in Thailand in 1969. The move to Bombay would give Aditya, twenty-seven, the independence and the confidence to emerge as the most successful industrialist of his generation over the next quarter century.

As B.K. Birla remarks: 'Aditya became the pioneer and leader of all our operations there. Bombay is the heart of India's trade, commerce and industry. Aditya came in touch with captains of industry and banking. Had he stayed on in Calcutta, he would have been just a member of the Birla family. In Bombay he became "The Birla".'

*

THE PERIOD BETWEEN 1971 and 1983 was critical for Aditya Birla. In those twelve years he would expand his overseas empire and consolidate his Indian operations, led by Indian Rayon and the new caustic soda unit at Nagda. He would also develop the ideas that enabled him to convert a domestic business inheritance into a global conglomerate within a decade. In 1971, when he arrived in Bombay, Aditya controlled a small group of companies with a turnover of less than Rs 20 crore. By 1983, when G.D. Birla died, passing his flagships Gwalior Rayon and Hindalco to his favourite grandson, Aditya was already on his way to becoming the biggest Birla yet. Shobha Ram and Shiv Narayan Birla had, in the nineteenth century, migrated from their Rajasthani village, first to Pilani and then successively to Ahmedabad, Bombay and Calcutta. Aditya's move to Bombay was in keeping with that Birla tradition—constantly seeking fertile new pastures to plant new businesses in—and would prove equally rewarding.

The flat Aditya and Rajashree chose in Bombay was a duplex apartment on the sixteenth and seventeenth floors of an imposing high-rise on Malabar Hill. It was the most exclusive condominium in Bombay's most exclusive neighbourhood. The building, Il Palazzo, commands a panoramic view of Bombay's Queen's Necklace, the gently curving south Bombay strip from Chowpatty to Nariman Point. Il Palazzo was constructed in the late 1960s on premises owned by the WIAA (Western India Automobile Association) Club. It was the perfect location for a married couple in their twenties with a young son. A *griha pravesh* ceremony was conducted at the flat on February 5, 1971. Dressed in a traditional saree and fine jewellery, twenty-two-year-old Rajashree was a picture of contentment as she sat beside her husband and three-year-old son.

Life in Bombay, says Rajashree, was dramatically different from Calcutta. 'In Calcutta we had been tense and troubled by the Naxalite violence from 1969 onwards,' she says. 'In Bombay, we enjoyed a feeling of greater security. Of course, we missed my parents-in-law and the rest of the family with whom we had lived at Basant Vihar from 1965 to 1971. We also missed our close circle of friends in Calcutta. But in Bombay we learned to enjoy our new independence as a family.'

Making new friends was not difficult either. B.K. Birla had long had a large office in Century Bhavan in central Bombay and the Birla family's headquarters at Industry House in south Bombay was also familiar ground for Aditya. Business associates of group companies, many relocated from Calcutta, made the transition easier and the couple settled down quickly in their new environment. 'The period from 1971 to 1974 was a period of adjustment,' reminisces Rajashree. 'We were settling down and making new friends. In the beginning my husband's first cousin, Bharat Taparia, kept us company. Other relatives also made us feel at home. My father-in-law's sister's son and another sister's daughter, Madhuri Dhoot, helped us settle down.'

Gradually, as if attracted to a particularly luminous constellation, Aditya's old friends in Calcutta followed him to Bombay. Lalit Daga was the first to shift, in 1973, followed by Ashwin Kothari, in 1977.[3] Aditya and Rajashree thus again built for themselves a close circle of friends who would remain an important part of their lives for the next two decades. 'Aditya was not fond of large parties,' says Rajashree. 'But he was very fond of the company of a few close friends. That is why we took along several of our Calcutta friends even for our honeymoon in Ranchi. Aditya loved the company of friends.'

---

[3] Ashwin Kothari studied chemical engineering at MIT with Aditya and was a director in Eastern Spinning.

Lalit Daga resumed his partnership with Aditya on the badminton court.[4] Three times a week, Aditya would leave his Industry House office at 6.30 p.m. to go to Bombay Gymkhana, a five-minute drive away, for a strenuous game of badminton with Daga and other club regulars. It was now the only exercise he got in a crushingly busy schedule. There was little time for cricket though he did, in later years, start regular evening walks in the compound of his building. Daga and Kothari, along with Rajender Lodha, Ganga Prasad Loyalka, Pradeep Jajodia and Suresh Tapuriah, remained Aditya's closest friends. Kothari lunched with Aditya at his private Industry House dining room every afternoon for the next nearly twenty years.

In 1971, Kothari's family-owned chemical export company was appointed the sole selling agent for Indian Rayon in Gujarat—a state that accounted for over 60 per cent of Indian Rayon's sales. The business relationship between Aditya and Kothari had begun in 1965 when he joined the board of Eastern Spinning (he remains a director) and helped Aditya set up the company's spinning plant. After 1970, Kothari accompanied Aditya on virtually every business trip he made to Southeast Asia as well as to Europe and the United States. Several years ago, Kothari bought a 22 per cent equity stake in Essel Mining & Industries Ltd, promoted by Aditya's group which held the balance 78 per cent. The company, located in Orissa, is extremely profitable. It is run by R.L. Bathwal, who today also looks after Aditya's first inheritance, Hindustan Gas.

Daga's business interests were less closely entwined with Aditya's, though he too flew several times with G.D. Birla and Aditya between 1973 and 1995 to Renukoot, where Hindalco is located, and later started his own company, Associated Aluminium Industries Pvt. Ltd. Stockily built, with a face that creases frequently into a broad smile, Daga was friend, confidant and colleague all rolled into one. He and his wife Sheela dined with Aditya and Rajashree every weekend, usually at Shri Sadan, a building on south Bombay's Nepean Sea

---

[4] Lalit Daga used to play badminton with Aditya and knew him since his college days when he was at City College while Aditya studied at St Xavier's College.

road where the Dagas had moved on their arrival from Calcutta. They later shifted to another building, Acropolis, across the road from Il Palazzo, to be nearer Aditya and Rajashree. And in 1987 they moved again, a few hundred yards away to a larger flat in Purshottam Bhavan at, Daga says, Aditya's insistence. 'He took great interest in the matter,' reveals Daga. 'The new flat was in a tenanted building and he personally spoke to the people concerned, obtained the necessary permissions and, when we took possession, even selected the furniture and artefacts.'

Aditya's friends and business associates speak of his 'humane' approach to men and matters. 'In the nearly thirty years that I worked for him,' says Bagrodia, 'he never once lost his cool or directed a harsh word towards me.' When the Dagas first arrived in Bombay in 1973, they stayed for several weeks with Aditya and Rajashree. 'They took us to plays, movies and weekend outings,' recalls Daga. 'Aditya wanted us to shift permanently to Bombay and was trying his best to make us feel happy and comfortable here. We finally moved in 1973.'

Despite his wealth, Aditya did not throw his weight around. 'At Bombay Gymkhana he was known in our badminton circle as just a good player, never as a big industrialist,' says Daga. 'He put on no airs and had a very humble, down-to-earth attitude towards people.' Aditya's business rivals do not share that opinion. 'He could be quite ruthless,' says one business journalist who knew him well, 'especially with people like the Modis[5] when they were trying to set up a competing VSF unit in collaboration with Courtaulds Ltd of the UK.'

By the mid-1970s—he was now thirty-two—Aditya had developed into a tough, single-minded businessman. He demanded the highest standards of performance from his executives. According to his senior managers, the most outstanding qualities he possessed were his uncanny judgement of people, his ability to break down problems into small quantum pieces in order to engineer solutions, and the extraordinarily strong management systems that he put into place in all his factories around the world. 'He was an extremely confident

---

[5] S.K. Modi—Chairman, Modi Global Enterprises.

man,' says Bagrodia.[6] 'He was also always very well prepared and had all the relevant facts at his fingertips. In the beginning Aditya babu would look in detail at the debtors' list, the daily price of raw materials and the sales figures. Later, as his businesses grew, he came to rely on monthly financial reports and performance reviews.'

The period between 1971 and 1983—the first dozen years Aditya spent in India's commercial capital—was to prove a formative one for a young businessman intensely aware of his formidable legacy. Aditya arrived in Bombay as a twenty-seven-year-old seeking to carve an independent identity as a businessman in his own right, outside the shadow of his illustrious grandfather and father. By 1983, on the eve of his fortieth birthday, Aditya had established himself as one of India's most extraordinary industrialists. If he had cut his teeth in Calcutta, it was in Bombay that he earned his spurs.

Even as he concentrated on building his Indian and overseas enterprises, Aditya spent as much time as he could with his family. Son Kumar was just over three and a half years old when the family moved to Bombay. 'My first memories of him,' recalls Kumar, 'were that he was a very caring father.'

AN UNEXPECTED END

In July 1993 Aditya was in Washington on the last leg of a barnstorming trip to market Hindalco's Euro issue. Accompanied by Rajashree, Aditya waited impatiently in the departure lounge of Washington airport to board a British Airways flight to London. The couple was

---

[6] Mahesh Bagrodia is one of the most senior executives in Aditya Birla Group.

looking forward to returning home to India after a short stopover in the British capital. As he and Rajashree walked towards the departure lounge, Aditya, carrying his trademark maroon briefcase and black leather pouch, glanced up at the plethora of colourful hoardings that dotted the airport's walls. One suddenly caught his eye. It said: 'If you are a man and over the age of 50, you should have a prostate check-up—you may be suffering from prostate cancer.'

Aditya stopped in mid-stride to read the hoarding again. He turned to his wife. 'I want to have a prostate check-up,' he said thoughtfully, adding: 'As soon as possible.' Rajashree glanced quizzically at her husband. There was an edge to his voice that she had not heard before. Aditya said he had been having difficulty relieving his bladder over the past few weeks. Rajashree was worried but did not show it. 'It's probably the tension of all the business meetings and travelling,' she said to her husband. 'But just to be sure why don't we get a check-up done in London?' Aditya demurred. 'We'll have it done in Bombay,' he said as they boarded the flight.

Within days of arriving in Bombay Rajashree phoned Dr Ajit Phadke for an appointment for her husband. She said it was fairly urgent and since her husband was experiencing bladder difficulties a full check-up should be done. Dr Phadke, the head of urology at Bombay Hospital, had previously treated several members of the Birla family, including G.D, L.N. and K.K.[7] He had also performed routine prostate surgery on L.N. and K.K. Birla in Calcutta in the early 1980s. However, he had not treated Aditya before.

'Mr and Mrs Aditya Birla walked into my rooms in mid-July 1993,' recalls Dr Phadke. 'We exchanged pleasantries and they told me about the short trip they had made to Egypt with their friends Lalit and Sheela Daga, as well as their Washington visit.' Dr Phadke then examined Aditya. 'The moment I felt Aditya babu's prostate,' says Dr Phadke, 'I realized there was a problem. I finished the examination quickly and told him we would need to do further tests. He looked

---

[7] Lakshmi Nivas Birla and Krishna Kumar Birla were sons of G.D. Birla. Basant Kumar Birla was their brother and Aditya Birla was their nephew.

at me straight in the eye and asked point-blank: "Dr Phadke, do you suspect cancer?" I replied that I couldn't say definitely one way or the other. "Your prostate feels different, but there could be many reasons for that—infection, fibrosis, not necessarily cancer." He then asked me: "But how do we rule out cancer?" I said, if he liked, we could do a sonography immediately. We then conducted an ultra sonography scan. The results showed excessive calcium deposits. To a clinician, that suggests chronic infection. Aditya looked at me when I told him this and asked, "Are you happy, Dr Phadke?" I replied that, unfortunately, we still could not rule out cancer though if there are calcium deposits there is a greater likelihood of the problem being caused by fibrosis or an infection.'

As Aditya dressed and prepared to leave the room with his wife, Dr Phadke told him to have a special blood examination called the PSA (prostate specific antigen) test as soon as possible. The results of the PSA test were borderline. 'Aditya and Mrs Birla came to my rooms with the results,' says Dr Phadke. 'Aditya babu asked me, "Now are you happy I don't have cancer?" I said, "I wish I could say that all the evidence so far points against cancer. But we must be sure. I want a second opinion."'

Dr Praful Desai, director and chief surgeon at Tata Memorial Hospital, is India's leading cancer specialist. He arrived at Dr Phadke's rooms on the fourteenth floor of Bombay Hospital on a wet late-July evening. He examined Aditya and agreed with Dr Phadke's verdict: the prostate felt extremely irregular. A soft-spoken, avuncular man, Dr Phadke today concedes: 'I suspected cancer the very first day I examined Aditya. And I think he instinctively knew that.'

After Dr Desai had left, Aditya, Rajashree and Dr Phadke discussed the next step. It was decided to do an immediate biopsy. The procedure involved putting a needle into the prostate and taking out a small piece. 'Aditya babu said he would like to have the biopsy done abroad,' says Dr Phadke, 'in order to avoid any possible rumours of his illness spreading in India. He was very conscious of the fact that lakhs of shareholders had invested their money in his companies and he did not wish to cause unnecessary alarm or panic.'

Within the next forty-eight hours, the famed Birla machinery swung into action. Group executives in the US and Europe fanned out to identify the best hospital in the world for specialized prostate cancer treatment. Three were shortlisted: Johns Hopkins Hospital in Baltimore, Mayo Clinic in Rochester (Minnesota) and Memorial Hospital in New York.

The next day, Aditya invited Dr Phadke to his Industry House office. There, in the boardroom, the pros and cons of each institution were discussed threadbare. Within an hour, the choice was made: Johns Hopkins. The key man at the world-renowned Baltimore hospital was the chairman of the department of urology, the legendary Dr Patrick Walsh, pioneer of 'nerve-sparing radical prostatectomy', a new surgical procedure used in treating prostate cancer.

Within a week, by early August 1993, all arrangements had been finalized. Aditya, Rajashree, Kumar, Neerja, Lalit and Sheela Daga, Rajendra Lodha and Dr Phadke boarded a British Airways flight to London. The party was to stay there overnight before flying to Washington. However, Rajashree developed a fever and the stay was extended by a day. To make up for some of the lost time, the Birlas took a Concorde flight from London to Washington.

From Washington airport—where ironically three weeks ago the hoarding urging men over fifty to undergo a prostate cancer check had sparked the current chain of events—the Birla entourage was whisked away in a convoy of three limousines to Baltimore, an hour's drive from Washington. Basant Kumar and Saraladevi had meanwhile flown into the city the same day on a Swissair flight. The group checked into the Hyatt Regency hotel, strategically located in the city's inner harbour and just across from Johns Hopkins Hospital.

The next day, Dr Walsh conducted a cystoscopic examination of Aditya. Simultaneously, a biopsy was done under local anaesthesia and sedation. Dr Walsh told the family that the results of the biopsy would be known in forty-eight hours. 'We returned to the hotel,' recalls Dr Phadke. It was August 10, 1993. Two days later, the hospital phoned: the biopsy report was ready; would the Birlas come over to meet Dr Walsh?

Dr Phadke accompanied Aditya and Rajashree into Dr Walsh's room. Basant Kumar, Saraladevi, Kumar, Neerja, the Dagas, and Rajendra Lodha waited in the visitors' room outside. Without preamble, Dr Walsh delivered the devastating news: 'Mr Birla, you have cancer of the prostate. We grade such cancers on a scale of 1 to 10 using Gleason's Score. Yours has a Gleason's Score of 8 and 9 which makes it among the worst types of prostate cancer.'

It was possibly the most wrenching moment in Aditya and Rajashree Birla's lives. As Dr Phadke escorted the ashen-faced couple out of Dr Walsh's room, Aditya's family and friends waiting outside knew instantly that their worst fears had been realized. Aditya, recovering his composure quickly, broke the news himself. Speaking in calm, measured tones he said simply: 'I have got cancer.'

Several members of the family broke down and wept. Unable to maintain his own composure, Aditya broke down as well. It was now evening. The family returned to the hotel. Meanwhile, preparations were made at the hospital to operate on Aditya within the next four days. Dr Walsh made it clear that the malignant tumour in the prostate would be removed surgically only if the cancer had not already spread.

'Amidst all the anguish,' says Dr Phadke, 'Mrs Rajashree Birla was incredibly brave. She never once lost her composure and she never once left her husband's side. Aditya babu was also very brave throughout the illness but I have in all my medical experience never seen such a courageous and composed lady as Mrs Birla.'

Dr Walsh operated on Aditya on August 16, 1993. Within minutes he knew the tumour was inoperable. To make sure, he sent the lymph nodes surrounding the prostate for frozen section examination. The report from the laboratory arrived in ten minutes: the cancer, it said, had spread beyond the prostate. Dr Walsh was genuinely distressed. Over the past week, he had grown fond of Aditya, Rajashree and their family. Now, as he stitched up the incision, he turned to Dr Phadke who was in the operation theatre with him. 'I am sorry you and the Birla family had to come all the way from India,' he said. 'But there is nothing I can do surgically.'

Dr Walsh then walked out of the theatre to meet the family assembled outside. 'I'm sorry,' he repeated. 'The cancer has spread. It is not operable.'

Several members of the family again broke down but composed themselves quickly. Dr Walsh consoled them: 'Not everything is lost. We can't operate on the prostate but we do have alternative treatments like hormone therapy.'

Meanwhile, Aditya had regained consciousness in the operation theatre. As he was being taken to the recovery room, he opened his eyes and saw Dr Walsh. 'Could you do the operation, Dr Walsh?' he asked drowsily.

Dr Walsh replied: 'No, I could not. I'm sorry, Mr Birla. However, we do have alternative treatments to offer. We plan to give you hormone therapy.'

Still heavily sedated, Aditya murmured: 'That means the disease has spread outside the prostate, doesn't it?'

'Yes,' replied Dr Walsh, unable to meet the Indian industrialist's eyes. Aditya nodded slowly. Then, shutting his eyes, he went to sleep.

The next day, Rajashree and other members of the family escorted Aditya back to the hotel. As they struggled to come to terms with the most devastating period of their lives, the Birlas also began to consider the impact the news of Aditya's illness could have back home. Apart from the tremors that could hit the AVB group's listed scrips, it was critical that the confidence of employees, investors and customers in the family's global businesses should not be undermined even fractionally. It was decided to announce officially that Aditya had gone to the United States for a routine prostate check-up and that everything was all right.

On the British Airways flight back to Delhi via London, a quiet young man shared the first class lounge with the Birlas. He was the younger son of Madhavrao Scindia, the former Congress Minister for Civil Aviation. When Aditya disembarked with his family at New Delhi's Indira Gandhi international airport, the first person he saw in the passenger lounge was Scindia who enquired solicitously:

'Hello, Mr Birla. I hear that you underwent an operation in America. I hope you are all right.'

As the family drove out of the airport, Aditya mustered up a smile as the irony struck him. 'Here we are,' he chuckled to Rajashree, 'trying to keep all this under wraps and the moment I set foot in India someone like Madhavrao Scindia knows all about it.'

However, over the next two years Aditya's illness would remain one of India's best kept medical secrets, with only a handful of close relatives, friends and business associates being fully aware of just how seriously ill he was. And throughout that period, Aditya would show extraordinary courage as he plunged back into his work with an energy and zeal that almost defied his ever-weakening body.

'He was incredibly brave about it,' says Rajashree. 'Once the diagnosis of prostate cancer was confirmed in America, and we were returning to India, Aditya told me: "God has not given me a very long life. But he has given me many other compensations." He continued working as hard as before. There was no increase in momentum but he now arranged his business affairs more systematically.'

Kumar inevitably now became the focus of attention. Ever the meticulous planner, Aditya tackled the task of Kumar's training with added urgency. 'The doctors told us my husband had about five years to live,' says Rajashree. 'What came as a shock was how quickly the illness progressed. In the end, he got only two years.'

Dr Phadke says the illness spread faster than anyone had anticipated. In mid-1993, Aditya knew that he was unlikely to live longer than another four or five years. But he recognized the growing possibility that the time he had left could be considerably less than that. Virtually every business decision Aditya took after 1993 was based on two strategies: first, strengthening management systems within the group's Indian and overseas companies to ensure that his absence would not affect their future performance; and second, inducting Kumar rapidly in senior management positions in key group companies. Kumar was already in charge of Indo Gulf and Vikram Ispat. Now, in rapid succession, he was appointed vice-chairman of all flagship AVB companies, including Grasim, Hindalco and Indian Rayon.

Back in Bombay, Aditya began the hormone therapy prescribed by Dr Walsh. The treatment consisted of one injection a month. By 1994, the illness seemed to have stabilized, giving Aditya and his family a glimmer of hope that the cancer had gone into remission. Meanwhile, Aditya despatched Rajendra Lodha to attend several international conferences on prostate cancer and scour the world for medical literature on the latest advances in its treatment. He read up virtually everything on the subject and was particularly interested in a revolutionary new anti-cancer gene therapy being experimented on animals in the United States.

In business, there was considerable expansion activity: the group's new telecom, petrochemical, power and financial services ventures were at various stages of implementation. Kumar rapidly began to assume a leadership role in negotiating the terms for several of these projects as well as supervising the expansion programmes of existing group companies. Aditya concentrated on broad strategic planning and raising capital abroad. He began to pass many of his trademark management precepts to Kumar. Aditya solved complex problems by breaking them up into small parts. He often floored highly qualified managers with innovative, instant solutions to problems they had unsuccessfully grappled with, sometimes for months. Kumar learned quickly and was soon making major decisions in all AVB group companies.

Aditya continued to visit Johns Hopkins Hospital for periodic check-ups. In Bombay, Dr Phadke carried out regular checks as well. One physical examination showed that the tumour was getting progressively larger. Aditya was now again beginning to experience urinary difficulties directly linked to the growing tumour. Dr Phadke was worried and suggested an immediate consultation with Dr Walsh.

The American specialist agreed that urgent action was called for. To control the tumour locally it was decided to administer radiotherapy. The treatment, Dr Walsh said, would last at least six weeks. Aditya was worried that a stay of that duration in a well-known cancer hospital like Johns Hopkins would raise eyebrows in India. He preferred to undergo the treatment in London where he had an apartment and where a prolonged stay would not appear unusual.

Once again, the Birla family prepared to fly abroad at short notice. Aditya received cobalt radiation treatment at Royal Marsden Hospital, a specialized cancer institution; he was put on a catheter and had a rubber bag strapped to his thigh for the entire seven-week duration of the treatment in London. Though the therapy progressed well, there were some side effects. Aditya lost his appetite and became weak.

On his return to India, in July 1994, Aditya developed measles. His granddaughter, Ananyashree, had just been born and owing to the infection he could not visit her in hospital. He would sit in his car in the hospital parking lot and later, when Ananyashree came home, he set up a video camera in her room so that he could see her on film. Once he had recovered from the measles, Aditya spent as much time as he could with his granddaughter. He knew better than anyone else that his time could be drawing to a close.

Though in some pain, and often under heavy medication through most of 1994, Aditya did not relent on his punishing work schedule. By October 1994, he had decided that the AVB group would forge a strong presence in the newly liberalized and privatized telecom industry. He strongly believed that telecom was a sunrise business in India and the Birla group's unmatched financial and management skills could create a successful environment for a telecom venture. As usual, he sought out a world leader in the field as a partner: AT&T, the American global telecommunications major. The joint venture—Birla–AT&T Communications Ltd—was launched in January 1995 and it was to be one of the last formal public occasions Aditya would appear at. The only other was the launch of the Birla Mutual Fund, also in January 1995, when Aditya gave a rousing speech to India's top stockbrokers and financial analysts.

A pressing agenda on Aditya's timetable at the end of 1994 was the twenty-fifth anniversary of his overseas business group. He had launched his international business career in 1969 in Thailand. That career had flourished beyond anyone's expectation. It had established him in the eyes of his peers and the international business community as the first Indian multinational industrialist. He had made a pioneering contribution to Indian industry in Southeast Asia with his now-sprawling empire. In the last week of November 1994, barely ten months before his death, that empire would be twenty-five years old and Aditya intended to mark the occasion fittingly. In Bangkok, where it had all begun, Mahansaria began preparations for the silver anniversary celebrations on a war footing. 'Aditya babu was running a temperature in mid-November and phoned to tell me that he might not be able to come to Bangkok,' says Mahansaria. 'I told him that it was impossible to hold the function without him. Finally, after many telephone calls and much persuasion, he agreed to come despite his fever.' Ironically, the fever was unconnected to his prostate malignancy.

Meanwhile, official messages of congratulations began to pour in. On November 4, 1994, President Shankar Dayal Sharma wrote to Aditya, complimenting him on the AVB group's achievements abroad: 'I am glad to learn that the Birla group is completing a quarter-century of its industrial presence in Southeast Asia. The Birla group is part of the industrial tradition of India and has made a major contribution to our national development. Through its numerous enterprises abroad, the group has substantially added to the nation's export earnings. As India seeks to participate more intensively in global economic activity, the success of these joint ventures acquires greater significance and helps shape India's image abroad. On the occasion of the silver jubilee celebrations, I send my best wishes to the Birla group.'

Before leaving for the celebrations in Bangkok, Aditya wrote a letter to his staff in Thailand in which he poured fulsome praise on their contribution and commitment. The letter set the tone for the coming week in which the AVB group planned not only several official functions but a series of plant visits for VIP guests across Thailand: 'On behalf of the Birla group, I wish to convey my warmest congratulations to the management team, staff and workers of our group of companies in Thailand on their outstanding performance. I wish them continued growth and success in the future. During the past twenty-five years, the Birla group has repeatedly demonstrated its strong faith, confidence and total commitment to the industrial development of Thailand by bringing in investments and advanced technologies. The products manufactured in the group's companies are of the highest quality, meeting the most stringent international standards. The group companies meet not just local requirements, but have also been in the forefront of the export efforts of the country.

'Since 1969, the Birla group has set up a large number of the most modern factories using the latest state-of-the-art technologies covering a wide range of sophisticated products in speciality chemicals, synthetic fibres and textiles. Most of these products have been manufactured for the first time in Thailand and even in the ASEAN region. Combining the best quality raw materials with the most advanced technology in its production processes, together with highly competent management and a skilled Thai workforce, the Birla group in Thailand has built a very strong reputation over the past two decades for the quality and reliability of its products matching international standards.'

As the AVB group's Thai workers and managers awaited them, the B.K. and Aditya Birla family prepared to celebrate the event in full strength. On November 16, Aditya, Rajashree, Kumar, Neerja and Vasavadatta flew to Bangkok directly from Bombay. B.K. Birla and Saraladevi arrived a few hours later from Calcutta with Manjushree and Jayashree. Aditya and Rajashree waited at Bangkok airport to receive them. 'Aditya was looking weak,' recalls Saraladevi. 'He had been visiting his various plants and seemed tired: Indeed, with his cancer spreading rapidly, and the fever sapping his energy, it took exceptional willpower for Aditya to go through the taxing schedule of ceremonies and dinners planned for the occasion.

The Birlas stayed at the Dusit Thani hotel in Bangkok. Kumar and Neerja had brought along their four-month-old baby daughter,

Ananyashree, and the young couple, accompanied by Rajashree, Jayashree and Manjushree, plunged into sightseeing and shopping.

Aditya, Kumar and their senior executives meanwhile concentrated on business. A year earlier, Aditya had launched a $40 million (Rs. 145 crore) carbon black unit in Alexandria, Egypt. Now he used the Bangkok silver jubilee celebrations to announce a $400 million (Rs. 1450 crore) investment package in new textiles and chemicals ventures in Thailand. Among these was the first-ever plant in Southeast Asia to produce epi-chloro-hydrin, a raw material for epoxy resins.

Thailand was the crown jewel of Aditya's Southeast Asian empire. In November 1994, the AVB group's eight industrial ventures in Thailand had a sales turnover of just below Rs. 2000 crore. The group's first company, Indo–Thai Synthetics, had begun operations in 1969–70 with 12,768 spindles. It now had 67,292 spindles and produced a variety of spun yarns. The group's largest Thai company, Thai Rayon, set up in 1975, accounted twenty years later for 20 per cent of the Thai textile industry's total exports. The AVB group employed 9000 people in its overseas plants, half of them in Thailand. S.S. Mahansaria, who spearheaded the group's growth since his arrival in Bangkok on April 10, 1969, sits in an elegant office at Mahatun Plaza, a top Bangkok business address. He says succinctly: 'There is no red tapism whatsoever in Thailand. In all my years here, no government agency has visited us, except perhaps for pollution checks. In Thailand one has to fight the world to do well. In India, one's fight is always with the government.'

On November 20, 1994, Aditya went to bed with mixed feelings. He had spent the last few days visiting his plants in and around Bangkok. He was tired but happy: the next day was to be one of the most triumphant in a career already studded with achievement. Rajashree insisted that Aditya sleep early; the fever and exertions of the past four days had enervated him.

On the evening of November 21, nearly 2000 of Bangkok's most powerful political and business leaders, including Prime Minister Kun Chuan Leekpai, arrived at the Dusit Thani's Lumpini ballroom to share Aditya's triumph. Watched by Rajashree and other close family members, Aditya rose to give what would be his most important but last major speech to an international audience. It was redolent with pride in the group's achievements overseas but tempered with the knowledge that much yet remained to be done. It was also a tribute to Thailand and its people of whom Aditya was genuinely fond:

'H.E. the Prime Minister of Thailand Kun Chuan Leekpai, H.E. the Deputy Prime Minister Kun Supachai Panichpakdee, H.E. the Finance Minister Kun Tarrin Niamhaeminda, H.E. the Ambassador of India, Mr Ranjit Gupta and ambassadors from all other countries, distinguished and honoured guests, friends, ladies and gentlemen. It is a great pleasure and honour for me to welcome all of you on this very special, memorable and, for me personally, a very sentimental and emotional occasion, the occasion of the Birla group reaching the glorious milestone of completing twenty-five not silver but golden years of operations in Thailand, leading to our silver jubilee. I would like to especially thank His Excellency the Prime Minister, whose very presence itself is a source of great inspiration. Thanks are also due to the honourable ministers for encouraging us with their presence here today. Let me also express my gratitude to the people and to the government of Thailand for their warm welcome, solid support and abundant affection showered on the Birla group in Thailand. This, more than anything else, has made it possible for us to achieve our outstanding success and to be where we are today.'

As the assembled audience applauded, Aditya turned to specifics. Speaking with only the barest glance at his notes, he declared: 'The A.V. Birla group, including its foreign ventures, is today India's largest industrial house. As stated in *Euromoney* magazine, it is also the only truly multinational Indian group. In India, we are the largest producer of:

— Rayon filament yarn;
— Flax yarn;
— Caustic soda; Rayon grade pulp;
— Aluminium metal (in the private sector).

'Worldwide, we are:

— The largest producer of viscose staple fibre and palm oil;
— The third largest producer of insulators;
— The sixth largest producer of carbon black.

'The Birla group has over 100 plants, extending across India, Thailand, Malaysia, Indonesia, Philippines, England, Canada, Kenya and Egypt. It has offices in several other countries around the world. The group is planning to start industries in Vietnam, Romania, Poland and Russia in the near future.'

As the assembled audience again broke into applause, Aditya turned on the charm. 'I am particularly proud and fond of our projects in Thailand,' he declared. 'Starting with a small synthetic textile plant, the Birla group has vigorously expanded and diversified into various high-technology areas. Over the years, we have set up plants in Thailand to manufacture synthetic cloth, rayon fibre, carbon black, sodium tri-polyphosphate, hydrogen peroxide, acrylic fibre, epoxy resins and sodium meta bi-sulphite. Each one of these plants was the *first* of its kind in Thailand. There were no manufacturing activities in these products in Thailand until we put up these plants. Ours was the pioneering effort. The products we make were earlier imported into Thailand, resulting in a substantial outflow of foreign exchange. We not only satisfied the total domestic demand but also turned Thailand into a net exporter of these products. We obtained the latest technology available in the world and put Thailand on the industrial map of the world, and a force to reckon with. With the dedicated efforts of a strong team of 4500 persons in Thailand, the Birla group's total revenue has reached Baht 10 billion, of which Baht 4 billion is from exports to all parts of the world. Our commitment to Thailand is demonstrated by the fact that we made the maximum investment at the peak of the Vietnam war, when several corporations were withdrawing from the country. This was an act of faith in the future and in the destiny of Thailand. It was a commitment born out of confidence. We are here to stay.'

And then, as if to demonstrate that beneath the serious visage of a businessman there lurked an impish sense of humour, Aditya quipped: 'My wife often warns that I may leave India and settle down in Thailand. When I used to speak in India to those in the government, praising the policies of the Thai government, they often light-heartedly remarked that more than a citizen of India, I was perhaps putting myself across as an ambassador of goodwill for Thailand. This reflects my strong sentiments and warm feelings towards this great country. In the last couple of years, during my discussions with those in the Government of India, I have revealed the pragmatic economic policies of the Government of Thailand, which has led to your success. In the wake of our reforms, several of these ideas are being implemented. Your Excellency, I do hope that for borrowing a leaf from your economic policies, I will not be charged with a violation of Intellectual Property Rights!'

The wit sat well with the audience. Aditya, who had celebrated his fifty-first birthday exactly a week ago in India on November 14, 1994, turned now to history. 'Trade relations between India and Thailand go back more than 2500 years. Trade by sea and along the old silk route occurred even before recorded history. Over time, trade led to religious exchanges during the third century B.C., when Emperor Ashoka sent emissaries to Southeast Asian countries and Siam, in particular, which ultimately led to the establishment of the Buddhist faith in Thailand. Thus we also share common religious bonds. In languages too, both the Hindi and Thai languages have their origins in Sanskrit. There are several words in Thai and Hindi which are similar. Our cultural and religious ties are further strengthened by the great epic *Ramayana* which is widely read, revered and idolized in both Thailand and India. Our geographic closeness is a fact of life. We, therefore, have strong links, through our religion, culture, language and proximity. All these factors make us natural partners.

'When my grandfather, G.D. Birla, visited Thailand in 1974, the then prime minister of Thailand remarked that despite the closeness and similarities, India and Thailand have yet to take notice of each other. Sir, the time is now ripe to forge economic alliances, to foster cultural relationship, to deepen our religious affinity and to bring our two great countries close, for the greater good of our people. The Birla group is proud of having played its role in strengthening the bonds that already exist between our countries. We are privileged to have played the role of a catalyst in achieving this worthy objective. I am confident that our association with your great country will continue to flourish and grow in the years ahead.'

He had now been speaking for over fifty-five minutes but the crowd in the ornate hotel ballroom had remained completely riveted. Aditya himself, despite the fever and the strain of the last few days, betrayed no outward signs of fatigue. His gaze swept across the audience as he said his final words: 'In conclusion, sir, I would like to add that the people of both our countries are God-fearing, religious and peace-loving. Both our countries believe in the Sanskrit saying which means "Treat your guest as God himself" and, believe me, Your Excellency, we have been treated here in this very spirit. We have no words to express our gratitude and sincere thanks for making us feel at home in Thailand.'

It was an extraordinary hour-long speech, possibly the best Aditya had ever given. And it underscored how a twenty-five-year-old's vision in 1969 at, as he pointed out, the height of the Vietnam war had been vindicated. Aditya received a standing ovation from the audience in the luxurious Lumpini ballroom as he sat down. After a few minutes, the formalities completed, dinner was announced. As the 2000 guests, a nice mix of Indians and Thais, nibbled on the jalebis, halwas, pulao, masala dosas and Japanese and Thai curry, the fragrant smell of rose petals and incense wafted gently through the air. Aditya, Rajashree, Kumar, Neerja and Vasavadatta, along with Basant Kumar, Saraladevi, Manjushree and Jayashree, mingled with the guests—Thai cabinet ministers, senior Birla executives and local business leaders—savouring an achievement that lent honour not only to the Birla family but, as Aditya had pointed out, to India itself. It was precisely the sentiment that had guided six generations of Birlas before Aditya and would guide the eighth—Kumar Mangalam—in the years to come.

The next day, November 22, after a press conference attended by the international media, Aditya and Rajashree flew to Singapore for a short holiday before returning home to Bombay. Aditya had much to do and many loose ends to tie up in the remaining few months of his life.

Over the next three months following his return from Bangkok, Aditya's battle with his cancer ebbed and flowed. There were weeks when he felt well; there were others when he was in agony and could relieve his bladder only with the greatest difficulty. By March 1995, the prostate tumour seemed to have grown larger. The radiotherapy in London had succeeded only in slowing down its growth and to Dr Phadke, who continued to examine Aditya periodically, the signs now seemed ominous.

The early months of 1995 had passed in a flurry of meetings and public functions for the launch of several new AVB group joint ventures, including the ambitious telecom project with AT&T and the mutual fund and asset management company with Marlin Securities and Capital International. Aditya had borne the growing pain caused by his illness with a stoicism that drew admiration from his family and close friends who alone were aware of the full extent of his suffering. 'In spite of being ill,' says Kumar, 'my father had a very positive attitude. He was very brave. He would tell us sometimes that he did not want us to be affected by his illness and that work should go on smoothly. He used to tell us: "Things might go wrong, I hope you are aware of that." He was in a way preparing us for the future. Obviously, as the pain grew worse, it was a very emotional time for all of us. We were upset but he told us to get on with things, not succumb, to carry on with enthusiasm.'

In March 1995, Dr Phadke removed the catheter that had been inserted during Aditya's radiotherapy in London the previous month and had been retained as a precautionary measure for most of the intervening period. A few hours after the catheter was removed, Dr Phadke received a call from the Birla residence that gladdened him: Aditya had relieved his bladder unaided for the first time in weeks and was delighted. 'I was relieved,' recalls Dr Phadke. 'I was going out to a dinner party that evening in Bandra. I left the telephone number of the host with Aditya in case he experienced any problems later in the night. This was the first time in several weeks that we had removed the catheter.'

Even as Dr Phadke entered the house of his host in Bandra an hour later, the phone rang. It was Aditya. He said, 'Dr Phadke, I'm very uncomfortable. I can't relieve my bladder.' Dr Phadke told him to go immediately to either Breach Candy Hospital or Bombay Hospital for an examination. He would join him there in forty-five minutes. Aditya demurred. 'Dr Phadke, I don't want to go to either hospital. Can we do the examination at your nursing home?' Dr Phadke agreed. He immediately phoned his private clinic, Colony Nursing Home in Matunga, and told the staff to keep the operation theatre ready. He phoned Aditya back and told him to meet him at the nursing home in thirty minutes.

Aditya and Rajashree descended from the seventeenth floor in the high-speed lift of their Il Palazzo residence. They drove straight to Colony Nursing Home in Matunga. At Haji Ali, disaster struck: their car broke down. As the chauffeur tried unsuccesfully to get it started again, Aditya and Rajashree climbed out. Aditya was now in acute discomfort, his bladder full. As motorists sped by the famous Haji Ali roundabout, Aditya and Rajashree tried to flag down a passing taxi. It was past 10.00 p.m. and few taxis were plying on the road. Those that were drove past without stopping. By a stroke of luck, an acquaintance of the family who was driving past spotted the Birla couple. He stopped his car and drove them to the Matunga clinic. By the time they reached, Aditya was in agony.

Dr Phadke and his assistants were waiting and immediately wheeled him on to the operating table. 'Dr Phadke', Aditya said, 'I can't bear the pain. If it carries on like this, I'll die.'

Dr Phadke inserted a catheter to drain out the urine. Within minutes, the pressure on Aditya's bladder was relieved. The pain eased. Dr Phadke advised Rajashree that Aditya should spend the night at the nursing home. By now, the rest of the Birla family and close friends had arrived at the clinic: Kumar, Vasavadatta, Basant

Kumar and Saraladevi (who were in town), Rajendra Lodha and the Dagas.

Rajashree, utterly composed despite the crisis, took Aditya home the next morning. 'He was now very comfortable,' remembers Dr Phadke, 'and very grateful. But this episode got me worried. If the radiotherapy in London had succeeded in reducing the size of the tumour in the prostate, why was Aditya experiencing so much difficulty relieving his bladder? To me it suggested that the nerves leading to the bladder were being affected. The disease was obviously spreading fast.'

A few weeks later Aditya developed sciatica. Spasms of pain radiated down to his lower back. Dr Dholakia, the city's leading orthopaedic specialist, was consulted. He suggested traction and rest. Aditya felt better after the treatment and the sciatica attack subsided. Within days, however, the shooting pain in his lower back returned. Dr Dholakia was now concerned. He discovered, to his shock, that a CAT scan on Aditya's back had not been done in London during the radiotherapy at Royal Marsden Hospital. He ordered an immediate X-ray of the spine. As it transpired, the periphery of the spinal X-ray also displayed parts of Aditya's lung. When Dr Dholakia looked at the X-ray closely his heart sank: there was evidence of deposits in the lungs. The cancer had spread far beyond the prostate.

On May 10, 1995, Dr Phadke took stock of the situation. His patient could empty his bladder only with the aid of a catheter due to the cancerous cells in the nerves surrounding the prostate gland; he could not walk because of the sciatica attack; he had constant back pain and was virtually immobilized. The position was critical.

Dr Dholakia suggested a magnetic resonance imaging (MRI) of the full spine. The test was done at Bhatia Hospital. Till now all the investigations into Aditya's illness had been conducted either abroad or in total secrecy in India. Now Rajashree put her foot down. 'I don't care who comes to know—he must get proper treatment,' she told the phalanx of doctors attending to her husband.

Aditya was driven the same day to Bhatia Hospital. The MRI showed that the disease had indeed spread, in Dr Phadke's words, 'far and beyond. It had affected the bones of the spinal cord and one of the lower vertebrae was totally destroyed. It had spread to the lungs and to the lymph nodes. It was obvious we were fighting a losing battle.'

Aditya, however, had not given up hope. Rajashree, constantly by his side, says he had great faith in the revolutionary new anti-cancer gene therapy that was being developed in the United States. Dr Phadke says Aditya was convinced that a breakthrough in gene therapy might just save him. He did not, however, want to undergo chemotherapy because of the harsh side effects. Aditya spoke to Dr Walsh in Baltimore several times on the phone, asking him about the progress Johns Hopkins's researchers were making in their work on gene therapy. Dr Walsh replied that the therapy was being tried out experimentally on animals but no testing had yet been done on humans. He told Aditya, who had by now read virtually every academic paper on cancer research and related subjects, that he was prepared, if it were warranted, to even use gene therapy on him for the first time. 'Aditya babu was now hoping for miracles,' says Dr Phadke thoughtfully. 'He could not accept that there was no hope.'

Aditya's health now began to deteriorate rapidly. A blood test in the third week of May 1995 showed abnormally high calcium levels—typical of advanced cases of cancer. If the calcium levels continued to shoot up, the heart could stop. Doctors immediately put Aditya on an intravenous drip to pump in cortisone and other specialized medicines to lower the calcium deposits. Within twenty-four hours, however, more complications arose. The damaged vertebrae caused partial paralysis below the waist. Aditya now could not move his legs. Panic set in. Doctors attending to him feared that if he even sat up, the vertebrae would collapse and he would be totally paralysed.

Emergency preparations were made to fly Aditya to Johns Hopkins Hospital. The first available British Airways flight was on May 27. Basant Kumar and Saraladevi would fly Swissair and join the rest of the family in Washington en route to Baltimore. Virtually the entire first class lounge of the British Airways aircraft was reserved to allow a stretcher on board and make room for the nearly one dozen close Birla family members, friends, three doctors and several attendants who were to accompany Aditya to Baltimore. Dr Phadke was joined by the family physician, Dr K. Rammoorthi, and an intensive care specialist, Dr Pravin Amin. Last-minute arrangements, including a saline drip placed on board the British Airways flight, were completed barely hours before departure.

On a sweltering Saturday night, May 27, 1995, Aditya Birla, in acute pain and virtually paralysed below the waist, left his Il Palazzo duplex apartment for the last time in his life. An ambulance drove him and Rajashree to Sahar International Airport; other members of his family, close friends and doctors followed in a convoy of cars. The British Airways flight took off in the early hours of the morning.

On board with Rajashree, who sat close by Aditya's side, were Kumar, Neerja, Vasavadatta, Lalit and Sheela Daga, Rajendra Lodha, Dr Phadke, Dr Rammoorthi, Dr Amin and several attendants. The journey to London was uneventful though Aditya's condition was deteriorating rapidly. Paralysis was setting in and he had lost control over his bowel movements.

During the short stop at Heathrow airport, Aditya's blood was sent by the pathologist-daughter of his London-based chief executive to the laboratory for examination. Though it was early Sunday morning, the report arrived before the plane took off for Washington. It showed that the calcium deposits were not rising. Other indications in the blood report were also better. The flight across the Atlantic passed relatively smoothly. Aditya, heavily sedated, was in pain but retained his composure. Seated nearby was a scion of the Ambani family; the news of Aditya's illness was known in select corporate circles and the first thing that awaited the Birlas at Johns Hopkins Hospital in Baltimore a few hours later was a large bouquet of flowers from the Ambani family.

At Washington airport, more bad luck dogged the Birlas. The ambulance which was to have been arranged by John Hopkins Hospital failed to turn up. To make things worse, the airbridge connecting the aircraft to the airport lounge was not available. The British Airways plane thus parked itself on the tarmac and disembarking passengers walked to the arrival lounge. Aditya, however, could not sit up and refused to be put in a wheelchair. The British Airways crew complained that Aditya was holding up the plane. Aditya suddenly lost his temper. 'If this is how you treat a British Airways gold card holder who is seriously ill and on a stretcher,' he told the crew furiously, 'then I don't want your gold card. Tear it up.'

Rattled, the British Airways ground staff arranged for an ambulance to come right up to the parked plane. Aditya, lying flat on his back on a stretcher with a saline drip on his arm, and Rajashree were driven in the ambulance to Johns Hopkins Hospital. The rest of the party followed in a cavalcade of limousines. It was late evening when they arrived at the hospital. Awaiting them outside the entrance were three of Johns Hopkins's seniormost specialists: Dr Walsh, the head of the department of urology, and the heads of the departments of radiotherapy and chemotherapy. 'It was unprecedented,' says Dr Phadke. 'It was the Sunday evening of a long weekend. In America senior doctors are simply not available on such days. I do not think the heads of three different departments at Johns Hopkins Hospital would have waited at the entrance on a Sunday evening for any patient other than the American President.'

Within an hour, the team of doctors had put Aditya on radiotherapy; they took deep X-rays of the spine to ascertain the damage to the vertebrae. The next day, they called a leading neurosurgeon to examine Aditya. He advised an immediate decompression operation to relieve the pressure on the nerves in Aditya's back.

As the family struggled to keep up with the rapid pace of events, Dr Walsh walked up to Basant Kumar and declared softly: 'I don't think your son will ever walk again.' Basant Kumar, who had maintained a brave front all these months, now broke down completely.

The back operation was planned for Tuesday, May 30. Aditya was on painkillers and heavily sedated. He still remembered to ask Dr Walsh: 'What about the gene therapy?' Dr Walsh replied:

'First, let us take care of the emergency.' Privately, Dr Walsh told Dr Phadke that gene therapy was not really an option. It had not advanced beyond testing on animals. The American doctors' strategy was to first operate on Aditya's back, eliminate the nerve pain and then start intensive chemotherapy as a last-resort attempt to stop the rampaging cancer.

The operation on Aditya's lower back on Tuesday was successful. A tumour was removed from the lumbo-sacral region of the spine and sent for examination. A shock awaited the American and Indian doctors when the report arrived. For nearly two years they had been treating Aditya for cancer of the prostate known technically as adeno carcinoma. This form of cancer is not very sensitive to chemotherapy but can be treated effectively with certain drugs. The report on the tumour taken out of Aditya's back, however, showed that the cancer had changed its character. It was now squamous—metaplasia of the adeno carcinoma. Squamous carcinomas are notorious for not responding to chemotherapy. The doctors' last hopes were now dashed. And yet chemotherapy remained the only option. Radiotherapy had failed; and surgery was ruled out since the disease was so widespread.

A side effect of advanced cancer is that fluid accumulates in the lungs, making the patient breathless. Doctors had been forced to put a needle in the pleural cavity of Aditya's lungs to remove two litres of bloodstained fluid. The rapidity with which the fluid had again begun to accumulate in the lungs now compelled the American doctors to start chemotherapy immediately. Within twenty-four hours of taking the first course of chemotherapy, Aditya became breathless. As his condition deteriorated, he told Rajashree that he might not survive the night. Rajashree, as she would for the next four months, kept vigil at Aditya's bedside through the night. Slowly, his condition stabilized. The excruciating pain in his back disappeared after the decompression operation. Aditya, however, remained paralysed below the waist and was confined to a wheelchair. The chemotherapy caused acute hair loss but, after the traumatic first dose, relatively few other side effects.

Kumar, Neerja, Vasavadatta, Basant Kumar and Saraladevi continued to stay at the nearby Hyatt Regency hotel, along with Rajendra Lodha and the Dagas. Rajashree stayed in a room next to her husband at the hospital. In July 1995, Kumar and Neerja celebrated Ananyashree's first birthday. Rajashree's room at the hospital was decorated with balloons and ribbons; Aditya was wheeled into the room and spent precious moments with his only grandchild.

By the last week of August 1995, with Aditya's condition unchanged, Dr Phadke returned to India. The head of Bombay Hospital's urology department had shut down his practice in Bombay for three months to be at Aditya's side. As he said goodbye, Dr Phadke recalls Aditya's innate courtesy despite his serious condition. 'He apologized for having caused me any inconvenience and wished me well in the future.'

Aditya had so far undergone three rounds of chemotherapy and had managed to spend a week in the hotel with family and friends. In early September 1995, however, his condition began to deteriorate again. He was rushed back to hospital and administered a fourth dose of chemotherapy.

In between treatments at the hospital, Aditya had kept in touch on the phone with his senior executives in Bombay, Calcutta, Bangkok and elsewhere. Bagrodia spoke to him frequently between June and September 1995, keeping him posted on the Birla–AT&T telecom venture as well as the Bina and Rosa power projects. 'I spoke to Aditya babu about once a week during his last four months at Johns Hopkins Hospital in Baltimore,' says Bagrodia. 'The last time we spoke was on September 13, 1995. He had phoned me at my Industry House office but I happened to be at our copper smelter office in Raheja Chambers at Nariman Point. It was 6.00 p.m. The operator at Industry House informed him that I was at Raheja Chambers. He called me and his voice somehow sounded different. I did not normally take liberties with him, but I said: "Babu, today your voice is not sounding good, you seem to be in a lot of pain." He said it was the drugs. We spoke mainly about MRPL. That was the last time I heard his voice.'

Aditya slipped into a coma a few days later. He never came out of it. The end came at midnight, American Eastern Time, on Sunday, October 1, 1995. It was 9.30 a.m. in India. Aditya was not yet fifty-two.

The shock that followed his death was due largely to the fact that few people in India even knew that Aditya was seriously ill. While the business press had speculated during his long absence from India that he was suffering from prostate cancer, there was no independent confirmation from the family. The official explanation given to the media since early 1995 was that Aditya Birla had a slipped disc which required specialized medical attention in the United States. Panic indeed could have set in had AVB group company shareholders known how ill their chairman was. When the news of Aditya Birla's death was front-paged in every major Indian newspaper on October 2, 1995, major AVB company stocks plunged. Grasim fell by 4 per cent, Hindalco by 3.5 per cent and Indian Rayon by 3 per cent. However, within days the shares recovered all their lost ground as investors realized that the strong, decentralized management structure Aditya had built would maintain the group's growth momentum.

Ironically, in a family renowned for its longevity, Aditya was the youngest to die of natural causes. His great-grandfather, Baldevdas, had lived to the age of 93. G.D. Birla died at 89. And father Basant Kumar is an energetic 76.

In India, the news of Aditya Birla's death was greeted with shock. Apart from the suddenness, there were few details immediately available about what had happened in faraway Baltimore. As Indians awoke to a late Sunday morning breakfast on October 1, 1995, teleprinters in newspaper offices around the country began flashing the news. Being a holiday, there were no evening papers that day and most Indians read about the industrialist's death only on Monday morning, October 2—ironically the birth anniversary of Mahatma Gandhi who had enjoyed a long and close relationship with the Birla family.

The first reports put out by news agencies were sketchy on detail. Most simply said: 'Aditya Vikram Birla died at a hospital in Baltimore,

USA, early Sunday morning following pneumonic fever and malaria. He was fifty-one. Birla was suffering from a back problem. Mahesh Bagrodia of the Birla group in Bombay said: "He had recovered from a slipped disc condition and was staying in a hotel in Baltimore when he developed pneumonia."'

Even the *Economic Times*, which usually had the inside track of India's largest business houses, was left groping in the dark. On October 2, it front-paged the news of Aditya's death with a report from its Bombay bureau:

After months of suffering, Aditya Vikram Birla passed away at the world-renowned Johns Hopkins Hospital in Baltimore near Washington, DC. He would have turned 52 on November 14. His father, Basant Kumar Birla, mother Saraladevi, wife Rajashree, son Kumar Mangalam, daughter Vasavadatta, and daughter-in-law Neerja were at his bedside when Birla breathed his last. His body will be flown to Bombay on Monday night or Tuesday morning for cremation.

Birla was admitted to hospital—according to the official version—for treatment of slipped disc. His muscles continued to weaken and he was virtually bedridden. The final blow came when he contracted pneumonic fever and malaria. He is said to have been under heavy sedation for the past one week. Family sources have consistently denied rumours that Birla was suffering from prostate cancer. Soon after he was admitted to hospital, Mr B.K. Birla, who has been virtually camping at the Hyatt Regency in Baltimore, had told the *Economic Times* that his son was 'speedily recovering' and would be returning to India in about a couple of weeks. But that was not to be. The recent annual general meetings of Hindalco and Grasim could not be presided over by him. At least thrice in these past few months, the stock market found itself gripped by rumours of Birla's death, all of them untrue and possibly the handiwork of bear operators keen to hammer down share prices of his group companies.

Aditya's body was flown to Bombay on a chartered DC-10 aircraft via Rome on Tuesday afternoon, October 3. The plane landed at Sahar International Airport at 2.00 p.m. Accompanying the body from Baltimore were Aditya's parents, Rajashree, Kumar, Neerja, Vasavadatta, Rajendra Lodha, the Dagas and the Kasliwals. Jayashree, Manjushree and Kumar's cousins Siddharth and Yashovardhan received them on the tarmac. Several dozen Birla executives swarmed around the airport lounge waiting for the coffin to be escorted to Sagar Lehri, Basant Kumar's residence in Prabhadevi.

Kumar Mangalam helped his grandfather Basant Kumar supervise the arrangements as the grim-faced passengers disembarked. Both maintained an extraordinary calm till they met Aditya's close friends in the airport lounge. Basant Kumar broke down and Kumar Mangalam was inconsolable. Within minutes, however, they had recovered their composure. Like them, Saraladevi and Rajashree maintained the dignified calm that has come to be the hallmark of the Birla family in times of crises.

Aditya's body was taken in a waiting ambulance to Sagar Lehri, where thousands of Birla executives, workers, and senior business and government leaders came to pay tribute. The body lay in state at Sagar Lehri till the next morning. Just after 8.00 a.m. it was transported to Century Bhavan to enable members of the public to pay their last respects. At 11.00 a.m. on Wednesday, October 4, Aditya's body, dressed in his favourite dark brown suit, was carried to Banganga, the centuries-old cremation ground near Raj Bhavan, in a flower-laden truck from Century Bhavan. Basant Kumar and Kumar Mangalam gently touched Aditya's face for the last time, controlling their anguish. Saraladevi and Rajashree had bade farewell hours earlier at Century Bhavan. Now the Birla menfolk steeled themselves for the last wrenching moments. Krishna Kumar, Ganga Prasad, Chandrakant and Sudarshan stood beside Kumar Mangalam and Basant Kumar, bonded in silent grief. Clad in a spotless white dhoti and kurta, and fighting back tears, Kumar lit the funeral pyre at 1 p.m. after performing the last rites. A group of saffron-clad priests chanted, 'Hare Krishna, Hare Krishna, Hare Rama, Hare, Hare . . .'

Basant Kumar was at his grandson's side as the leaping flames consumed Aditya's body.

Among the mourners was the cream of Indian business and government. Ratan Tata, chairman of India's largest business house, came in his office clothes, though he removed his jacket and loosened his tie. Others were more traditionally dressed. Virtually every major industrialist as well as the heads of financial institutions—all large shareholders in Aditya Birla group companies—were present. In an unprecedented step, the Bombay Stock Exchange began trading ninety minutes late on October 4 as a mark of respect for a man whose companies had a collective market capitalization of Rs 14,000 crore and an impeccable reputation among millions of shareholders.

The Federation of Indian Chambers of Commerce and Industry (FICCI), which Aditya's grandfather G.D. Birla had co-founded, paid a particularly fond tribute: 'India has lost a most distinguished and world-renowned industrialist, visionary and philanthropist.' The FICCI president, A.K. Rungta, called Aditya 'the jewel of Indian industry'. Assocham president S.M. Dutta, then chairman of Hindustan Lever, said Aditya was 'a young and dynamic industrialist who had made a mark in the industrial development of the country'. Rajive Kaul, president of the Confederation of Indian Industries, added: 'In Aditya Birla's death, Indian industry has lost a leader of tremendous vision, great sense of humour and strong clarity of thought and conviction.'

Individual business leaders were even more fulsome in their praise. R.P. Goenka, chairman emeritus of the Rs. 5000 crore RPG group, said: 'In the passing away of Aditya the country has lost a prized son. Industry has lost its leader. And I have lost a brother.' Keshub Mahindra, one of India's most respected industrialists, declared that 'Aditya Birla was a man of great vision. This is a tremendous loss to Indian industry and to friends like me. He was a man of several great qualities. His biggest virtue was that he was never opposed to any suggestion made by anyone. He listened to even the smallest person in his organization. His contribution to the business world remains unique.'

Dr Manmohan Singh had always enjoyed an excellent relationship with Aditya, in sharp contrast to the distrust previous finance ministers—especially V.P. Singh—shared with Indian businessmen. Dr Singh had involved Aditya in official work right from the time he was governor of the Reserve Bank of India in 1982. Aditya was inducted into the RBI as a director and he was also on the board of the government-run Air India. Besides, he was one of the most frequently invited industrialists on official trade delegations. On one such delegation to Japan in 1992, Aditya accompanied Manmohan Singh and became especially close to him. The cordiality grew into mutual respect and Aditya's was the opinion the erudite finance minister valued the most at pre-budget industry–government conferences.

Dr Singh was scheduled to fly abroad on the evening of October 4 but still made a point of visiting Bombay first the same afternoon to personally condole the Birla family. He was accompanied by RBI governor C. Rangarajan and declared emotionally: 'Aditya Birla was younger to me but he was my friend and advisor. Right from the days when I was governor in the Reserve Bank of India, I had a strong relationship with him built on respect and ability.'

Dhirubhai Ambani, chairman of Reliance Industries, who almost never makes a public appearance except at his own company's AGMs, made an exception for a man he said he had 'respected immensely'. In a gesture that was not lost on the Birlas, Dhirubhai came to Basant Kumar's residence with his wife Kokilaben and elder son Mukesh Ambani in a car driven personally by younger son Anil Ambani. The irony, though, was lost in the emotion of the moment: Dhirubhai walked in to pay his last respects just as Manmohan Singh was leaving Sagar Lehri. The Indian finance minister and Dhirubhai had never enjoyed the kind of easy relationship that Manmohan Singh shared with the man they had both come to mourn.

J.R.D. TATA

Excerpts from *The Creation of Wealth* by R.M. Lala

I t was in the first decade of the century.

Two young boys spent their summer holidays at Hardelot, a beach resort near Boulogne in Northern France. One was the son of the legendary Louis Bleriot, the first man to fly across the English Channel in 1909. The other was the son of an Indian industrialist, R.D. Tata. As they played, the boys would occasionally see Bleriot's chief pilot Adolph Pegoud land a plane on the beach. Pegoud was the first man to loop-the-loop in a plane. He was a hero, especially for Tata's young son Jehangir.

In such small beginnings lie the seed of history. The exploits of the Frenchman stirred the heart of the young Indian. At the age of fifteen, after taking a joy ride in a plane at Hardelot, Jehangir decided to become a pilot and if possible to make a career in aviation. Young Jehangir had to wait nine years. He was twenty-four before a flying club opened in his home town Bombay, India—5000 miles away from that wind-swept beach in northern France. Though not the first to register, he was the first Indian to pass out with 'No. 1' endorsed on his flying licence. And so it came to pass that India's first pilot was to pour most of his creative genius into building an airline for his country, giving his nation wings.

Those were years of adventure. In 1930, the Aga Khan announced a prize of £500 to the first Indian who would fly solo between England and India, starting at either end. Among the competitors was a young man called Manmohan Singh. His spirit was willing but his navigation was weak. Twice he left England with a flourish to fly to India. Twice he lost his way over Europe and had to fly back to England to start all over again. C.G. Grey, editor of the *Aeroplane*, observed: 'Mr Manmohan Singh has called his aeroplane "Miss India" and he is likely to!' Another hopeful from the England end was eighteen-year-old Aspy Engineer. Still another to enter for fun, taking off from the Karachi end, was the now twenty-six-year-old Jehangir R.D. Tata. At Aboukir, near Alexandria in Egypt, JRD ran into Aspy, who had left England a week earlier and who was stranded for want of spark plugs. JRD gave Aspy his spare spark plugs, and they took off in opposite directions. Aspy reached Karachi a few hours before JRD reached England, winning the prize. On the strength of his performance, Aspy was admitted into the Indian Air Force, which had just been created. Aspy Engineer was the second Indian to be Chief of the Air Staff. JRD, meanwhile, had another ambition and he did not have long to wait.

> On an exciting October dawn in 1932, a Puss Moth and I soared joyfully from Karachi with our first precious load of mail, on an inaugural flight to Bombay. As we hummed towards our destination at a 'dazzling' hundred miles an hour, I breathed a silent prayer for the success of our venture and for the safety of those who worked for it. We were a small team in those days. We shared successes and failures, the joys and headaches, as together we built up the enterprise which later was to blossom into Air India and Air India International.

When JRD landed on the Juhu mud flats that October day in 1932, India's first air service was inaugurated. He does not take the credit for it. He gives it instead to a far-seeing Englishman—a former officer of the RAF called Nevill Vintcent, who a year earlier had come to India barnstorming the country, giving joy rides. Nevill Vintcent offered J.R.D. Tata a project to start an airline. Sir Dorab Tata, then chairman of Tata Sons, was not a bit enthusiastic about the proposition. But the initial investment was small—Rs 2,00,000—and he was persuaded by JRD's mentor and colleague John Peterson to give his approval.

'We had no aids whatsoever on the ground or in the air,' JRD recalls, 'no radio, no navigational or landing guides of any kind. In fact we did not even have an aerodrome in Bombay. We used a mud flat at Juhu (fishing village-cum-beach resort near the city). The sea was below what we called our airfield, and during the monsoon the runway was below the sea! So we had to pack up each year, lock, stock and barrel—two planes, three pilots and three mechanics, and transfer ourselves to Poona (Pune) where we were allowed to use a maidan as an aerodrome, appropriately under the shadow of the Yeravada Jail!'

The annual report of the Directorate of Civil Aviation (DCA) of India for the year 1933–34 stated:

> As an example how airmail service should be run, we commend the efficiency of Tata Services who on October 10, 1933, arriving at Karachi as usual to time, completed a year's working with 100 per cent punctuality . . . even during the most difficult monsoon months when rainstorms increased the perils of the Western Ghat portion of the route no mail from Madras or Bombay missed connection at Karachi nor was the mail delivered late on a single occasion at Madras . . . our esteemed Trans-Continental Airways, alias Imperial Airways, might send their staff on deputation to Tatas to see how it is done.

Karachi was chosen as the starting point because Imperial Airways terminated there with the mail from England and the route chosen by Tatas was Karachi–Bombay–Madras. Tatas requested the government for a small subsidy for carrying the mail as was the normal practice in other countries. The subsidy asked for was small but the government declined. Tatas reduced the figure to a bare minimum. The government still declined. So Tatas decided that they would just give the service to the country collecting the little stamp surcharge which the addresser put on the envelope to connect it with the Imperial Airways at Karachi. When asked why they did so, JRD replied, 'Vintcent and I had faith in the future of aviation and believed that if we came in at the beginning of an era we had a better chance ultimately to achieve growth and leadership in the field.'

The unfolding years were to justify that faith. In 1936 the all-up Empire Mail Service was launched by the British Government, under which all first-class mail travelled by air without surcharge, and Tata Airlines' revenues soared. At the beginning the aeroplanes used were so small that the service was restricted to mail, but a single passenger was occasionally allowed to sit on top of the mail bags— usually with his heels higher than his head!

In 1936, larger aircraft, though still single-engined, were introduced. Tatas felt the need to give more sophisticated training to their pilots and hired an instructor from England to start a training centre for pilots. The Bombay–Delhi service was inaugurated in 1937. Then came the World War II and all services, including Tatas', were commandeered by the Government of India.

With their airline operations severely restricted and controlled, Nevill Vintcent and J.R.D. Tata looked for alternative avenues for their brimming enthusiasm and their growing expertise. A specially exciting opportunity, they felt, offered itself in the field of aircraft manufacture. Whereas the construction of metal aircraft would have involved an elaborately equipped factory, the De Havilland Mosquito, an outstanding twin-engined fighter-bomber made of wood, could, they felt, be put quickly into production in India. Tatas, therefore, submitted in 1942 a project to the British government for the large-scale manufacture of Mosquito aircraft in a factory they would build for the purpose in Pune. The project was approved by the British government and a new company, Tata Aircraft Limited, was formed to give it life. Land was acquired and a large factory building constructed. Had this plan come off, Tatas would have gone into aircraft production.

The British government had second thoughts and decided instead that invasion gliders should be built under the project. This change was reluctantly accepted by Tatas as the work of building the factory, recruiting staff and organizing manufacture had already gone too far to be abandoned. The project was revised accordingly.

Nevill Vintcent was a man of great physical courage and resourcefulness. More than once he flew to England for discussions with the British authorities. Usually flying by Imperial Airways long-range aircraft, he was flown by a sufficiently circuitous route to keep out of range of German fighters. Tragically, however, on one occasion Vintcent, as an ex-RAF officer, arranged to get a lift on an RAF Hudson bomber on the first leg of a flight from England to Gibraltar. The plane never reached Gibraltar and was reported to have been shot down off the coast of France. The loss of Vintcent was a grievous blow to Tatas and to JRD personally, for apart from being the able and moving spirit behind Tata Airlines and Tata Aircraft that he was, Vintcent and JRD were close friends. This tragic blow was followed by the cancellation of the project itself by the British, who in response to Tatas' own enquiries on the subject, discovered that invasion gliders made by Tata in Pune could not be used in the war because there were no aircraft to tow them! Thus came to a tragic end a project on which JRD had set his heart and which, if it had gone through, as originally planned, would probably have resulted in another invaluable addition to India's industry.

In 1946, Tata Air Lines, a division of Tata Sons, went public and became a joint-stock company. It was called Air India Ltd. The age of passenger travel had arrived and there was to be plenty of competition. Even during wartime Tatas were working on a scheme to extend their services to London. In October 1947, in the turmoil of the post-Partition period, Tatas proposed to the Indian government a service to Europe. They placed an order for three Lockheed Constellations, on faith that this venture would be approved. It was a measure of their faith in the newly independent India, then in the convulsions of the partition of the subcontinent.

Tatas proposed that the Indian government take 49 per cent of the capital, Tatas 25 per cent and the rest be publicly subscribed. The government had the right to buy a further two per cent from Tatas taking their share to 51 per cent and giving them total control. This was the first ever proposal of a joint enterprise between the public and private sectors in the country. The proposal was made by J.R.D. Tata at a most inopportune time, when communal strife raged in Delhi. To his astonishment, which still lingers, JRD got acceptance to his joint sector proposal from the government within weeks. Many years later he asked a senior Cabinet Minister, Jagjivan Ram, why a decision could be made so speedily in those days when today it took the government at least two years 'not to make a decision.' Mr Ram replied, 'We did not know any better then!'

The proposal provided for a new company to be called Air India International. It was to be managed and provided with its staff, its maintenance and its services by Tatas' domestic airline Air India Ltd. On 8 June 1948 Air India International with its famous Maharaja spread its wings to Europe. The fledgling airline soon established itself as one of the finest air carriers of the world.

Meanwhile India's domestic airlines were heading for a crisis. At the end of the War, planes were disposed of by the American Tenth Air Force in India at throwaway prices. For political reasons the government sanctioned every airline applicant, and India soon found itself with eleven airlines while there was room for only two or three. As a result they all ran into rough weather for there were not enough traffic routes to allocate amongst them. Except Air India all the airlines lost heavily. In 1953 the government took a decision to nationalize the airlines, proposing to merge them into a single state corporation with JRD as chairman. Mr Tata advised that the domestic and the international airlines of India should be kept apart and two separate corporations be formed. The suggestion was accepted and he was invited to head the international airline, a task he accepted. For the next twenty-five years he was to be the chairman of Air India, and a director on the board of Indian Airlines.

The international-airline business is ferociously competitive and JRD, chairman of some of the largest companies in India, had to give more and more time to the running of Air India. He carried this burden happily, for aviation was his first love. He did everything he could to make Air India as good as the best among the world's airlines. Its planes were lavishly decorated. He insisted that even if a plane was used for twenty years, it should always look as if it had come out from its factory—new, inside and outside. And it did. With Air India efficiently run, JRD saw no reason why all public undertakings could not also be run to the world's best standards and be profitable.

As chairman, JRD believed in personalized attention. He was dubbed a perfectionist for he called upon his staff: 'Always aim at perfection for only then will you achieve excellence.' On every flight on which he travelled he kept detailed notes of his observations and would painstakingly take action on them on return to base. He gave India pride in its national airline. His forty-six-year aviation career spanned an era from the wood and fabric of the little two-seater Puss Moth to the gleaming 400-seater giant Boeing 747. He insisted that there should be no compromise on operating and maintenance standards or on service. One of the airline's publicity chiefs recalls how he once received a midnight phone call at his home from the chairman suggesting how to improve the wording on a publicity hoarding. 'We had to give so much of ourselves because he gave so much of himself,' said this executive.

Air Marshal Nur Khan, former head of the Pakistan Air Force, and later chairman of Pakistan International Airlines, when asked by an Indian magazine what he thought of his neighbour airline, Air India, and its then chairman J.R.D. Tata, replied: 'A great airline and JRD is an epic figure.' In recognition of this epic figure's services to air transport, JRD was made the recipient of the Tony Jannus Award in 1979, named after the founder pilot of the first scheduled airline in the world, which began in Tampa, Florida, in 1912. Amongst its recipients are the inventor of the jet engine, Sir Frank Whittle; the developers of the Concorde SST, and the founders of the Douglas Aircraft Corporation, Pan-Am, Eastern and United Airlines. Other awards followed. In 1989, the Daniel Guggenheim Medal Award, first conferred on Orville Wright, was presented to J.R.D. Tata.

BHAI MOHAN SINGH

Excerpts from *The Ranbaxy Story* by Bhupesh Bhandari

CRACKS IN THE FAMILY

In 1989, Bhai Mohan Singh split the family business between his three sons—Dr Singh,[1] Bhai Manjit Singh and Analjit Singh. The business had grown and each of them wanted his own space. Corporate India had just seen two very unpleasant family splits: one in the Birla family and the other in the Modi family. The nasty infighting had leaked to the media, which fed salacious details to readers. Bhai Mohan Singh wanted to avoid a similar situation. Till then, there were no family fissures that were visible to outsiders. Besides, few in his family had survived beyond sixty-five years and he wanted to divide the family assets amicably during his lifetime.

Thus, Dr Singh got control of Ranbaxy, Manjit of Montari Industries and Analjit of Max India. In addition, Manjit got the family properties at the posh Golf Links and Prithviraj Road in New Delhi and Analjit got Ranbaxy's Okhla factory. The Aurangzeb Road property had been divided into four parts—one part for Bhai Mohan Singh and one each for the three sons. Since Ranbaxy was the largest company of the lot, Manjit and Analjit also received cash compensation of around Rs 1 crore each.

Bhai Mohan Singh had brought up his family in a traditional way. The drawing room of his house had impressions in henna of six pairs of hands—that of each son and his wife. The impression is put soon after marriage as a mark of solidarity with the family and respect to the parents. What people did not know was that things had changed. In the end, there was much rancour within the family and

---

[1] Dr Parvinder Singh, the eldest son of Bhai Mohan Singh.

the split was so bitter that the corporate world had not seen any like it. Each of the three brothers had embarked on a different destiny.

Manjit was born in January 1947, four years after Dr Singh and three months before the family moved from Rawalpindi to New Delhi. He had a happy childhood, divided between school at St Columba's, swimming and playing lawn tennis at the Delhi Gymkhana and bicycle rides to Khan Market to buy books. During summer every year, the family would go to Kashmir for four weeks. In 1958, Manjit was sent to Doon School, where Dr Singh was already studying. Amongst Manjit's classmates were future stars of Indian politics like Sanjay Gandhi, Kamal Nath, Naveen Patnaik and Akbar 'Dumpy' Ahmad.

After clearing his Senior Cambridge examinations in 1964, Manjit returned to Delhi to study in St Stephen's College and completed his graduation in 1968. While his father wanted him to enrol in a business school abroad, he himself had other plans. He had fallen in love with Maheep, an acquaintance, and wanted to marry her. His plans would go awry if he went abroad. So he decided to stay on in Delhi and enrolled in law college.

But destiny had something else in store for him. The Lepetit crisis[2] happened and Manjit ended up joining Ranbaxy in 1968 as a management trainee on a monthly stipend of Rs 1500 (he was allowed to have lunch with his father at work). Over the next twenty-odd years, he went on to handle several functions ranging from purchase, exports and imports, and overseeing the consumer products division which included products like Naturelle shampoo, Garlic Pearls and vitamin tablets for children.

Manjit was inducted into Ranbaxy's board of directors in 1977 along with his elder brother. But Dr Singh rose through the hierarchy faster: in April 1982, he was promoted as managing director of the company for a period of five years and, in April 1987, he was made

---

[2] The Milan-based pharmaceutical company Lepetit had entered into a joint venture with Ranbaxy to form Lepetit Ranbaxy Ltd in 1959. The joint venture died an early death and Bhai Mohan Singh bought the stake of his Italian partners.

the vice-chairman and managing director for five years. All this while, Manjit continued as the commercial director.

Manjit, by his own admission, had differences with Dr Singh right from his first day at work. While Dr Singh was focussed on pharmaceuticals, Manjit wanted to diversify into other areas and began scouting for opportunities. As far back as the early 1970s, he had developed a passion for setting up a hotel in the heart of Delhi. In 1972, Ranbaxy bought shares in a company called Tara Hotels, which then became its subsidiary. The 1972 directors' report to the shareholders of Tara Hotel noted that the company was negotiating with a foreign party for collaboration, and it was hoped that the company would be able to take up the project that year itself.

By now, the family had moved from the Prithviraj Road residence to the complex of four houses on Aurangzeb Road. All the four houses were interconnected, so that everyone could have the comfort of being with the family along with the required privacy. The construction laws at that time said that at least two acres of land was required for a hotel. The Aurangzeb Road plot had 2.7 acres between the four houses. Manjit suggested that a hotel could be constructed on the site in a joint venture with a global hospitality major. The land would be the family's equity contribution. Everybody agreed and the land was parked in a new company called Delhi Guest Houses Ltd in which Bhai Mohan Singh and his three sons were equal shareholders.

After negotiating with a host of global hotel chains, Manjit tied up with Hong Kong–based Regent International, a new and upcoming chain of luxury hotels. The architecture of the hotel, along with the design of the rooms and the layout of the restaurants, was finalized and submitted for the local administration's approval. While most of the other approvals did not take much time to come through, the Delhi Urban Arts Commission objected to the plan on the grounds that it did not conform to the Master Plan for Lutyens's Delhi (the zone falling in the area designed by the architect of New Delhi, Edward Lutyens). The hotel was to have eight floors and it was argued that the top floor would overlook the Mahatma Gandhi memorial on Tees January Marg located nearby.

Manjit made numerous representations to successive governments, but in vain. This was one of the rare instances where Bhai Mohan Singh's awesome political connections did not work.

Then, in 1980, Manjit convinced his school friend Sanjay Gandhi that the proposed hotel conformed to the Master Plan in all respects. Sanjay Gandhi promised to help. Finally, there seemed to be light at the end of the tunnel for Manjit and the dream he had pursued for over a decade. But Sanjay Gandhi died in an air crash soon after and Manjit was back to square one. Meanwhile, there were murmurs within the family that, in the light of all this, the hotel was not a very good business proposal. The project was given a burial.

Delhi Guest Houses continued to exist and own the four properties. Ranbaxy held shares of the company till 2001 when the stock was taken over by a private company owned by Malvinder Singh and Shivinder Singh, Dr Singh's sons.

Almost twenty years after the project was abandoned, Manjit continued to maintain that corporate rivalry did it in. A hotel on Aurangzeb Road would have cut into the business of two hotels in the vicinity—Claridges Hotel, which was right opposite Bhai Mohan Singh's house, and Taj Mahal Hotel run by the Tata-owned Indian Hotels. But more than the corporate rivals, Manjit blamed his elder brother for not supporting the project sufficiently because he did not want to diversify into areas unrelated to pharmaceuticals.

After the jinxed hotel venture, Manjit again started looking around for opportunities. He examined various business options ranging from sponge iron to two-wheeler tyres, leather and pharmaceutical intermediates. He finally zeroed in on pharmaceutical ingredients. A few products were shortlisted and the technology to produce them identified. But the business plan turned out to be too expensive for Manjit and this plan too had to be scrapped.

The only option left for Manjit was chemicals and he, therefore, opted for pesticides. The family invested in a new company called Montari Chemicals (Mon from Bhai Mohan Singh and Tari from Avtar Kaur's nickname), which put up a plant for basic chemicals inside the sprawling Ranbaxy complex at Bhai Mohan Singh Nagar in Punjab. A Chandigarh-based formulations company, Kisan Chemicals, was also taken over for this purpose. Its plant was subsequently shifted to Bhai Mohan Singh Nagar and the company was merged with Montari Chemicals to form Montari Industries. On 1 October 1988, Manjit was appointed the managing director of Montari Industries, as a part of the family settlement. As a result, he resigned from the post of commercial director at Ranbaxy and became a non-executive director. Things were going well for Manjit.

In 1988, Naina Lal, granddaughter of legendary industrialist Lala Karam Chand Thapar and investment banker with ANZ Grindlays (now with HSBC), approached Ranbaxy with a proposal. Bausch & Lomb, the United States–based eyewear major which owned the famous Ray-Ban brand of sunglasses, was keen on starting a venture in India to make contact lenses. Would Ranbaxy be interested? Bausch & Lomb was interested in the eye-care liquids market more than Ray-Ban sunglasses. It wanted to sell its products through chemists and not opticians. That is why it was on the lookout for an alliance with a company like Ranbaxy.

Bhai Mohan Singh accepted the offer and talks between the two parties began. As Dr Singh did not show much interest, Manjit expressed his interest in becoming a partner in the venture. Bhai Mohan Singh told Bausch & Lomb that Montari, and not Ranbaxy, would be their partner. Bausch & Lomb had no choice but to agree. The talks had progressed too far ahead to pull back now and start fresh negotiations with another party. Besides, Bhai Mohan Singh gave the assurance that Montari was a part of the same group and the venture could count on Ranbaxy's full support. Ranbaxy was indeed involved in giving shape to the joint venture. As the family separation was under way at that time, the agreement with Bausch & Lomb was signed by one of the investment companies that were to go to Manjit Singh. Bhai Mohan Singh roped in key Ranbaxy officials like Vinay Kaul to work out the details.

Soon, Manjit was on his way to Rochester to meet the Bausch & Lomb brass. The proposal he made at Rochester was nothing short of outrageous. As production of foreign brands like Ray-Ban was not allowed in India at that time, he said that the brand could be launched in the Indian market using either a prefix or a suffix! (Pepsi, for instance, was launched as Lehar Pepsi.) Surprisingly, Bausch & Lomb agreed. Meanwhile, back in India, hectic lobbying had started bearing fruit, and the government agreed to amend the rules on local manufacturing of foreign brands. Ray-Ban was to become the first foreign eyewear brand to be launched in India. Both Montari Industries and Bausch & Lomb took 40 per cent each in the joint venture, Bausch & Lomb India Pvt. Ltd, while 20 per cent equity was placed with the public.

This was perhaps the high-water mark of Manjit's career. Though his pet hotel never saw the light of day, the pesticides business was off the block and he had brought one of the biggest brands in the world to India. A footwear export business was also on the anvil. Prompted by export incentives, Manjit set up Montari Leather in the late 1980s in technical collaboration with Bally of Switzerland for manufacturing footwear. The British Shoe Company of the United Kingdom had agreed to pick up the products for marketing in Europe. Again, Montari Industries was chosen to invest in the equity capital of Montari Leather.

As per the shareholders' agreement of Bausch & Lomb India, while Manjit became the managing director of the company, the president was to be jointly appointed by the two partners, the chief financial officer (CFO) would be a Bausch & Lomb nominee, and Montari Industries would provide secretarial services. By appointing his own man as the company secretary, Manjit could keep tabs on who was selling and buying into the company, a common practice amongst Indian businessmen. Both the partners had equal representation on the board of directors.

The good-natured and affable Manjit was able to attract people from multinational corporations and top Indian companies to work for Bausch & Lomb India. He liked to talk of his business as the Montari Group, of which Bausch & Lomb India was the crown jewel. Manjit knew that Bausch & Lomb India was different from his other two home-grown companies. In fact, he admired Bausch & Lomb's culture and had struck a good rapport with the company's top brass. He was particularly close to Bausch & Lomb's head in Europe, India-born Alex Kumar. As a result, he never tried to impose the Montari culture on this company and gave its president, Jaspal Bajwa, a free hand to run the company. Senior Bausch & Lomb India executives would say that Manjit shielded them from interference by the Montari management. On the contrary, for important meetings with bankers, he would take senior executives from the company along in order to showcase the managerial talent in his group.

But the honeymoon proved short-lived. Within the first year itself, it became evident that the company's breakeven projections were too ambitious. As its equity base was capitalized at just Rs 10 crore, the company ran short of money in the first year itself and had to go for a rights issue to stay afloat. Losses started mounting by the day as the company invested heavily in developing the market for its sunglasses. Soon it was time for more money to be pumped into the company. While Bausch & Lomb was prepared to infuse more money, Manjit found his hands tied. Montari Industries had started making losses and Montari Leather was headed in the same direction. The implication was clear: if the company was to become financially strong, he would have to reduce his stake. That would have meant the end of Manjit's dreams. Thus all Bausch & Lomb proposals for a rights issue got delayed.

Meanwhile, there was no improvement in the company's fortunes. By 1996, its net worth had eroded by 50 per cent and it faced the prospect of reporting to the Board for Industrial & Financial Reconstruction (BIFR) as required by the law. This would have affected Bausch & Lomb's image in the country and dampened the morale of its marketing team. The company however managed to ward off the crisis and get a reprieve of fifteen to eighteen months. While the losses would be arrested within this time, Bajwa and his men were hopeful that the two promoters would come to an understanding and money would get injected into the company.

But the relationship between the two partners was deteriorating fast. To further complicate matters, Bausch & Lomb India terminated its contract with a Manjit-owned company called Vimoni (named after his children Vikramjit, Mohanjit and Niyamat) for the supply of bottles and grinding of lenses on the grounds that it was no longer viable. The upshot was that when Manjit's five-year term as managing director came to an end in 1997, it was not extended.

With the disagreements persisting, Manjit finally agreed to sell out of the company. All his nominees on the board gave undated resignation letters.

As news of Manjit's sell-out leaked to the media, the price of Bausch & Lomb India shares skyrocketed. Manjit had pledged almost his entire stock to raise funds. So with rising prices, the creditors sold the shares in the market, recovering their investments and returning the remainder to Manjit. Thus, even after buying him out of the joint venture in 1998, Bausch & Lomb's stake in the company went up only marginally from 40 per cent to 43 per cent.

To make investments in Bausch & Lomb, pesticides and leather, Montari Industries had decided to go for a rights issue of Rs 43 crore in March 1991. The stock markets were booming and it was decided to price the rights issue at Rs 35 per share as against the stock market price of Rs 70 per share. Unfortunately for Manjit, two days after the rights issue opened for a month, the markets crashed and the Montari Industries share price plummeted. The issue was grossly undersubscribed and against a target of Rs 43 crore, the company could muster only Rs 25 crore.

This put Manjit in a spot. Bausch & Lomb had already sent its share of money for the rights issue three months earlier and the money was lying in the bank. Other investments too had been committed and there was no way he could have backed out. Manjit decided to make up the deficit by raising debt from the market. Montari Industries borrowed almost Rs 25 crore through inter-corporate deposits at interest rates of up to 25 per cent per annum. The financial burden proved too much for the company and it soon became a sick company. Montari Leather too met with the same fate.

Manjit became a bitter man, blaming the family settlement for his ills.

*

Dr Singh and Manjit had very little in common. While his elder brother was serious and cold to all except his close friends and relatives, Manjit was fun-loving and fond of the good life. He loved to entertain and throw expensive parties. Dr Singh, on the other hand, would use very little of his entertainment allowance, as Raizada[3] discovered while managing the finances at Ranbaxy. Two months before his death in July 1999, Dr Singh wanted to take one final vacation in Italy with his family. He called up his close friend Vivek Bharat Ram to make arrangements for his stay. Vivek, who had a joint venture with Italian clothing major Benetton, agreed but protested that Dr Singh's budget was too frugal for a decent hotel. Reminding him that it was a private holiday, Dr Singh raised the budget by $50 a day. This, at a time when he was one of the richest men in the country!

In many ways, Dr Singh was similar to his youngest brother, Analjit. Both were visionaries with a modern worldview and were capable of thinking ahead of their times. In addition, both of them were deeply spiritual; while Dr Singh was a follower of the Radha Soami Satsang, Analjit became a lifelong devotee of the Chinmaya Mission. Yet, the two also drifted apart.

*

Analjit was born in January 1954. He was deeply attached to his parents and his brothers in his formative years and the attachment grew as the years passed. There was a gap of eleven years between Analjit and Dr Singh. So, while he always looked up to him, he was also a little scared of him. On his part, Dr Singh was very fond of his youngest brother; he and his friends would call him 'Monkey'

---

[3] Bimal Raizada, who studied Chartered Accountancy in London, was one of the first professionals hired by Ranbaxy.

instead of calling him by his pet name Mannu. (His passport records his name as Analjit Singh a.k.a. Mannu Mohan Singh. The addition to his passport was made in the 1970s when he was studying in the United States.)

He was more relaxed and friendly with Manjit. Analjit was like a handyman to his elder brother and his friends, running errands for them. In 1967, when Dr Singh returned from the United States, Analjit left for Doon School. His friends there included journalist Karan Thapar and Rajiv Khanna, grandson of hotelier Mohan Singh Oberoi. At school, Analjit excelled as a table tennis player and was a part of the school orchestra.

When in Delhi, Analjit would act as his father's secretary-cum-housekeeper at home. He would type out Bhai Mohan Singh's telegrams and try to find out why he was travelling abroad. Even at that time he was aware of his father's awesome network of contacts. 'Bhai Mohan Singh knew everybody and everybody knew Bhai Mohan Singh,' Analjit would recount decades later. Bhai Mohan Singh rarely had time for home and family. When Analjit was eighteen years old, Bhai Mohan Singh took him along on some of his overseas business trips to make up for the absence from home. On these visits, while Bhai Mohan Singh would be busy in business meetings during the day, Analjit was left on his own to explore and sightsee.

After passing out of Doon School in 1972, Analjit joined the Shri Ram College of Commerce in Delhi. Those were very good years for Analjit. Both his brothers had got married within a space of ten days. The whole family used to stay together, though a couple of years later, Dr Singh and Manjit moved to their new houses in the Aurangzeb Road complex. Analjit was particularly close to Dr Singh's wife, Nimmi. Whenever Dr Singh would go abroad, Analjit would be a devoted younger brother-in-law and look after her. In 1975, Analjit left for the United States to get an MBA degree. On his second visit home in December 1978, he was introduced to Neelu, a girl from Dehradun. He returned the next summer to get engaged to her and they were married on 30 December 1979, Bhai Mohan Singh's birthday.

Though Analjit worked with the Miami-based North American Biologicals Inc. after completing his studies, Bhai Mohan Singh had different plans for him. Thus, the notice sent to Ranbaxy shareholders for the company's twentieth annual general meeting scheduled for 16 June 1981 at Mohali had an interesting item on the agenda—the appointment of Analjit as an executive in the senior cadre of the company from 1 June 1981.

Analjit made a lateral entry into the high-profile executive committee of Ranbaxy as director (projects), though he was not given a berth on the company's board of directors. This is when life took a U-turn for him.

The stupendous success of ampicillin, launched in 1977, required the company to go in for backward integration of its operations. Ranbaxy was still importing 6APA (6 amino-penicillic acid), the main ingredients of semi-synthetic penicillins, but it had started thinking in terms of manufacturing it as well. Though the 1977 annual report had mentioned that 'laboratory-scale work for the manufacture of 6APA has been completed and the process is now being up-scaled for commercial production', two years later, there was still no sign of the project being implemented.

By 1982, it was decided that the 6APA project would be Analjit's baby. Ranbaxy, in association with the Punjab State Industrial Development Corporation, promoted Max India Ltd, which put up a plant in the Hoshiarpur district of Punjab, a Centrally Notified Backward Area, for the manufacture of 6APA. The technology was provided by a Japanese company, Toyo Jozo Co. Ltd. It was seen as a major import substitution effort, potentially leading to substantial foreign exchange savings.

The 6APA project had become a matter of critical importance for Ranbaxy. The 1983 directors' report had noted that the company suffered heavily on account of the canalization of 6APA from January 1983. The government did not fix prices or arrange to procure stocks and release the intermediate to the industry till September 1983. The non-availability of 6APA affected the company's production of ampicillin.

Analjit had not been keen to join Ranbaxy after his return from the United States as he had seen Manjit floundering there. He was aware that Manjit had been trying out the hotels business but was getting very little support from his father and his eldest brother. Yet, because of his strong attachment to his parents and brothers, he wanted to work for the family. Within two days of his arrival in India, Analjit was ushered into Dr Singh's office at Okhla. Over the next hour or so, he was educated about 6APA and its critical importance for Ranbaxy's business of anti-infective drugs derived from semi-synthetic penicillin. At the end, he was told that nothing could be more appropriate for him to start his innings in business.

Less than a week after this meeting, Analjit found himself in a small cubicle as manager (new projects). It had a red phone, a red carpet and a red thermos, and a file marked 6APA lay on his table. He was assigned a secretary, Raghu, who eventually became like a member of the family. Analjit's salary was fixed at Rs 3000 per month with no other financial emoluments.

Over the next year or so, Analjit realized that the 6APA project was fraught with difficulties. To begin with, production required an industrial licence. The government had already given out licences for all projected 6APA capacities. So there was no question of a new licence being issued. Second, technology to produce 6APA was not available in the country and it could only be procured from abroad. However, government rules of the time set a limit of $50,000 to acquire the technology. Third, Ranbaxy could not have imported penicillin, the raw material for 6APA, as it was on the negative list of imports. Analjit also realized that even if he did manage to get a special import licence for penicillin, the high customs duty would make the price of his 6APA three times the price of the ampicillin for which it was meant. The only option was to buy penicillin from the local producers—the public sector Hindustan Antibiotics Ltd and IDPL. But the quality of their penicillin was poor; instead of sparkling white, it was pale yellow in colour.

The first challenge before Analjit was to get a licence to produce 6APA. Here, he got Bhai Mohan Singh's help. The two argued with the licencing authorities that none of the companies which had been given 6APA licences had begun production. Moreover, as Ranbaxy was the country's largest producer of ampicillin, the project was all the more critical for it. Finally, the government relented and a licence was given to Analjit. By then, Analjit had also identified Toyo Jozo as a technology partner. To implement the project, he formed a new company called Max India. The M in Max stood for Bhai Mohan Singh, A for Avtar Kaur and X for all others.

But the biggest challenge was still awaiting Analjit. The cost of the 6APA venture was estimated at around Rs 5 crore. As he had no personal wealth, Analjit had no option but to ask the family and Ranbaxy to bankroll the project. To his surprise, he was told that the family would not invest more than Rs 25 lakh in the project, and Dr Singh told him that Ranbaxy would not put in more than Rs 40 lakh. That left a yawning gap in finances. Undaunted, Analjit persevered with the project, taking personal loans to bridge the equity gap. The 6APA plant was set up at Taonsa. It took Analjit almost eighteen years after Max India started in 1985 to repay the loans he had taken. The sum of Rs 65 lakh is the only financial help from the family or Ranbaxy that Analjit received in his life.

Having been in the pharmaceutical business for over fifteen years, Dr Singh could not have been unaware of the pitfalls in the project. Then why did he push his brother into the project knowing that he had no work experience in India? The only explanation Analjit could come up with was that Dr Singh did all this to toughen his youngest brother. Or did Dr Singh not want his brother to succeed? After all, Manjit too had not been able to realize his dream of building a hotel because of stiff resistance from Dr Singh. Nobody doubted the fact that the hotel project would definitely have come about if Dr Singh had thrown his weight behind it.

More importantly, why did Bhai Mohan Singh not come out in support of Analjit, especially when it came to funding the 6APA venture? In his eyes, his eldest son, who was in the process of single-handedly turning around the fortunes of Ranbaxy, could do no wrong.

In spite of the odds stacked against him, Analjit pressed on. He introduced certain technical changes in the 6APA plant which resulted in considerable productivity improvement. Two years later, in 1987, he had added a 7ADCA (7-aminodeacetoxycephalosporanic acid) unit to the plant. 7ADCA is a key intermediate for the production of cephalexin, cefradine and other cephalosporins. This drove the profitability of the company.

Though he got little support from the family, Analjit was fortunate to have a loyal band of executives working for him, led by Ashwani Windlass. By the end of his innings at Max India, Windlass came to be known as one of the finest strategists in the corporate world. Windlass had started his career in 1978 as a management trainee with Delhi-based DCM Ltd. In 1981, he had joined Ranbaxy's finance department. Soon he was attached to Analjit for the 6APA project. When Max India was formed in 1984, he was made the company's CFO at just twenty-seven years of age. Apart from looking after the finances of Max India, he was soon advising Analjit on new business possibilities, given the tough nature of the 6APA business.

One business on Analjit and Windlass's shortlist was electronics. Once again, the proposal met with stiff resistance from the family, which argued that any investment outside pharmaceuticals would be suicidal. Instead of getting bogged down by criticism, Analjit decided to go ahead on his own. As a foray into electronics would require substantial investments, he decided to get into duty-free trading which would generate capital for the electronics venture. He floated a company called Dove Corporation in the mid-1980s, which was soon representing over twenty famous liquor and fashion brands in India's duty-free shops. Once it had started generating profits, the company got into distribution of equipment and components for the electronics industry.

The next business Max India got into was BOPP (Biaxially Oriented Polypropylene) films. Analjit and Windlass were convinced that as the Indian economy grew, demand for synthetic packaging material would also go up. Their projections were accurate. When the economy opened up, BOPP films became hugely popular and the business raked in profits for Analjit for many years to come. This was not the first time that the two were able to look beyond the immediate future. This time also, Analjit was told that he would not get any financial support from the family and that he would have to fend for himself. Analjit had floated a new company called Maxxon India in 1992. The cost of the project was estimated at Rs 30 crore. With investors reluctant to put their money into a greenfield venture, Analjit and Windlass devised an issue of convertible bonds in 1993. Investors would get a fixed return till the project materialized, after which they could convert the bonds into equity shares.

When Maxxon was on the drawing board, the family assets were divided between the three brothers. Whatever little hopes Analjit had of receiving support from the family got dashed in 1989. Things took a turn for the worse soon.

*

Ranbaxy was the largest buyer of 6APA and 7ADCA in the Indian market, accounting for around 30 per cent of the total production in the country. Max India got almost 60 per cent of its business from Ranbaxy. In 1991, Ranbaxy pulled the rug from under Max India's feet when it set up its own 7ADCA unit at Mohali. Ranbaxy was facing pressure on cephalosporin prices as several companies abroad, including Antibioticos in Spain, Dobfar in Italy, Royal Gist-Brocades (GB) in The Netherlands and a handful of Indian companies like Lupin and later Orchid, had gone in for backward integration and set up 7ADCA facilities. Ranbaxy's competitiveness in cephalosporins was under threat and the only way to restore profitability was to manufacture its own 7ADCA. Max India was plunged into a severe financial crisis. Analjit charged his brother of reneging on his commitment to support Max India. But Dr Singh refused to budge. Analjit had no choice but to bring the profitable Dove Corporation within the Max India fold. It was made a division of the company and re-christened Max Electronics.

Meanwhile, the BOPP films business also started totting up losses. The 1991 Gulf War had caused raw material prices to rise sharply. At the same time, as the economy was going through a slump, there was intense competition at home resulting in prices being slashed. Maxxon had to function with another handicap: while rivals like Cosmo Films with its unit at Aurangabad and Gujarat Propack in Gujarat were close to the ports, its unit was located in Punjab, requiring huge investments in logistics. A stage was reached in 1991 when bankruptcy was staring at Maxxon.

Once again, Windlass showed the way out. He proposed a reverse merger of Max India into Maxxon. This would give Maxxon a new lease of life. The reverse merger was done in 1993 and Maxxon was subsequently renamed Max India. Still, the struggle was far from over for Analjit. Relations between the two brothers only deteriorated in the days to come.

*

GB or Royal Gist-Brocades had emerged as the world's leading producer of penicillin and its derivatives like 6APA and 7ADCA over the years. It knew that it needed to locate cheaper sources of supply of 6APA, if it wanted to maintain its leadership position in the long run. It was facing competition from Max in the European markets. GB was selling 6APA at as high a price as $400 per kg. Once Max entered the market, it was forced to drop its price to $150 per kg. Hence, it began to scout for opportunities in India. It spoke to a number of companies, including Ranbaxy, but finally tied up with Max in 1994. The 6APA and 7ADCA business was now parked in a new company called Max GB, in which both the partners held a 50 per cent stake.

More importantly, from Analjit's point of view, the joint venture agreement said that Max GB would pay Max India Rs 6 crore a year as 'rights to use' fees for the USFDA approved 6APA and 7ADCA plant at Bhai Mohan Singh Nagar. It was a great deal for Analjit. He had not given up control of the business and had ensured that Rs 6 crore got added on to Max India's bottom line every year.

Max India, by now, had emerged as the largest buyer of penicillin in the country. While it was procuring 30 per cent of its requirement locally from Hindustan Antibiotics,[4] it was importing the remaining 70 per cent. It only made sense for Max India to get into penicillin production in order to control costs and get a better grip on the quality of its products. Meanwhile, by 1989, it had become clear to the government that the policy of restricting the production of penicillin to the public sector had lost its relevance. It thus handed out almost a dozen licences to the private sector, including one each to Max India and Ranbaxy.

Analjit first proposed a three-way joint venture to produce penicillin between Max India, Ranbaxy and Antibioticos. But Ranbaxy was cold to the proposal and the venture did not materialize. Ranbaxy had actually decided against getting into penicillin after carefully studying the matter. One, the prices were slated to fall with new capacities coming up. Two, Ranbaxy by now had embarked on an ambitious programme for global expansion and saw little merit in investing in a penicillin plant at the time.

Around the same time, Hindustan Antibiotics realized that it needed to upgrade its penicillin facility in order to survive once private sector players got into production. It approached GB for help, which said that all its business in India would be carried out by Max GB. This brought Max India in touch with Hindustan Antibiotics.

Analjit had now come to realize that a greenfield penicillin venture could be very expensive. The cost of putting up a new plant of a decent size was estimated at nothing less than Rs 150 crore. Given the imminent fall in global penicillin prices, it did not make sense to invest large sums of money in new plant and machinery. Again, Analjit proposed something that was not on anybody's radar screen: a joint venture with Hindustan Antibiotics to take over its penicillin facility. This was much before the country had even started thinking in terms of divesting the government's stake in the public sector. Analjit threw a sweetener into the deal and said that the joint venture company would pay Hindustan Antibiotics a sum of Rs 17

---

[4] Hindustan Antibiotics Ltd was a PSU set up by the government to make penicillin.

crore every year for using its facility. He also assured that he would double the production of penicillin from the facility and reduce costs by half without making any significant investments.

Hindustan Antibiotics could not have asked for a better deal. It would get GB technology to upgrade its facility and Rs 17 crore every year as lease rental, all without making any financial commitment. All hurdles appeared to have been cleared for the formation of the fifty–fifty joint venture, Hindustan Max GB Ltd. Analjit, who was then living in a suite in Claridges Hotel because his house was being renovated, was confident that the joint venture had come through. After a particularly fruitful meeting with the government, he had even uncorked a bottle of champagne for his close friends. He had not anticipated the unpleasant turn the whole affair was set to take.

Two days after Max GB and Hindustan Antibiotics signed the agreement in 1995, Torrent moved a public interest litigation (PIL) in the Delhi High Court alleging that the deal lacked transparency. As Hindustan Antibiotics was a public sector undertaking, it should have invited tenders for selecting a partner rather than strike a deal privately, the PIL said. Soon, Chennai-based Spic Pharmaceuticals and Delhi-based JK Pharmaceuticals too had moved similar PILs and the Delhi High Court decided to club the three petitions into one.

All the three applicants had committed investments in excess of Rs 150 crore each for new penicillin plants. Torrent had even raised money from the market for the venture. The Max GB–Hindustan Antibiotics deal put a question mark on these projects as, with high interest rates prevailing at that time and depreciation, these companies would never be able to match the prices of the joint venture.

Soon the media was full of reports that the government had sold out to Max India and GB. The matter came up before the Parliamentary Standing Committee on chemicals. The smear campaign against Analjit and Hindustan Antibiotics managing director, A.K. Basu, had begun. Analjit had reasons to believe that the campaign against him was being orchestrated by Ranbaxy. His close aides would say that several unsigned notes that were circulated those days, ostensibly in public interest, originated from Ranbaxy.

Several such faxes were found to bear the Ranbaxy address. Ranbaxy, on its part, denied any involvement. But that didn't matter as Analjit was convinced of its involvement. 'My brother loved to push a chilli up my back every day,' Analjit would recount many years later.

The perfect gentleman that he was, Analjit still refrained from badmouthing his brother in public. Yet, he decided to hit back. Operating out of his suite in Claridges, his team soon joined the trial by media. Journalists covering the slugfest had a field day.

Analjit and Windlass had done their homework quite well. All decisions related to the deal were properly documented. The final court verdict went in their favour and Hindustan Max GB commenced operations. Still, the mudslinging and the court battles took their toll on Analjit. He aged dramatically during those years, worry lines marking his otherwise youthful face. He became more spiritual, placing immense faith on divine justice.

Analjit's aides from those days insist that Ranbaxy's ire had been provoked due to another factor. Max was looking at spreading its wings in pharmaceuticals beyond 6APA and 7ADCA. In the family settlement, Max India had acquired the Okhla factory complete with its 600 workers. On its sixth founder's day celebrations in 1991, it gave awards to employees of the Okhla factory for completing twenty-five years of service! Still, by the early-1990s, Analjit was able to trim the workforce substantially through voluntary separation schemes. He now started making a wide range of formulations here. He quickly became a fairly large player in generic medicine. He had also launched a publicity campaign, 'Take Good Care of Your Body', in the media, which was well received in the medical fraternity. Next on the cards was a bulk drugs plant in the southern state of Karnataka.

The big moment came when Max India tied up with United States–based Upjohn Co. Ltd for distributing its products in the country. It went on to launch Upjohn's controversial injectable contraceptive for women, Depo-Provera, in the country. The product had received USFDA's clearance only a year earlier. The launch caused an uproar, especially amongst women's rights activists, but the company went ahead.

Meanwhile, the relationship between the brothers had touched a new low. To his close aides Analjit would call Dr Singh cold and calculating, devoid of any emotion. But as a businessman, he was always full of respect for Dr Singh. 'Ranbaxy had an unbeatable team: Bhai Mohan Singh built the brand, Dr Singh gave the vision and corporate governance and Brar is the best in execution,' he said of Ranbaxy's success years later. When Dr Singh fell ill, he told his close aides that both companies could have achieved so much more had the two brothers decided to work together.

Analjit gradually exited from the pharmaceuticals business. He ceded a controlling stake to GB in Max GB (this also took away Hindustan Max GB away from him), sold the formulations business, including brands and stock-in-trade to Rhone-Poulenc and finally sold the bulk drugs plant to Delhi-based Jubilant Organosys (earlier known as Vam Organics) promoted by Shyam and Hari Bhartiya. The Bhartiyas engaged Jag Mohan Khanna, the former research and development chief of Ranbaxy, to steer their pharmaceuticals business. Analjit was to find his riches elsewhere.

*

By the late 1980s, Dove Corporation (before it became Max Electronics) was supplying components to consumer electronics companies, the defence services and a host of telecommunication companies like EPABX system manufacturers and the government's Centre for Development of Telematics (C-DOT). Almost 60 per cent of the business came from the telecom companies.

Windlass was convinced that India was headed for a telecom revolution. Thus, in 1991, much before the government came out with its National Telecom Policy, Max India, along with United States–based telecom major Motorola and Mumbai-based Arya Communications, a distributor of Motorola components, applied for a nation-wide paging licence. It was the first case to come up before the newly formed Foreign Investment Promotion Board (FIPB). Radio paging had taken the world by storm in the late 1980s. Much before anybody else could even think of it, Max

India had sought government permission to bring the service to India.

However, Analjit and Windlass realized that, the world over, telecom was a services business and they had tied up with Motorola, an equipment manufacturer. If Max India had to enter the sector, it would have to tie up with a telecom service provider. Thus began Max India's search for a telecom partner. In the end, it was Motorola that helped Max India sign up with Li Ka-shing of Hong Kong.

*

Born in 1928, Li Ka-shing was the chairman of Cheung Kong (Holdings) Ltd and Hutchison Whampoa Ltd. Li Ka-shing had founded Cheung Kong Industries in 1950, which started as a plastics manufacturer and later evolved into a property investment company. The group acquired Hutchison Whampoa in 1979.

By 2003, Cheung Kong Group's business straddled such diverse areas as property development and investment, real estate and estate management, hotels, telecommunications and e-commerce, finance and investment, retail and manufacturing, ports and related services, energy, infrastructure projects and materials, media, and biotechnology. Based in Hong Kong, the combined group ranks among the top 100 corporations in the world.

Hutchison Whampoa's origins can be traced to 1828 when a small dispensary company called A.S. Watson opened in the Guangzhou province of China. By 1841, it expanded its operations to Hong Kong. In 1863, the Hongkong and Whampoa Dock Company (HWD) was established to acquire docks and repair yards at Whampoa, on the Pearl river in China, and at the then newly constructed dry docks at Aberdeen on Hong Kong Island.

In the late 1800s, a young Briton by the name of John Duflon Hutchison, who had come to Hong Kong, set up the John D. Hutchison and Company Ltd, laying the foundation of the Hutchison business empire. In the 1960s, Hutchison International Ltd began an acquisition programme, which gave it control of, among others, HWD. Hutchison Whampoa Ltd was born in 1977 as a result of a merger between the two companies. In January 1978, Hutchison Whampoa Ltd became a listed company in Hong Kong. In 1979, Li Ka-shing acquired a substantial shareholding in the company from the Hongkong and Shanghai Bank, thus becoming the first Chinese to take control of a British-style 'hong' (business empire). Li Ka-shing was amongst the first to spot the opportunity in cellular services. In 1985, he ventured into cellular telephony and the Hutchison Telephone Company Ltd was established to launch Hong Kong's first cellular mobile telephone system. In 1989, Hutchison Telecom entered the British and Australian mobile telecommunications markets.

Meanwhile, the Indian government had opened up cellular services, inviting bids for the four metros of Mumbai, Delhi, Chennai and Kolkata. Hutchison and Max India officials got together to draft their bid document. Bidders were required to give the broad parameters of their proposed service, on the basis of which the government would award the circles. Nobody knew what weight the government would assign to the various parameters. While the bid document was being prepared, Windlass insisted that it be mentioned that consumers would be charged zero rental. It so happened the government had decided to give maximum weightage to rentals. As a result, when the bids were opened, Hutchison Max was right on top with a score of ninety-two out of 100. It was on its way to getting a licence to operate cellular services in Mumbai, the commercial capital of India.

However, owing to a slight oversight in the bid document, Hutchison Max was disqualified. But the company went to the courts and got a favourable judgement. The day after the judgement, Mumbai woke up to thirty-one hoardings put up at prime locations by Hutchison Max, saying 'Hello Bombay'.

Cellular telephony is a capital-intensive business. The choice before Analjit was to keep on pumping money or encash his stake. In 1997, on Janmashtami, the day Hindus celebrate the birth of Lord Krishna, Analjit decided on the latter course of action. The divestment exercise was aptly named Project Krishna. In April 1998,

Max India offloaded 41 per cent of its stake in the company to its joint venture partner for Rs 549 crore. Analjit's business finally was flush with funds.

Once the money from the Hutchison deal was in the coffers of Max India, Analjit decided to just relax for the next six months. That is the time Windlass, his trusted aide, who did not want to miss out on the action in telecom, decided to leave Max, though he continued to serve on its board of directors. The question confronting Singh was, what next?

At that time, all Singh knew was that he had had enough of manufacturing and chasing bureaucrats. 'I knew the name of every guard in Shastri Bhawan. With the telecom venture, the babus in Sanchar Bhawan (the headquarters of the department of telecom) got added to the list. *Pagal kar diya tha* (they drove me mad),' Singh would recall. To help him make up his mind, the consultancy firm McKinsey was called on board. A McKinsey executive asked Analjit to write his obituary in 800 words—what did he want to be remembered as. The trick worked. Analjit wrote the obituary and, at the end of it, knew what he wanted to do. 'I want to make Max the country's most admired company in service excellence. I want to do what Naresh Goel has done with Jet (Airways) or what the Oberois have done (in the hotels business),' Singh told himself.

He identified three areas of growth: healthcare delivery, life insurance and information technology. The vision was further narrowed to healthcare and life insurance by 2002. In-between, he also made a foray into clinical research. He began by setting up three companies to this effect: Neeman Medical International Plc in the United Kingdom, Neeman Medical International Inc. in the United States and Neeman Asia Ltd in India. In 2001, Max India acquired a 75 per cent stake in Instituto Costarricense De Investigaciones Clinicas, a clinical research firm based at San Jose, Costa Rica, at a cost of $6.5 million. This company had fifty-three people on its rolls and its list of clients included Pfizer, Eli Lilly, Roche, Johnson & Johnson and GSK. The acquisition was to become a springboard for an entry in the clinical research business in Latin America.

Analjit also felt that Max India required a new corporate identity. Thus was born the new logo of Max India—a blue earthen lamp with a saffron flame accompanying the lettering, Max. The saffron flame was a symbol of the country's spirituality and represents power, strength and knowledge.

*

Still, Analjit remained unhappy and resentful of the family situation. Over the years, he became a votary of keeping families away from business. At the Young Presidents' Organization, he constantly spoke on how joint families destroy wealth.

Sometime in the late 1990s, when his son, Vir, broached the topic of joining the family business, Analjit asked him to fetch the atlas. With the family huddled round it, he told Vir: 'Son, there is this whole world outside and all you want to do is work with Papa?'

BITTER SEPARATION

It was called the Aurangzeb syndrome. Mughal emperor Aurangzeb had seized the kingdom after a bloody conflict with his father, Shahjahan, and his brothers. Shahjahan had been imprisoned in the Red Fort of Agra and he died in captivity.

In the 1980s, there had been several instances of bitter corporate rifts in India, where business associates had almost come to blows with each other. There were also cases of cousins and brothers at each other's throats. But never had a son risen against his father. However, in the early 1990s, two such family spats stunned the corporate world.

The first was between Raunaq Singh of the Delhi-based Apollo Tyres and his son Onkar Singh Kanwar. Raunaq Singh had risen from humble origins in pre-Partition Punjab. After Partition, he moved to Delhi and built up a steel tubes business brick by brick. He joined the big league in the mid-1970s when he ventured into the tyres business with Apollo Tyres. In the next few years, his son turned it into one of the country's premier tyre companies, getting Continental AG of Germany as a technology partner. Father and son got into a confrontation over the control of Apollo Tyres, which had emerged as the family's cash cow by the late-1980s. The fight was soon out in the open and there was much mudslinging from both sides. Finally, Raunaq Singh was ousted from the company and Onkar Singh Kanwar gained full control of Apollo Tyres.

However, in terms of sheer unpleasantness, this fight was nothing when compared to the one between Bhai Mohan Singh and Dr Singh. It generated more sadness, bitterness and pain than any other family separation in India Inc.

Even Ranbaxy insiders and those who knew the family well were taken by surprise. After all, Dr Singh was Bhai Mohan Singh's favourite son, a fact he made no secret of. In an article published in the *Tribune of Chandigarh* in 1984, Bhai Mohan Singh was quoted as saying: 'I feel particularly blessed that I have a brilliant son who has done in two years, against the three years taken by others, his PhD in pharmacy from a US university. He has been particularly helpful to me in the launching of one unit of our company in Nigeria and another in Malaysia.' Though the newspaper called it 'more an acknowledgement of fact than an expression of parental pride', everybody knew who was the apple of Bhai Mohan Singh's eye.

Bhai Mohan Singh was particularly proud of his son's academic achievements—nobody in his family or in his circle of friends could boast of such educational qualifications. The two of them seldom had differences. Dr Singh was respectful to his father and Bhai Mohan Singh doted on his son.

One summer day in the late 1970s, IPS Grover from Ranbaxy's research and development department had gone to the office wing where the rooms of Bhai Mohan Singh and Dr Singh were located. The whole family was holidaying in the cool environs of

Kashmir, except for Bhai Mohan Singh, who was in Delhi. Just then, Dr Singh's secretary received a call: it was Dr Singh from Kashmir and he wanted to speak to his father. On hearing this, Bhai Mohan Singh ran from his office barefoot to take the call, afraid that something may be wrong. Fortunately, that was not the case. Grover could see that Bhai Mohan Singh was a bundle of nerves and his eyes were moist. He had never seen such a display of emotions.

Others too could see the special bond between father and son. Soon after he had joined Ranbaxy in the early 1980s, Windlass was sitting with Dr Singh in his office taking instructions. Just then, Bhai Mohan Singh walked in. He was going abroad and had come to see his son. He put his hand on Dr Singh's head, took out Rs 500 from his wallet and pressed the money into his son's hand. The amount was small, but the gesture was heartwarming. Though Dr Singh was a big man by now, his father still treated him like a small child.

As late as in 1990, Prem Bhatia, then editor-in-chief of the *Tribune* and a close friend of Bhai Mohan Singh, wrote: 'Bhai Mohan Singh's happy family life has been one of the main assets which have made his three score years and ten not only eventful and rewarding but which also helped him to live up to the definition of "goodness" as understood by me.'

Dr Singh too respected his parents. Being the first child of his parents, he was closer to his mother. Whenever he was in Delhi, he would meet her every morning—a habit he kept till his last days. He gave both his sons the middle name Mohan—Malvinder Mohan Singh and Shivinder Mohan Singh. The two boys would meet their grandparents every morning before leaving for school to take their blessings. Since Dr Singh was strict and would not let them eat chocolates very often, Bhai Mohan Singh would give them sweets during these early morning meetings on the condition that they did not tell their parents. Every Saturday, Avtar Kaur would lay an elaborate table at lunch for all her grandchildren, pampering each with his or her favourite preparation.

*

Soon after the three brothers split in 1989, Ranbaxy's profitability went up substantially. While the turnover more than doubled from Rs 199.11 crore in 1989–90 to Rs 460.67 crore in 1992–93, the profit after tax shot up from Rs 8.09 crore to Rs 35.34 crore during the period. The company's net worth too increased from Rs 40.64 crore in 1989–90 to Rs 124.56 crore in 1992–93.

At the same time, Manjit's Montari Industries was turning into a financial mess. Analjit's Max India, though profitable, was still small. It had received a blow when Ranbaxy decided to make its own 7ADCA in the early 1990s. Analjit's other venture into BOPP films was close to shutting down. Though Analjit had accepted the division as his destiny, faint murmurs to the effect that the division of assets between the brothers was 'fixed' could now be heard. Manjit alleged that Ranbaxy's financial numbers were deliberately suppressed at the time of the division in order to get himself and Analjit out of Ranbaxy. This was when Manjit first levelled the charge that Analjit and he were shortchanged by at least Rs 20 crore each. 'I would rather have a smaller company with a share for all in the family,' Bhai Mohan Singh one day told the management guru Mrityunjay Athreya, while reflecting on the rapid progress made by Ranbaxy in the mid-1990s.

Ranbaxy was now being completely run by professionals. The only members of the family in the new-look executive committee were Bhai Mohan Singh and Dr Singh. Brar had been promoted as president (pharmaceuticals) in 1991, the second-most important position in the company. It was now clear to one and all that Brar was one day going to head the company. Dr Singh trusted his genius totally and would consult him while taking all decisions.

While dividing the assets between his sons, Bhai Mohan Singh had transferred all his Ranbaxy shares to Dr Singh. There was an agreement in the family settlement that Bhai Mohan Singh would be involved in important matters and the company would take care of his expenses on things like housing, medical treatment and travel. Dr Singh's deep attachment and respect for his father gave Bhai Mohan Singh no reason to believe that the transfer of shares could one day result in him being stripped of all powers.

Ranbaxy was more than just an enterprise for Bhai Mohan Singh. To his close friends like Srichand Chhabra, the mercurial chief of the New Delhi Municipal Corporation in the early 1970s, he always referred to the company as his fourth son. He had always been firmly in the saddle. As late as in 1989, when the Bausch & Lomb deal was being negotiated, it was Bhai Mohan Singh who was talking on behalf of Ranbaxy. The sons were nowhere in the picture in the early stages. It was only when Dr Singh expressed his reluctance to go ahead with the venture and Manjit decided to grab the opportunity that the negotiators from Bausch & Lomb got to meet other family members.

The fact that his wings had been clipped soon started preying on Bhai Mohan Singh's mind. And he blamed Dr Singh for it. Life had come a full circle for father and son. From being inseparable, they now got into a bitter struggle for power. It started as a boardroom battle. But once the news broke out, Bhai Mohan Singh was not averse to washing dirty linen in public. Soon, he started telling his friends that Dr Singh was violating the family agreement that Bhai Mohan Singh had the right to veto any matter that was not to his liking. He also complained that Dr Singh was showing no signs of fulfilling his promise of setting up a trust to enable Bhai Mohan Singh to carry out his charitable activities. Throughout his life, Bhai Mohan Singh had been a generous donor to social and religious causes but now he no longer controlled the purse strings. For the first time in his life, he had to turn back people who sought his financial help. This bruised his ego very badly.

The charge that the separation was fixed did not hold much ground. The valuation of the family's assets was not done by Bhai Mohan Singh or Dr Singh. It was carried out by professionals; Bansi Mehta, the renowned Mumbai-based chartered accountant, had been engaged for this purpose. It was done in a completely transparent manner. Besides, if Ranbaxy numbers had been deliberately suppressed, it is unlikely that the fact would have gone unnoticed by the other brothers, especially Manjit. Though both the brothers were on the executive committee, Manjit was also the company's commercial director with an insider's view of the company's finances.

Dr Singh's friends maintained that the allegations that he had doctored the figures were ridiculous, considering he maintained the highest ethical standards at work. He had been brought up with a very strong sense of values which was reinforced when he became a member of the Radha Soami Satsang.

What had happened was that right through the 1980s, the government exercised a strict price control on drugs and this restricted the profitability of all pharmaceutical companies, including Ranbaxy. In the mid-1980s, when the rupee started falling against the dollar, things took a turn for the worse for companies like Ranbaxy, which still imported the raw material for a host of its products. The company's profitability was getting eroded.

Around the time the brothers split in 1989, the business environment started improving due to several factors. After the severe drought of 1987, a good monsoon in 1988 perked up the economy, which led to an improvement in the liquidity in the markets. Besides, there was a progressive implementation of the Drug Price Control Order, 1987, which removed price controls on several drugs, thus enabling companies like Ranbaxy to raise their prices and, in the process, shore up their bottom line.

Moreover, the launch of Revital and Cifran in 1989 proved extremely successful, with both logging a turnover of Rs 10 crore each within the first year of launch. Soon afterwards, Ranbaxy clinched the cefaclor deal with Eli Lilly. This was really the turning point for the company. Money was flowing into its coffers like never before. Dr Singh could hardly be blamed for the timing of the upturn in business.

That professionals had come to occupy the centre stage is also unlikely to have provoked Bhai Mohan Singh. After all, he had given Dr Singh a free hand when the first wave of professionals were recruited in the early 1970s. Besides, there were well-entrenched professionals in Montari as well as in Max India. If Bhai Mohan Singh's ire was against professionals, he would also have objected to the growing stature of Windlass within Max India. He had come to be called the D.S. Brar of Max India. But he chose not to do so.

The differences between Bhai Mohan Singh and Dr Singh ran deeper. It was a clash between two ways of doing business—the master of the licence-permit-quota raj came into confrontation with the votary of a new, global vision.

*

Bhai Mohan Singh never missed a chance to make friends. 'Everybody was Bhai Mohan Singh's friend and Bhai Mohan Singh was everybody's friend,' Analjit would recall of his father. From bureaucrats to financiers and social activists, Bhai Mohan Singh had time for everyone. He never missed a chance to help his friends. It was a lesson Bhai Mohan Singh had learnt very early in life.

'Do not be angry. Don't quarrel even if you are unhappy. Never shout at others,' Bhai Gyan Chand would often tell his adolescent son. When Bhai Mohan Singh refused to reply to a stranger who greeted him, Bhai Gyan Chand would admonish him, saying he would have got the stranger's blessings if he had replied. Though he had brought up his son as a Sikh, Bhai Gyan Chand would take him to Hindu temples and taught him not to be a religious bigot. The message was driven home quite well—never miss the opportunity to get into the good books of people.

Once Bhai Mohan Singh had joined his father's construction business, he saw another facet of his father's pleasant manners and benevolent disposition. Bhai Gyan Chand had donated Rs 1,50,000 for the construction of a swimming pool for British army officers. The family firm had also put up a refreshments stall at Rawalpindi railway station during the Second World War to cater to soldiers passing through the station. Soon, army officers at Rawalpindi would head straight for Bhai Gyan Chand's house whenever they needed to be bailed out of a tight spot. This was the time that the family had started bidding for army contracts as the government was spending large sums of money on construction during the war years.

Bhai Mohan Singh's father-in-law, Bakshi Dalip Singh, was an equally influential man. Thanks to him, Bhai Mohan Singh had come to be associated with the tuberculosis sanatorium at the picturesque hill station of Murree (now in Pakistan). As a result, Bhai Mohan Singh could get surplus petrol in those days of rationing to drive his family to Murree very frequently. Thanks to his rising reputation with the army officers and the civil administration, Bhai Mohan Singh was even made an honorary magistrate at Rawalpindi.

Once he had shifted to New Delhi, Bhai Mohan Singh was again quick to make friends. Within no time, he became very close to some of the senior bureaucrats of that time like Abid Hussain, who later became the Indian ambassador to the United States, and Naqi Billgrami, a senior Indian Foreign Service (IFS) officer.

When the first government of Delhi was formed under Chaudhary Brahm Prakash, Bhai Mohan Singh was invited to join the New Delhi Municipal Corporation. He continued to serve the corporation for many years. Finally, in 1971, the government awarded him the Padma Shri in recognition of his services. This brought Bhai Mohan Singh in close contact with senior political leaders, and none less than the then president of India, V.V. Giri, inaugurated Ranbaxy's Mohali factory in 1974. It stunned the business world since the factory involved an investment of only Rs 1 crore. The foundation stone of this plant had been laid by the then chief minister of Punjab, Giani Zail Singh, who went on to become the president of India in the 1980s. In November 1978, the chloroquine plant at Mohali was inaugurated by Sardar Prakash Singh Badal, then chief minister of Punjab, and the function was presided over by Jaisukhlal Hathi, who had become the governor of the state. In 1981, the company's new plant for the manufacture of bulk doxycycline was inaugurated by the then Union minister for petroleum, chemicals and fertilizers, P.C. Sethi, and in 1983 the chief minister of Madhya Pradesh, Arjun Singh, laid the foundation stone of the company's new pharmaceutical formulations plant at Dewas.

Once his pharmaceutical business was in full swing, Bhai Mohan Singh became active in the field of public health. He first started working with the Tuberculosis Association of India. Every year, the association kicks off its campaign with the blessings of the president of India. As Bhai Mohan Singh was always a key functionary of the association, this guaranteed him at least one audience with the president every year. By the time he was ready to launch imported diazepam in the country, he had built enough contacts to safeguard himself against any legal problems Roche might raise. In fact, he had taken the government into confidence on the issue. At that time, the Union health minister was Rajkumari Amrit Kaur, who used to refer to Bhai Mohan Singh as 'son'. Bhai Mohan Singh had floated an organization called the All India Society for Prevention of Blindness. While Rajkumari Amrit Kaur was its president, Bhai Mohan Singh was the vice-president and general secretary. She had assured him that he would receive all possible help from the government should Roche decide to create trouble.

A booklet published in January 1974 lists no less than thirty social and religious associations with Bhai Mohan Singh as a key functionary. He was a member of the health ministry's Drugs Technical Advisory Committee for twelve years. When he retired from the committee, Dr Singh stepped in to fill the slot. Thus, the family had a presence on this all-important committee for eighteen years without a break. When Bhai Mohan Singh was elected president of the Indian Drug Manufacturers' Association in 1974, Inder Kumar Gujral, the then information and broadcasting minister, sent a letter calling him a friend. Those were the days when industrialists were viewed with suspicion and politicians did their best to dissociate from them. Gujral and Bhai Mohan Singh had grown up together at Jhelum.

Government patronage was the key to a successful business in those days. Nobody knew this better than Bhai Mohan Singh. Pleasing the political masters of the day was central to business planning. The company's 1971 annual report had, on its first page, a photograph of Bhai Mohan Singh presenting a box of Ranbaxy medicines for the National Relief Fund to Prime Minister Indira Gandhi. The picture shows the prime minister flashing a benevolent smile, a slightly bent Bhai Mohan Singh standing next to her, his hands folded, while P.C. Sethi looks on. The message was clear to all who saw the annual report: Bhai Mohan Singh had access to the Prime Minister's Office. The picture made a reappearance on the first page of the company's 1973 annual report as well.

Bhai Mohan Singh also made several top bureaucrats of the country members of the board. Businessmen always found ex-officials handy during the licence-permit-quota raj when enormous powers of decision-making were vested in the hands of the bureaucrat. Thus, B.P. Patel, a bureaucrat from the elite Indian Civil Services, was brought on the Ranbaxy board as an additional director in October 1974. Patel had served as Secretary in the Union ministry of health and family planning, the managing director of the State Trading Corporation, the government body responsible for 'canalizing' all pharmaceutical imports, and the chairman and managing director of the State Bank of India, the country's largest bank. Three years later, in 1977, another retired bureaucrat, Narottam Sahgal, joined the Ranbaxy board.

Dr Singh, in contrast, was hardly a public relations man. He was more comfortable dealing with scientists than with bureaucrats. Unlike Bhai Mohan Singh, who loved to throw parties and entertain the high and mighty at his residence, Dr Singh would seldom call power brokers home. When it became absolutely necessary, he would organize a party at the Ranbaxy guest house at Sunder Nagar.

However, there was often speculation that he was extremely close to Rajiv Gandhi and exercised considerable influence over the young and energetic prime minister.

Dr Singh and Rajiv had met courtesy Vivek Bharat Ram, who was in the same class as Indira Gandhi's elder son in Doon School. Before Rajiv became the prime minister in 1984, the two would meet often at parties at Vivek Bharat Ram's house. They took an instant liking to each other as both of them were forward-looking and wanted India to take rapid strides in science and technology. Even after becoming prime minister, Rajiv would always take time out for Dr Singh.

However, Dr Singh did not know Rajiv well enough to curry favours with him. Still, Dr Singh was grief-stricken when Raizada informed him of Rajiv's assassination in 1991. He was in the United States when he was given the news, and he broke down on the phone.

By the late 1980s, before anybody else in India, Dr Singh knew that things were going to change in the pharmaceutical business. The protection offered by the patent regime would have to go as India integrated with the global economy. He was aware of the drift of the patent negotiations at the multilateral trade negotiations, the precursor to the World Trade Organization (WTO) and knew that the days of unprotected product patents were numbered.

His close associates like Bimal Raizada first got to know of his changed views around 1988, when he ordered that Ranbaxy stop funding the National Council for Patent Laws, a voluntary organization managed by one B.K. Keyala, which was arguing that India did not require patents of any kind. Keyala was funded by both Ranbaxy and Cipla. Once Dr Singh realized that Keyala was fighting a lost cause, he pulled out. Cipla, however, continued to fund Keyala for many more years. Cipla's Hamied was always bitterly opposed to any change in the patent laws, arguing passionately against India's commitment to reintroduce product patents from 1 January 2005.

Though he had started discussing the matter with friends and colleagues, it was only in his management review for 1993–94 that Dr Singh first made public his changed views on the subject:

> For the Indian pharmaceutical industry, the GATT (General Agreement on Tariff and Trade) treaty signalled the emergence of a new era with the acceptance of product patents. Although some in the industry have misgivings on the issue, we at Ranbaxy believe that this can provide new opportunities. With the new Intellectual Property Rights regime that India has agreed upon, focus must now shift to innovation. Industry has not been investing adequately on research and development, as profit margins have remained low on account of a rigid price control mechanism. The future belongs to those companies who will invest and enhance their research capabilities, initiate change and avail themselves of the emerging opportunities.

This meant that Ranbaxy had to alter its style of functioning. To begin with, the top decision-making body of the company had to have the best brains within Ranbaxy. After the 1989 split, Dr Singh got the opportunity to restructure the executive committee. While the earlier twelve-member committee had five family members—Bhai Mohan Singh, his three sons and Jaswant Singh—and one diehard loyalist in Sawhney, the new committee of six had only two family members, Bhai Mohan Singh and Dr Singh, while the other four—Sheth, Raizada, Brar and Chakroborty—were professionals. The next year, Jag Mohan Khanna was co-opted into this high-powered body.

The next imperative was that Ranbaxy had to take risks in research and development. Money would have to be pumped into research to develop new products with no guarantee that the investment would one day pay off. Dr Singh was convinced that for Ranbaxy to do well abroad, it had to first consolidate its position at home. Ranbaxy was not even present in all segments of the Indian market. It was largely an anti-infectives company and it needed to expand its product portfolio in double quick time. This could be done only through acquisitions and mergers, which called for a total change in mindset. An all-stock acquisition deal or a merger could dilute the family's stake in Ranbaxy. Also, all the expansion plans drawn up by Dr Singh required fresh infusion of capital into the company. This, again, would have called for a dilution in the promoter's stake in the company. All this was too radical for Bhai Mohan Singh.

*

Bhai Mohan Singh had little contribution to make to the new Ranbaxy. The P.V. Narasimha Rao government had opened up the Indian economy in 1991, sounding the death knell of the licence-permit quota raj. The skills of environment management, which Bhai Mohan Singh had honed to perfection, were rendered redundant overnight. In a break from the past, management discussion would now focus on global pharmaceutical trends. Bhai Mohan Singh felt alienated.

Dr Singh was only too aware of his father's dilemma. But he still had a role cut out for him. He wanted Bhai Mohan Singh to be Ranbaxy's face at business forums and industry associations. But this alone was unacceptable to Bhai Mohan Singh.

The differences slowly started appearing during board meetings. Dr Singh could sense resistance from Bhai Mohan Singh and some of his friends on the company's board. He knew he was running a race against time, and it was only natural for him to feel frustrated. Initially, it appeared that Dr Singh was going to lose the boardroom battle.

One day he called his friends from the executive committee and told them that it was soon going to be all over. He offered to give them some financial compensation out of his own pocket, once he was ousted from the board. These top professionals of the Indian pharmaceutical industry threw in their lot with Dr Singh. They gave him undated resignation letters to be used as the final gambit if he was cornered. Though the father and son were fighting inside the boardroom, it had not affected the company at all as the day-to-day running of the company was entrusted to professionals. If these people were to pull out of the company, Ranbaxy would come to a grinding halt.

Others in the company too had come out in support of Dr Singh. During a board meeting at Ranbaxy's office in the Nehru Place commercial complex in south Delhi, some fifty executives marched to the boardroom, shouting slogans in favour of Dr Singh. They were led by Sanjiv Kaul, who had started his innings at Ranbaxy in 1983, when he joined the company's international division. (He later went on to become in-charge of Ranbaxy's operations in China, the head of the India region and then the head of corporate affairs.) When he opened the door of the boardroom, he paused to look back at his other colleagues. There was no one there. Kaul's heart sank. Yet, he said his bit and walked back. Soon, some of the directors were baying for his blood but Dr Singh's intervention saved the day for him.

The fight started turning in Dr Singh's favour when Prof. Veda Vyas, Rustom P. Soonawala, Narottam Sahgal and D.D. Chopra resigned from the company's board of directors, effective from 18 September 1992. In their place, Dr Singh was quick to appoint Mumbai-based businessman Tirath R. Mulchandani, Vivek Bharat Ram, Vikram Lal of the Eicher group and the journalist Suman Dubey; all of them were his friends. (By now, Vivek Bharat Ram and Dr Singh had grown very close to each other.) They would speak to each other every day. In a move that would strengthen Dr Singh's position further on the board, Brar and Sheth were appointed as alternate directors between September 1992 and November 1992. Dubey, however, resigned soon after joining when he became in-charge of Dow Jones, the financial news agency, in India. The boardroom strengths of the two warring factions were now evenly matched.

Soon, sparks began to fly. Dr Singh rarely uttered a word against his father, but his friends did not hold their punches. They targeted Bhai Mohan Singh's friends on the board. Though professionals were invited to join the Ranbaxy board even as early as in the 1960s, Bhai Mohan Singh was not averse to packing the board with relatives and friends; Avtar Kaur served on the Ranbaxy board till 1983. When the fight with his son erupted, there were three board members, apart from Manjit, who decided to side with Bhai Mohan Singh: Dan Singh Bawa, Air Marshal O.P. Mehra and M.M. Sabharwal.

Bawa, a Delhi-based businessman with interests in construction and real estate, had joined Ranbaxy after Lepetit exited from the company. Air Marshal Mehra had studied with Bhai Mohan Singh in Government College, Lahore, and joined the Ranbaxy board in 1987. There was a tacit understanding that if he did not agree with Bhai Mohan Singh on any resolution that the latter was seeking to pass at the board meetings, Mehra would abstain from voting.

Sabharwal had first met Bhai Mohan Singh in 1980 as they were both members of the PHDCCI (Punjab, Haryana and Delhi Chambers of Commerce and Industry). Sabharwal's first impression was that Bhai Mohan Singh was an extremely cordial man with excellent contacts in government as well as diplomatic circles. It was clear to Sabharwal that, in a very pleasant way, Bhai Mohan Singh wielded a lot of influence in the corridors of power and that the mild-mannered Sikh had used the licence raj to ensure Ranbaxy's growth. In 1984, Bhai Mohan Singh invited Sabharwal, who had by then earned a reputation as a fine corporate director, to join the Ranbaxy board. If Sabharwal had a high opinion of Bhai Mohan Singh and how he had developed the craft of 'environment management' to perfection, the Ranbaxy chairman too had every reason to be impressed with the tall and elegant technocrat.

After graduating from Delhi's St. Stephen's College in 1942, Sabharwal chanced upon a job advertisement put out by Dunlop, the tyre company, for management trainees on a salary of Rs 75 per month, and decided to apply. However, the British employment manager there tried his best to dissuade Sabharwal from joining. He relented only when he learnt that Sabharwal's father had been awarded the Order of the British Empire (OBE). Little did the employment manager know that he was interviewing the future executive chairman of Dunlop and that in 1998 Sabharwal too would receive an OBE for his role in promoting Indo-British partnership in social welfare.

Sabharwal retired as the executive chairman of Dunlop in 1977. Soon afterwards, he was co-opted into the board of several multinational companies in India like Bata India, Britannia Industries, Indian Oxygen and a few public sector undertakings like Oil India and the National Aluminium Company. In the early and mid-1980s, Sabharwal was to once again earn a name for himself as the non-executive chairman of Britannia as well as Bata.

During a Britannia board meeting in 1981, he found that the company's opening stock for a month did not tally with the previous month's closing stock. Inquiries revealed that all was not well with the company's finances and Sabharwal realized that the only way out was to remove the managing director, the finance director and the marketing director of the company. He got permission from the principal shareholder of Britannia at that time—the United Kingdom–based Huntley and Palmer Foods. On consulting some lawyers, Sabharwal realized that secrecy was of utmost importance in such an operation. He went about the task in a manner that verged on the Machiavellian, and managed a smooth purge.

A few years later, Sabharwal once again played a stellar role in defusing a crisis, this time as the non-executive chairman of Bata. The shoe company had imported some raw material and exported footwear made from it, against which it got a refund of the import duty it paid. One day, a Bata India employee informed the government that the company was claiming duty drawbacks on exports that did not use imported raw material at all. The law enforcement agencies immediately raided the company's offices and factories all over the country. The managing director of the company was taken into custody. This was the time when V.P. Singh (who was to become prime minister in 1989) was the finance minister in Rajiv Gandhi's government and was cracking down on economic offences by corporate bodies.

Sabharwal called a meeting of the Bata board in Kolkata to discuss the whole issue. At the meeting, he offered to help the company in getting out of the jam, provided the board passed a resolution giving him the sole authority to handle the crisis. With no other solution in sight, the board had no option but to agree. Back in Delhi, Sabharwal sought a meeting with the Cabinet Secretary, P.K. Kaul. After their meeting, Kaul called up Vinod Pande, the Finance Secretary, asking him to see Sabharwal. Pande told Sabharwal bluntly that the only way out for the company was to accept that it had violated the law, tender an apology and give back to the government the excess duty drawbacks it had got.

It was not an easy choice for Sabharwal. The admission of wrongdoing by Bata could be used against the company in the future. There was not enough time to call the Bata headquarters in Canada for advice. Not knowing what to do, he telephoned Kaul who also asked him to submit an apology. Sabharwal sent an apology on behalf of Bata and, later in the day, was informed by Pande that the government had decided to drop the investigations but would give publicity to this case.

The next morning, Sabharwal got a telephone call from John Elliott, the local *Financial Times* representative, who told him that the government had announced Bata's apology at a press conference and asked Sabharwal if he would like to comment. Sabharwal had to decide quickly. This particular report had the potential to damage Bata's reputation globally. He gave a simple statement: 'If we make a mistake at Bata, we set it right immediately.' The Bata image was saved. Thomas Bata himself acknowledged Sabharwal's efforts in handling this crisis.

When Sabharwal joined the Ranbaxy board in 1984, there was no tacit understanding with Bhai Mohan Singh that Sabharwal would toe his line. Though the two of them were fairly well acquainted, Bhai Mohan Singh did not know Sabharwal well enough to extract such a commitment from him. Sabharwal had Dr Singh's respect too and the latter would often consult him on important matters. So why did Sabharwal side with Bhai Mohan Singh in the fight? Sabharwal felt that while Dr Singh was a man in a hurry, Bhai Mohan Singh was more conservative and wanted to ensure that the plans for rapid growth should not end in disaster. After all, Sabharwal had been witness to what had happened at Dunlop. The company had borrowed heavily to bankroll its ambitious expansion plans. Once the projected cash generation did not take place, Dunlop got mired in a financial crisis. He was apprehensive that Dr Singh's ambitious plans could similarly spell doom for Ranbaxy.

Still, Bhai Mohan Singh's supporters could feel the tide turning against them. As recounted by several board members present there, tempers ran so high that at one particular meeting, Capt. Amarinder Singh, who had studied with Dr Singh and who had joined the Ranbaxy board in 1983, told Bhai Mohan Singh that he would physically pick him up and remove him from the boardroom. Capt. Singh, who belonged to the former royal family of Patiala and later became the chief minister of Punjab, would not attend Ranbaxy board meetings regularly on account of his political engagements. Yet he strode into this board meeting to make a point in his own very emphatic style. Having made his statement, he snapped a pencil into two. The message was not lost on those present.

*

By now, Bhai Mohan Singh and Dr Singh were no longer on talking terms. Dr Singh would go to meet his mother every day, but Bhai Mohan Singh refused to see him. The fight took its heaviest toll on Avtar Kaur. She was torn between her husband and her favourite son. This was the time her health started failing and she never regained her energy. She died in July 2004 after a prolonged illness. But Dr Singh continued to meet her till he could stand on his feet. During his last days, when he knew his time was up, Dr Singh assured his mother that after him Malvinder would look after her and she would not feel his absence.

Several friends of Bhai Mohan Singh as well as Dr Singh tried to resolve the crisis but in vain. Sabharwal and Avtar Kaur went several times to counsel Dr Singh when father and son were not on talking terms. But he refused to relent. Bansi Mehta also tried to bring them together. But relations between the two had soured to such an extent that Bhai Mohan Singh wrote a letter to Dr Singh saying that there was no need for him to attend his funeral. Athreya's bid to help patch things up too met with no success. 'It is not easy to get Punjabis to compromise,' he would remember years later.

Air Marshal Mehra too tried to broker peace between father and son. A decade after the spat, sitting on the lawns of his home in New Delhi, he would recount how all his efforts were gently blocked by Dr Singh. 'He told me that he appreciated my concern, but this was a matter between him and his father. The words were chosen very carefully. He didn't say it was a matter between him and the chairman of the company. I got the message and did not pursue the matter any further,' he said.

Perhaps the most sincere efforts to bring the warring father and son together were made by Prem Pandhi, an old friend of Bhai Mohan Singh, from their college days. Pandhi went on to become the executive chairman of Cadbury India. Bhai Mohan Singh had offered him a berth on the Montari board. Pandhi told Bhai Mohan Singh several times to let things go. But his old friend would not listen. 'He was extremely worked up and was boiling from inside,' Pandhi was to recall. He even tried to reason with Dr Singh by telling him that all that his father wanted was some importance and not to snatch the business from him. But their efforts came to naught.

It was more than a personality clash for Dr Singh. He had to win against his father if Ranbaxy had to be put on the path to high growth. The ambitious plans he had drawn for the company would all be scrapped if he lost the battle. Ranbaxy would have remained an India-focussed company. He couldn't let it happen.

On 6 February 1993, Bhai Mohan Singh, Air Marshal Mehra, Sabharwal, Bawa and Manjit resigned from the Ranbaxy board of directors. The same day, Dr Singh took over as the chairman and managing director of the company. Bhai Mohan Singh was made chairman emeritus. The previous night, Manjit had come to know that there were plans to oust Bhai Mohan Singh in the board meeting scheduled for the day. He disclosed this to his father. Rather than be ousted unceremoniously, Bhai Mohan Singh chose to resign. Along with him, his friends also resigned. The boardroom battle was over, though the fight between father and son would continue.

Bhai Mohan Singh now took the fight to the courts, charging Dr Singh with reneging on the commitments made in the family settlement to give money for his charities. When Dr Singh died in 1999, Malvinder and Shivinder got embroiled in the legal cases. Even when Dr Singh was diagnosed with cancer, there was no thaw in relations. Though Bhai Mohan Singh did visit his son while he was undergoing treatment at the Sloane-Kettering hospital in the United States, the meetings were frosty and the uneasiness between the two was not lost on all who were present. It was not a meeting of father and son in the traditional Indian way. 'The normal empathy for a son dying so young was not there,' Dr P.S. Joshi, director of the Radha Soami Hospital at Beas, who was present during these meetings, would remember later.

But the fight did upset Dr Singh. In his last interview to the media, about a month before his death, he mentioned the ugly spat with his father as the only regret he had. He would invariably tell his close friends how going against his father had hurt him.

Once Dr Singh died, Bhai Mohan Singh made one last attempt to regain control of the company. Though he did not make any formal demand, he told the media that the promoter family should be represented on the Ranbaxy board and, therefore, Malvinder and Shivinder, should be inducted into the board right away. But Dr Singh had made it very clear that his sons would join the board only on their merit, when they had developed enough skills and knowledge to add value to all boardroom discussions. The conviction was as strong as ever during his final interview a month before he died. Though his body was frail, his eyes shone like those of a determined warrior. There was no mistaking that not even death could shake his belief. Both the sons were in their mid-twenties and did not have much work experience at the time of their father's death. They understood that whatever Dr Singh had willed was in the best interests of the company. Once Bhai Mohan Singh started voicing his demand, they promptly issued a statement saying that they would abide by their father's philosophy of separating ownership of an enterprise from its management. That put paid to Bhai Mohan Singh's last efforts to get the family back in the driving seat.

XERXES DESAI

Excerpts from *TATAlog* byHarish Bhat

TANISHQ ALMOST SHUTS SHOP

Clara Lobo manages the beautiful Tanishq showroom on Turner Road, a busy high street in the upscale Bandra area of Mumbai. Inside the store, a family is buying gold jewellery for their daughter's wedding in a few weeks' time. A young couple has just walked in to look at engagement rings. Saleswomen, dressed in elegant brown sarees, are navigating the couple through an assortment of styles. At another counter, two women look visibly excited while making a selection of a set of diamond-studded bangles. Soft music plays in the background. Lobo explains to me how the scenario has changed.

> All Indian women want to own Tanishq jewellery today. Our brand has connected so well with them. We have the happiest customers in the world. But it was so different when we began, for many years. I joined Tanishq fifteen years ago, in 1997, just a year after the brand had been launched. We would wait for hours together for a single customer to walk in. Often, a whole week would pass by in silence, and we would feel very depressed. Our performance was so poor that sometimes we even heard that this brand would be shut down.

Two thousand kilometres from Lobo's store, in the garden city of Bangalore, sits Xerxes Desai, the man who founded Tanishq. Now retired, he speaks slowly but clearly in his refined Oxford accent.

> Yes, for some years there certainly was pressure to hive off this business. There was mixed support from some people in the

Tatas. There was also an opinion that the jewellery business could only be run by family jewellers, that it never could be corporatized.

But I was firm in my view, and I said that any such hiving off or closure would happen over my dead body. We saw the huge opportunity, we had belief and we persisted.

Tanishq is the largest and most successful brand of jewellery in India today, serving nearly a million people (mostly women) each year and generating annual revenues of approximately Rs 10,000 crore, making it one of the glittering jewels in the Tata crown. It is a much-celebrated success that is steadily transforming the second-largest consumer sector in the country. In terms of sheer size, only the food industry beats jewellery.

This is the story of Tanishq, the vision and courage that powered it, and how it overcame all its early errors and struggles to set the gold standard for India.

WRISTWATCHES AND JEWELLERY

Titan Industries, the company which launched Tanishq, was founded in 1984 as a joint venture between the Tata Group and the Government of Tamil Nadu. In April 1987, it launched Titan watches in India. Built on the back of quartz technology and a range of fabulous designs, these watches took the market by storm.

Within a few years, Titan had established a formidable market share of more than 50 per cent in the organized market, frequently walking away with awards for superlative marketing. Titan had become a household name in the country. Even the first movement of Mozart's Twenty-Fifth Symphony, which Titan used in much of its advertising, became as popular as Bollywood songs in many Indian households. Given that very few Indians have any interest in Western classical music, this was a spectacular achievement by itself. Here was a brand that could do no wrong.

Desai, a long-time Tata veteran who founded the company and became its first managing director, recalls, 'Titan was doing extraordinarily well in the market. Sales volumes of our watches were jumping far beyond initial expectations. We revelled in our success.'

At that stage, Titan Industries entered the jewellery business for reasons that could be termed unconventional. In 1991 India faced a serious problem when its foreign currency reserves were severely depleted. The Government of India had to pledge several hundred tonnes of gold from its national reserves to help resolve that crisis. It is ironic that a jewellery business that today uses hundreds of tonnes of gold each year was born at that exact moment.

Titan used many imported components in its watches, even as it rapidly ramped up indigenous production, and the cash-strapped government insisted that it earn foreign exchange to fund these imports. The company was therefore on the lookout for a suitable project that could earn foreign currency through exports.

Desai says, with a mischievous smile, 'We looked at several other ventures before we finally chose to make and export jewellery. For instance, a granite business was actively considered for several weeks, before it was dropped. Indian granite was in huge demand those days for making Japanese tombstones. Fortunately for us, that bizarre idea was speedily buried in its own graveyard.'

The reasons for choosing to pursue the jewellery business were quite simple. World over, at the premium end of the market, jewellers were also watchmakers, and vice versa. Both watches and jewellery were objects of exquisite design and personal adornment. The same stores retailed both in Europe and America. And both participated in the same exhibitions worldwide.

So, Titan Industries invested in a factory and the expertise for manufacturing jewellery. The plant was established in Hosur, an industrial town in Tamil Nadu, at a distance of approximately forty kilometres from Bangalore. It was also in close proximity to the original unit that manufactured wristwatches. Beautifully landscaped and designed, the factory looked as sublime as the jewellery it would make.

Since the objective was to export all this jewellery and earn foreign exchange, the initial designs that were created in this factory were entirely Western and European in their inspiration. European designers were hired to achieve this. Jewelled watches were also created. However, two things happened soon thereafter that created immediate uncertainty for the viability of the project.

The demand patterns for gold jewellery in Europe and the United States changed dramatically. Due to a global economic downturn, the ostentatious spending of the Thatcher–Reagan era gave way to a new austerity, and women moved towards the more inexpensive steel-and-gold looks. Titan's fine jewellery was just not competitive enough in this new reality. It seemed that the export game was not worth the candle.

With the onset of the 1991 reforms the Indian economy recovered to a remarkable degree a year later. Other industries such as IT built large export surpluses. Imports were freely permitted, and the need to earn foreign exchange through exports disappeared. Suddenly, for Titan, selling jewellery to Europe was no longer essential.

Desai continues:

So, here we had a big jewellery factory, and no overseas market worth the effort of developing. This was an expensive plant, with expensive people. The European market for gold jewellery had shrunk, demand from those quarters had declined and it no longer made sense to compete in that space. That is when we turned to the Indian market, and thought of Tanishq.

THE BIRTH OF TANISHQ

Xerxes Desai had also spoken to J.R.D. Tata in the initial exploratory phases, and sought his views on entering the Indian jewellery market. JRD, who was in his final years as chairman of the Tata Group, was almost childishly excited by the prospect, and quite positive in his response.

'There's a very big market in India for jewellery,' JRD said. 'Given our technical skills and reputation, we should be able to do well.'

But JRD left the final decision to the managing director of the company, like he always did. 'He would hardly ever say no,' Desai recalls, 'unless it was something that he felt was not ethically or morally correct. Only then would he tell me: "Xerxes, in the Tatas we don't do it that way."'

Jamshed Bhabha, a senior Tata director on Titan's board, was even more vocal in his support for a jewellery business. He proudly showed Xerxes Desai a picture of his aunt, Lady Meherbai Tata, wife of Sir Dorab Tata, standing next to Queen Mary of England and wearing the monumental Jubilee diamond that weighed an amazing 245 carats (49.07 g). It was sold by the Tata family in the 1930s to Cartier, then on to Harry Winston, who sold it to a French billionaire, who in turn sold it to diamond czar Robert Mouawad, the current owner. Perhaps there was some fond hope that Titan's jewellery business, if it indeed began, would, some day, reclaim this coveted diamond for the Tatas!

While J.R.D. Tata's and Jamshed Bhabha's views were positive, this was not the response from other directors in the Tata Group. There was deep scepticism that jewellery, a trade that flourished in the unorganized sector, could ever be successful in the hands of a corporate body.

Ishaat Hussain, finance director of Tata Sons, has been a member of the board of directors of Titan Industries for more than two decades. He recalls, 'Jewellery stores in India had always worked with the owner/proprietor model, where the owner knows each customer and builds close personal contact with clients and their families. It was difficult to imagine at that time that this model could be corporatized, that it could change so fast.'

Within Titan too, there were several pockets of cynicism, particularly within the prosperous watch business. Why venture into an unknown industry, when Titan watches were performing so splendidly? Wouldn't it make far more sense to strengthen the watches portfolio by adding new brands or markets, which could further enhance its success?

It is in such moments that one's mettle is tested. Desai reflected on these views calmly, and also discussed them with his senior team, but time and again one indisputable fact leapt out at him. The Indian appetite for jewellery was huge—the size of the market exceeded Rs 50,000 crore annually (today, it is closer to three times that size). The opportunity was too enormous to ignore. Titan's proven manufacturing, marketing and design skills, and its Tata parentage, could be leveraged to crack open this market. Yes, it would not be a cakewalk like the watch business has been, but the rewards in time to come were worth the likely struggles of the initial years, as Tanishq sought to change consumer behaviour and loyalty to the 'family jeweller'.

Leaders of nations and large businesses have to often make lonely decisions, and Desai did, encouraged by the enthusiasm of those who led the jewellery project. In 1996, he decided to launch the first retail showroom of Tanishq in India.

Even as he took this call, he may have looked one last time at a colourful painting of a *bindu*, by the famous Indian artist Syed Haider Raza, which hung in the offices of Titan. The bindu is a dot, which is the source of all energy. Xerxes Desai's decision was on the dot, and here the source of his energy was his belief in the Indian consumer.

NAMING THE BABY

Marketers spend enormous time trying to create a new brand name. They commission quantitative and qualitative consumer research studies. They appoint experts to analyse the subliminal messages that a brand name conveys. They do many other things that supposedly convey scientific rigour in this area.

However, history tells us that the best brand names are often not born in this way. They just need to have a nice, catchy ring to them, an authentic origin and, if possible, a simple meaning as well. The name Tata is a good illustration: it is the family name of the founder of the group. Similarly, the brand name Apple was chosen because Steve Jobs worked in an apple farm one summer and it came before Atari (a competitor) in the phone book.

The name Tanishq, chosen by Desai and acknowledged today as a masterstroke by everyone, has a similar history. Here is his own version of the story:

> Anil Manchanda [who was leading the jewellery project in the company] was keen on the name Aurum. But this would look like a piece of the periodic table, and no one would really understand it, so we said no. We had previously used the brand name Celeste in the European market, during the early days of jewellery export. But we soon realized that Celeste had already been trademarked by another company.
>
> So, I thought of the word Tanishq. I was clear that the word should possess a feminine and Indian feel to it. It would also be useful for the names of our two promoters to be reflected in the name. So, *ta* stands both for Tata and Tamil Nadu, the promoters of our company. And *nishq* means a piece of jewellery. The name sounded even better when Fali Vakeel of our advertising agency, Lintas, pointed out to me that Tanishq, when sliced differently, is a combination of *tan* (body) and *ishq* (love). These are words which go very well with jewellery.
>
> But what is really interesting is how the name Tanishq jumped into my mind at the very beginning. I am fond of dogs, and I owned a Harlequin Great Dane at that time, called Monishqa. Also, the young daughter of a close friend, whose brains we had picked in the early days when working on Titan's marketing strategy, was named Monisha. So, I used these names often, and I think they triggered Tanishq, which sounds quite similar! When I tossed it around in my mind after that, it sounded very poetic and beautiful.

Marketers may wish to bear this story in mind when they commission research firms to search for brand names.

AN INDIAN SUMMER

Tanishq was launched in India in 1996, as a brand of precious gem set (studded) jewellery. Plain gold jewellery was a very small part of the product offering. As Desai mentioned in a speech many years later, the idea was to make Tanishq 'a composite Indian avatar of Cartier, Tiffany, Asprey and even Ernest Jones all rolled into one'.

Bhaskar Bhat, the current managing director of Titan Industries, explains why this choice was made:

> Plain gold jewellery offers little opportunity for differentiation (or so we felt at that time). With everyone sourcing from the same pool of *karigar*s (artisans), new designs are quickly copied. Also, everyone knows the price of gold. The customer then adds labour and wastage charges, and establishes the base price, leaving the jeweller with no pricing power. You make money by focusing on volumes and faster inventory turns.
>
> Studded jewellery is a different story altogether. Customers don't really know how to accurately value gems. Even with diamonds, where we have a clear evaluation process based on the four Cs of cut, colour, clarity and caratage, it is not easy to peg down a price. There is also the opportunity to be innovative in design, since people are less likely to copy them, given the low volumes. As a result, the jeweller has more price flexibility, and margins are much higher in studded jewellery.

The decision to get primarily into studded jewellery created a constraint because it meant that Tanishq could not offer any significant variety in 22 carat gold to consumers, despite this caratage being the standard in the Indian market. Eighteen carat gold would have to be used to make Tanishq jewellery, since 22 carat gold is too soft to hold diamonds or other gemstones. Simultaneously, there was also an effort to move the market for plain gold jewellery to 18 carat, with the belief that this offering would enable consumers to spread their budgets over larger or more pieces, since 18 carat gold is less expensive than 22 carat gold. It would also benefit customers because 18 carat gold is more scratch-proof and dent-proof.

The company knew that by doing this it was taking on the risk of trying to change long-standing consumer behaviour. Moving consumers from 22 carat gold to 18 carat jewellery was fundamental to the success of this strategy. However, Desai and team were supremely confident. They had successfully transformed the watch market. They were inspired marketers, recognized repeatedly as the best in the land. There was no reason to doubt that they would not do it again.

In July 1996, the first Tanishq showroom opened for business at Cathedral Road in Chennai. The showroom looked like a highly exclusive five-star hotel. Fitted with green marble, low counters, works of art and some show windows, there was very little jewellery on display compared to other Indian jewellery stores. Staff was hired and trained extensively in the art of customer service. An advertisement campaign was launched with a view to create mystery around the brand and also communicate that the showrooms were as precious as the Tanishq jewellery itself. Now the only thing that needed to happen was for customers to walk in. So they waited . . .

The Indian woman remained totally unmoved.

Gold jewellery was not merely a piece of adornment for her; it was her personal wealth, traditionally called *stridhan*. She was not willing to dilute this important aspect of her life by buying 18 carat gold, which was, in her perception, far less valuable than 22 carat gold. In her view, 'less than precious' 18 carat jewellery was eminently unsuitable, particularly for precious occasions such as weddings and Indian festivals. The few women who overcame this adverse perception and stepped into Tanishq showrooms were promptly intimidated by the opulent surroundings and the Western-style jewellery. 'Not for me' was the most common reaction, which did not change even after several months of intense marketing efforts.

With a bang and a thud, the marketers who could do no wrong were brought down to earth. The expensive jewellery factory in Hosur continued to incur losses, because there was little being sold. Tanishq was in distress.

WHEN IT RAINS, IT POURS

During the period 1996 to 2000, even as Tanishq was failing miserably to attract consumers, the parent company, Titan Industries, suffered many other setbacks as well.

The watch business made a foray into Europe, which turned out to be a misadventure. The losses incurred on this account ran into more than Rs 150 crore, which was a huge amount for the company to bear. A relatively new business in table clocks and wall clocks had to be discontinued, because its potential size and profitability was not attractive enough. The clocks bore the stamp of beautiful design, and the few remaining pieces are still sought after by connoisseurs, but the financial returns were completely inadequate. In addition, the company had invested in a joint venture with Timex Watches of the USA, which was also running into major financial and operational challenges.

Bhaskar Bhat recalls, 'We were deep in debt. Our initial successes in the watch market had given us an aura of invincibility, which was now peeling away. Media speculated that we would sell the jewellery business. Some reports even said that the Tata Group was very unhappy with our entry into this sector. The going was getting really rough.'

Indeed, there were several frowns and worried faces whenever the future of the jewellery business came up for discussion. It had already lost more than Rs 100 crore. Some observers reckoned that the brand was stuck in no man's land, and there was no light at the end of the tunnel. To make it worse, the company had to bear these huge losses at a time when nothing else seemed to be going well.

Desai also knew that the core watch business was earning much less money than originally planned, which is why the cash required to support the jewellery segment, on which the project and its borrowings were based, was rapidly evaporating. Several debates erupted now on the future of this business. Some of these debates occurred in Bombay House and were also thereafter tabled at the board of directors of Titan.

A protracted and sharply worded correspondence between Desai and Ishaat Hussain (who represented the Tata Group on Titan's board of directors) was typical of this period. Hussain was concerned about the mounting losses, and he took up the matter in no uncertain terms. The exchange of letters appeared to be veering into a deadlock.

Xerxes Desai says:

> Ishaat and I were good friends; in fact, my son had worked with him in earlier years. He was doing his job as a man of finance, but I entirely disagreed with his point of view on the jewellery business. I was convinced the business had big potential; perhaps we had made errors in execution leading to the losses, but we could change that around.
>
> There was also a view in some quarters in the Tatas and elsewhere that jewellery was not our core competence. These people said we were a watch company; that is why we were failing so badly in this new venture. But I ask you, if the Tatas had focused only on their core competence, wouldn't we have remained a textiles and trading group for the past century?

It is to the credit of the Tata Group that though there was significant impatience and discomfort with the jewellery business in the offices of Bombay House, they left the final decision to Desai and the board of directors of Titan Industries.

An interview with Ratan Tata, published in *Businessworld* magazine in December 2000, highlights this approach.

The interviewers, Tony Joseph and Radhika Dhawan, ask him if Titan had entered the jewellery business against the wishes of the group, and was then not delivering. Ratan Tata responded, 'You referred to the case of Titan going into the jewellery business, and the GEO's [group executive office's] contrary view on this. Ideally, where is this kind of issue to be discussed and debated? At the boards of these companies.'

He went on to say that the boards of companies had to be more concerned with their businesses than they had been in the past, and that the CEO should take his directions from the board, which is the requisite authority.

Notwithstanding Ratan Tata's viewpoint, pressure mounted on Desai to hive off the jewellery business into a separate company that could be sold, if necessary. This was in essence an exit plan, and the Tata Group appeared to have lost faith in Tanishq. Within Titan Industries, there was indifferent support from many segments in the prosperous watch section, which considered the jewellery business a bottomless and useless sink for funds. However, there was strong support for Tanishq from the manufacturing unit, which had discovered a passion for making fine jewellery, the sales and marketing team of the jewellery business, directors representing the Tamil Nadu government and some senior Tata directors such as Jamshed Bhabha.

Desai again consulted his senior management team, which included Jacob Kurian, Vasant Nangia and Bhaskar Bhat. He then decided that he would take the pressure head-on—the consumer opportunity in jewellery was as large as ever, despite the initial lack of success and the current financial stress. The need of the hour was a sound consumer proposition and good execution, and then it was just a question of giving the venture the time to succeed.

Desai says his knowledge of the pioneering history of the Tata Group gave him the confidence to shut out the noise and march ahead.

ENTER THE KARATMETER

Tanishq now made two big changes to its consumer offering. In 1999, bowing to the voice of the Indian woman, it abandoned its primary focus on 18 carat studded jewellery, and introduced a wide range of 22 carat gold jewellery. Many of these were designs inspired by an Indian look. This was built on a limited pilot offering of 22 carat jewellery that had already been launched. With this change in offering, many more Indian women opened their minds and wallets to Tanishq.

It also pioneered what will be remembered forever as one of the greatest innovations in the Indian jewellery market, the karatmeter.

This machine used the science of spectroscopy to measure the purity or caratage of gold in three minutes. It did this using rays of specified frequency without destroying the piece of jewellery. Karatmeters were placed in Tanishq showrooms where customers could see them in operation. Now, the karatmeter could instantly certify the purity of the jewellery at the point of sale.

'This was a masterstroke by the team,' says Desai. 'An obscure scientific laboratory instrument suddenly became the touchstone of our age.'

Tanishq then launched an aggressive marketing campaign highlighting that a lot of the jewellery sold in India actually offered less caratage of gold than promised, enabling jewellers to cheat the consumer and make a quick buck in the bargain. The advertisements highlighted the impeccable quality and caratage of Tanishq, invoking the Tata tradition of trust and the modern quality controls it used. The advertisements also invited consumers to walk into Tanishq showrooms and check the purity of their gold jewellery on the karatmeter at no cost.

Within days, thousands of women had walked into Tanishq showrooms to check their jewellery, and over 60 per cent of them had found that their gold was well below the stated caratage. In other words, they had been cheated by their jewellers, whom they had trusted all along.

As news of this spread like wildfire, women formed queues in front of Tanishq showrooms to check the purity of their gold. In many showrooms, including the early flagship store at Dickenson Road in Bangalore, many women broke down and wept inconsolably when they checked their gold on the karatmeter and saw that it was impure. This meant that their savings of a lifetime, much of which was in gold, diminished in value.

Tears gave way to rage and we all know hell hath no fury like a woman scorned (or cheated by her jeweller).

Such fury at family jewellers who cheat also translated into trust in Tanishq, which offered a written guarantee of 22 carat gold, backed by the Tata name and stringent quality controls.

C.K. Venkataraman, the current chief operating officer of the jewellery business, says that Tanishq has built on this promise of trust by not only offering the highest standards of purity in gold and diamonds, but also by being transparent with customers. 'Purity is concretely supported by the karatmeter, but you will find transparency in every bit of Tanishq,' he says, 'product, pricing, exchange policies, advertising—we take pride in being very clear and very customer-friendly.'

Trust continues to remain the foremost consumer proposition of Tanishq.

BELIEF, FOCUS AND INNOVATION

The introduction of 22 carat gold jewellery corrected an initial error of judgement, and the karatmeter had proved a game changer. But Tanishq was still seen by many women as too Western, too pricey and therefore 'not for me'. These remaining barriers had to be broken if the brand had to perform to potential.

In the year 2000, there was an unfortunate exodus of senior management from the stables of Tanishq. Vasant Nangia, the man who had introduced the karatmeter, and several members of his team, left to form their own jewellery-retailing venture. Tanishq was still losing money. Into this vacuum stepped a new team headed by Jacob Kurian, who had worked with the Tata Group for over fifteen years.

The need of the hour was to infuse belief in the business and make it profitable. This would also mean convincing several lakh women that Tanishq was the best jewellery they could buy.

I had the good fortune of working as a senior member of Jacob's team in Tanishq during this phase of the business, before I eventually took charge from him as head of the business. Jacob was a charismatic leader who could never stand fools, and he relentlessly drove several waves of growth. He gathered a bunch of fine people around him and led them with rare energy, empathy and intellect. In those hectic days, we were a small team determined to make a big success of this business, and we were also aware that the sword of Damocles still hung somewhere from the ceiling.

Jacob infused belief in the future of Tanishq. One particular team event called 'I Believe' served to rally the troops by dramatically showcasing several reasons why Tanishq would succeed magnificently. It ended with all those present lighting candles in a dark conference hall, to reiterate their faith and confidence in the success of Tanishq.

From that period, three specific initiatives in the areas of marketing, financing and product innovation deserve mention here.

The first was was a gold jewellery exchange scheme called '19 = 22'. Women could bring in their gold jewellery and get it tested on the karatmeter. If the purity of their jewellery was lower than 22 carat and higher than 19 carat, they could exchange it for Tanishq's pure 22 carat jewellery of their choice, by paying only the manufacturing charges. The scheme again built on the karatmeter idea, and was a wild success. It resulted in several thousand women turning to Tanishq and away from their existing jewellers.

The second was the introduction of a new funding mechanism, by which gold for making jewellery could be procured on lease from international banks. Therefore, the need to invest hard cash in buying gold disappeared instantly, and Tanishq's working capital requirements came down significantly. This threw open the vistas for rapid growth, and was the second great innovation for Tanishq after the karatmeter.

The third was the creation and marketing of lightweight gold jewellery, which maximized the surface area of the piece but minimized the weight of gold used. This appealed greatly to budget-conscious women and also conveyed the key message that Tanishq was affordable.

Riding on the back of these initiatives, Tanishq crossed business revenues of Rs 500 crore by the year 2005. This was tremendous progress, as it marked a twenty-fold increase from the revenues of Rs 24 crore achieved in 1998. Most importantly, under Kurian's leadership, the business turned profitable. The Tata Group's senior management's conviction—lacking so far—went up significantly.

Hussain says his own view of the jewellery business was transformed by these developments. 'Tanishq was appealing to the mainstream now; the model now was quite different from the elitist 18 carat jewellery premise with which the business began. Execution was excellent, the karatmeter had made its point, and "gold on lease" was a game changer.'

An article titled 'Glittering Again', published on the Tata website in October 2003, now praised Tanishq as a trailblazer: 'Pioneering can be a poisoned chalice. Tanishq, as much a trailblazer in the jewellery industry as its parent Titan was in the watch industry, knows this better than most.'

THE NEW FACE OF TANISHQ

An even more spectacular phase of growth began in the years thereafter. In 2002, Bhaskar Bhat had become the managing director of Titan Industries, and had defined economic success and consumer affection as the twin objectives of the company. In 2005, C.K. Venkataraman (Venkat) replaced me as the head of the jewellery business.

Venkat describes a magical moment of transformation:

After a fundamental piece of consumer research, we understood that the evolving Indian woman has a new sense of self. She plays by the rules, but modifies them in a way which suits her. She seeks a harmonious coexistence between tradition and modernity. We seized on this insight to position Tanishq as a progressive Indian brand that combined tradition and heritage, a brand that offers new tales of tradition.

The brand had found its new face. The insight led to a coherent product strategy and several appealing advertising campaigns, which ushered in over half a million women into Tanishq showrooms. If the karatmeter had rescued the brand from failure, this new brand promise was a tipping point towards stupendous success.

Tanishq's first 'new tale of tradition' was a television film whose backdrop closely resembled the settings of a popular and award-winning Hindi film called *Parineeta*. In the film, a beautiful and very traditional Indian bride, bedecked in her fabulous Tanishq jewellery, goes out for a formal drive with her groom. When they are just out of sight of the family home, she quickly exchanges places with him, and gets into the driver's seat of the car with equal ease. The film appealed immediately to all Indian women who respect tradition, yet desire freedom and modernity.

Tanishq also emphasized its Indian heritage by designing jewellery for period Bollywood films such as *Paheli* and *Jodhaa Akbar*. In *Jodhaa Akbar*, a love story involving the famous Mughal emperor Akbar and the Rajput princess Jodhaa, Tanishq created not merely the jewellery for the royal couple, but also the jewelled armour and magnificent swords. It was a fabulous display of the craft of traditional jewellery. The brand simultaneously highlighted its modern appeal by creating distinctive crowns for winners of the glamorous Miss India contest.

Venkat also mentions Tanishq's assiduous efforts to woo the large Indian middle class, with schemes such as the Golden Harvest programme, where consumers could buy jewellery through advance instalments, with an attractive free instalment thrown in by the company. Several focused efforts went into targeting the wedding jewellery market, as well as the high-value jewellery segment.

Tanishq retail showrooms across India, managed for the most part by competent franchisees, offered consumers one of the best shopping experiences in the country. Rigorous retail workshops were conducted with these franchisees each year to ensure that each element of the brand's plans were fully in place. Venkat says the idea of these workshops was a seminal moment in the story of the brand, particularly since retail is all about detail.

Tanishq developed a new focus on transforming its customers into passionate fans of the brand. Thousands of women customers and their spouses were also invited to visit the jewellery factory at Hosur. Here, for the first time in their lives, they saw for themselves the process of jewellery making, and also held in their hands a ten-kilogram ingot of pure Tanishq gold!

The brand also launched marketing campaigns to educate consumers about diamonds. In 2011, the legendary Bollywood actor Amitabh Bachchan paired up with his wife, Jaya Bachchan, in a memorable advertisement to showcase the virtues of diamonds marketed by Tanishq. Women responded by streaming into Tanishq stores, and sales of diamond jewellery shot up beyond expectations.

This was a dream run. Tanishq crossed annual revenues of Rs 5000 crore with ease and hurtled towards its next big milestone. It also notched up rapid growth in profits. In his presentation at the Tata Group's Annual General Managers' Meeting (AGMM) in 2012, Ratan Tata highlighted the relative financial performance of various businesses in the group. All major Tata businesses were grouped into four performance quadrants, for ease of understanding. The jewellery business, which had virtually been written off a decade earlier, now featured in the topmost quadrant of profitability.

TRANSFORMING THE JEWELLERY INDUSTRY

Behind the glamour of the Indian jewellery industry lie hidden some of the most primitive working conditions for the artisans who make handmade jewellery. They come from traditional jewellery-making areas and families, and their valuable skills are often passed on from one generation to the next. Yet, they have mostly worked in appallingly cramped conditions, exposed to heat, sweat, dust and hazardous chemicals. Because they are unorganized, they are exploited by crafty middlemen, who tend to pocket much of the profits, giving the artisans little in return. Readers of Charles Dickens's novels will find a lot of similarity between his descriptions of the poorest parts of London and the insides of these poorly lit jewellery workshops.

Tanishq, after achieving excellent growth and business success, has now set about transforming these industry conditions. It has established 'karigar parks' that bring these artisans together and provide them with comfortable working conditions. Venkat says:

> We have an ambitious programme called Mr Perfect, which modernizes these facilities and injects respectability, prestige and glamour into the manufacturing of jewellery. From dingy workshops, we have created well-ventilated, clean environments that are comparable with modern offices. This will encourage artisans to happily remain in this profession for generations to come. We hope many more enlightened jewellers will follow in our wake.
>
> Jewellery always brings beautiful smiles to the faces of women. We want to bring equally broad smiles to the faces of the artisans who create these wonderful pieces with their own hands.

Bhaskar Bhat, the managing director of Titan Industries, speaks about the next phase of transformation that Tanishq should drive. The jewellery industry is often seen in poor light, he says, because of the perception that unaccounted or 'black' money is involved in large purchases. The government has recently initiated some action on this front, and Tanishq will once again be at the forefront of setting the right example. He says, 'Our vision is not merely to be a large and very successful player in jewellery, but to be an engine of transformation—only then can we be creators of wealth in the tradition of the Tatas.'

LOOKING BACK, LOOKING AHEAD

In March 2012, Titan Industries hosted a gala dinner in the Taj Vivanta Hotel at Bangalore to celebrate twenty-five years of the company's existence. The board of directors, current and past members of senior management had turned up in strength. The dress code for the evening specified a touch of silver, but a number of elegant lady invitees chose to wear Tanishq gold and diamond jewellery instead.

Xerxes Desai, whose vision and courage had created Tanishq, was present. So was Ishaat Hussain, his friend from Tata headquarters, with whom he had debated the future of this business many years ago.

When Ishaat Hussain stood up to speak, he was gracious and aristocratic, as always. He said, 'On the jewellery business, I must admit that I was wrong. Xerxes's conviction has turned out to be quite right, and we must applaud him for having created such a magnificent enterprise.'

These are generous words, and they will do much to encourage future pioneers within the Tatas.

But Desai is not yet happy with Tanishq. He feels that while the brand may be a big commercial success, it will become iconic only if it sharpens its appeal and regains the high ground on design.

'Tanishq must segment the jewellery market based on designs and price points. It must go back to the design concept as a differentiator. A work of art is known by its concept, and jewellery is such an expansive art form. Look at what Faberge did with a blooming egg!'

S. RAMADORAI

Excerpts from *The TCS Story . . . and Beyond* by S. Ramadorai

The success of America's Silicon Valley can be attributed to several factors but one that is irrefutable is a supportive ecosystem that encourages creativity, innovation and entrepreneurship.

In contrast, in the India of the 1970s when TCS[1] had just started up, an ecosystem was non-existent, and as a matter of fact the regulatory environment was not even pro-business.

When TCS went public in 2004, we were into our thirty-sixth year of existence. Often people would ask me where TCS had been all this while, and I would tell them that our first twenty years were spent building the foundations of the IT industry, clearing the hurdles with the government, and catalysing the regulatory framework which till then had never catered to importing computers or exporting software. We consciously made investments of time, money and expertise in academic partnerships with a view to building a talent base in the nation, and we did this quietly and without fanfare. Too quietly perhaps did we wear the mantle of a pioneer, something for which we paid a price in later years. Let us not forget that for all other companies that followed, TCS's initial investment created a springboard to take off from.

Four decades ago, there were many challenges for a private sector company in dealing with the Indian government. Indira Gandhi was the prime minister and was determined to carry on the Nehruvian socialist model. Jawaharlal Nehru's education at Trinity College, Cambridge, had been influenced by the Fabian socialist movement and he had come to believe that in a poor and populous country like India, the public sector should occupy the commanding heights of industry.

---

[1] Tata Consultancy Service, part of the Tata Group, is a global IT software and services company.

Indira Gandhi fervently followed the same path, creating a centrally controlled economy based on the Soviet model. Under her rule the banking and insurance sectors were nationalized and India adopted a policy of five-year national plans. Everything that the private sector did required permission from the government in the form of a licence. The list of licences was almost endless: private sector companies needed industrial licences, capital goods licences and import licences to name just a few; this eventually led to this period being known as the licence raj.

The government strategy was driven in part by the lack of foreign reserves in our coffers. Precious foreign exchange had to be used to create food reserves, fund oil imports and pay for defence equipment etc. It was to be used sparingly for other purposes.

This had a direct impact on TCS because we wanted to bring mainframe computers and state-of-the-art technology into the country and use it to train our people, just like we had been trained in the US. Obviously, we needed foreign exchange to pay for these purchases.

The second factor working against us was a view that computers were labour-saving devices. As a result there was an inherent resistance to computerization, particularly in bigger public sector corporations and the government sector which had very strong, entrenched unions which felt that automation would take away jobs. There was also a widespread feeling that the government looked at profit-making with suspicion. Clearly we were on a path that was tangential to the Indian government.

The Indian private sector and foreign companies that were present in the Indian market felt a great sense of constraint. At the time the government had the power, through licences, to dictate to businesses when and where they could increase capacity and what products they could make. No company could expand annual revenues beyond Rs 20 crore without specific clearance under the Monopolies and Restrictive Trade Practices (MRTP) Act.

In fact, many large industrial groups felt that the government's restrictive policies prevented them from serving the country and enriching its economy to the full extent of their capacity and will. An exchange between P.N. Haksar and J.R.D. Tata provides a good insight of the frustration felt at that time by industrialists.

Haksar was a brilliant lawyer who after two decades of outstanding diplomatic service was recalled to serve as secretary, and later as principal secretary to Prime Minister Indira Gandhi. He was a big influence on the shaping of India's domestic and foreign policies.

On JRD's eightieth birthday, Haksar wrote him a congratulatory note and urged him to reflect constructively and creatively on the state of the country. JRD, who probably saw this comment as salt on his wounds, could not resist responding with an unabashed forthrightness.

He wrote:

In the 100 years prior to Independence, opportunities created by the Industrial Revolution were denied to Indian merchants, financiers and affluent members of the bourgeoisie. The advent of Independence brought about a dramatic change in the situation which would normally have provided the same vital base as in other countries for great projects, ventures and adventures by Indians.

An essential pre-requisite however would have been a freedom of choice, of investment and of action which it took no time at all for our politicians and our burgeoning bureaucracy to block or stifle in the process of concentrating of all economic power in the government.

Instead of releasing energies and enterprise, the system of licenses and all pervasive controls imposed on the private sector in the country combined with confiscatory personal taxation, not only discouraged and penalized honest free enterprise, but encouraged and brought success and wealth to a new breed of bribers, tax evaders and black marketers.

In a single generation, great fortunes largely transferred abroad were built at a time when personal incomes of Rs 1 lakh per year were taxed at 98 per cent. The nationalization, on expropriatory terms, of insurance and banks, conveniently created a virtual monopoly of investible and lendable funds while fiscal policies combined with the use made of the Companies Act, the Industries Development & Regulations Act, the Monopolies and Restrictive Trade Practices Act and innumerable other enactments, regulations and administrative decisions, effectively concentrated all real economic power in the hands of politicians in power and bureaucracy. Under such conditions efforts at promoting and bringing to fruition large projects however desirable became a nightmarish and time-consuming one or ended in outright rejection.

JRD's words were to echo strongly later with TCS. We too felt extremely constrained. While we saw how the West was leveraging mainframe computers and information technology to achieve efficiency through bulk data processing in sectors such as defence and banking, India was missing out on the IT revolution.

But we were persistent. In just the same way that the Tatas had been pioneers in steel, energy and engines, we believed that TCS could be a pioneer in IT. We had confidence that if we could bring these new technologies into India, they could change the course of the nation and some day be a very important parameter for growth.

To serve an overseas market, we needed the latest learning, the latest generation of computers to be imported and we needed to explore top-of-the-line partnerships. So the first task was to find a way to import the equipment into India. This meant crossing swords with the government and the mighty licence raj.

At that time every industry had an administrative ministry in the central government. We came under the department of electronics (DoE) which was headed by Professor M.G.K. Menon. Prof. Menon was also the chairman of the electronics commission, the secretary of the department of electronics, and the scientific adviser to the government on defence.

As a scientific department, the DoE reported directly to the prime minister, and unfortunately the department was very wary of our intentions. In addition, since TCS was a division of Tata Sons, and the Tata Group was listed under MRTP as a dominant company because of its size and market share, any expansion which resulted in a capacity increase of 25 per cent or more required approval from the Monopolies and Restrictive Trade Practices Commission (MRTPC). In practice this meant another round of bureaucratic torture.

The process for importing a computer was mind-bogglingly complex and every stage had its own challenges, mostly because this was all being done for the very first time in India and the existing laws were open to interpretation by government officials who were unfamiliar with computers.

The process went something like this:

1. First we had to submit an application for an import licence to the DoE. This included an application for import of capital goods as well. As part of this process we had to justify what we wanted to do with the computer. Towards this we would produce a letter of intent from Burroughs placing an order for software services from TCS. Also included was the pro forma invoice with model numbers of the machines; sometimes technical literature was also sent.

2. Eleven copies were required as copies would be sent to various ministries including finance, commerce and industries. The DoE would then obtain the capital goods permission.

3. Next we had to obtain approval from the MRTPC as we belonged to a 'large' business house.

4. Then we had to navigate the complicated import tariffs and estimate the customs duty, which as it turned out was more than the cost of the machine itself.

5. We also had to get approval for free foreign exchange (to pay in US dollars for the import) from the government.

6. We had to justify the import by undertaking an export obligation to export twice the import cost (CIF) over a five-year period after the import. Failure to do so would involve

confiscation of the machine in addition to severe financial penalties.

7. We also had to obtain an export licence from the US department of commerce and provide an 'end-user certificate'. This was a problem when we had an order for a defence laboratory. Even so, the exporting nation had the right to monitor the use of the machine and confiscate it and begin criminal proceedings against us should there be any misuse.

8. Once we had secured all the above licences and approvals we weighed several tons; for large systems we had to charter a B707 freighter!

9. When the equipment arrived in India we had to clear it through the stringent custom procedures.

10. Finally we had to transport the bulky yet delicate equipment to the data centre and install it. This posed other problems as roads could be bumpy, underpasses not high enough to allow trucks with tall tape drives to pass under without getting jammed, lifts not large enough, false floor tiles not strong enough to take the load without buckling, etc.

Once we decided to import our first mainframe, we quickly found ourselves caught in the maze of government departments and their regulations. It is no exaggeration to say that TCS was faced with a totally unprecedented situation.

In the early 1970s Burroughs, then the second-largest computer manufacturer after IBM, saw India as a potential market and was willing to share its technology. In 1973 TCS signed an agreement with Burroughs. We agreed to distribute and sell Burroughs computers in India and they agreed to sell us a new Burroughs B1728 'small-system' computer.

Though advanced for its day, the B1728 would not be categorized as a mainframe today because it had only 128 Kb of memory and 8 Mb of disk space to start with. The memory sticks in our pockets today have larger storage capacities.

Our strategy was to import the machine, train ourselves to program and write software applications for it, and then to sell these services to markets outside India in order to earn foreign exchange. But we had not anticipated just how difficult it would be to import a new mainframe into India.

At that time, nobody in the private sector had imported a brand new mainframe. There were about 300 mainframe computers in the country that had been imported by university research departments, government agencies or the Ministry of Defence, but none of them had to pay import duty. Similarly there was also no precedent for customs duty computation for import of new systems in the private sector, because till then no one in the private sector had imported a brand new computer. The practice till then was that IBM and ICL used subsystems and parts, which they refurbished in their factories in India before making them available to Indian customers. These imports were treated as 'project' imports which had a different duty computation. So when TCS imported a new mainframe it was a whole new matter.

The Indian government said it would give us permission to import a new mainframe, but only if we exported twice its value over a five-year period. It was a bold step for TCS to make this commitment at that stage because we hardly had any export revenue to speak of.

That is how the Indian software industry was born, not by any grand design but by an accident of history because India was short of foreign exchange and we had to earn foreign exchange to pay for the importation of a new Burroughs mainframe.

The government's foreign exchange was reserved exclusively for defence and other government projects. Others seeking foreign exchange were referred to two institutional banks, IDBI and ICICI. Both institutional banks had access to foreign exchange through the World Bank and could provide this to Indian companies in the form of loans. But our owners, the Tatas, did not want to go down this route because the loans came with a convertibility clause that meant if the borrower defaulted, the bank would have an option to convert their money into equity. Tata Sons was a privately held limited company with charitable trusts as the owners, and the trusts did not want any outsiders to have a stake in the company.

So instead of tapping the institutional banks when we wanted to purchase the Burroughs mainframe in 1973, we approached Citibank. The US bank agreed to provide us with a loan in New York at 1 per cent over the London Interbank Rate (Libor) so the interest rate was about 3 or 4 per cent compared to the 8 or 9 per cent we would have had to pay in India.

We planned to service the loan through Tata Inc. in New York using the foreign exchange we earned in the US. Tata Inc. was a company originally set up to procure spare parts for Air India, but later it became an arm of Tata Steel. The arrangement with the Tatas was that when any Tata group company purchased material from the US, it was routed through Tata Inc. which in turn received a commission for handling the paperwork.

It was a perfectly good idea, but the Indian government rejected it because the bureaucrats said, 'We do not allow Indian companies to borrow abroad.' We enlisted the support of the Secretary of Economic Affairs because he was the contemporary of the father of a TCS colleague when they had been at the Reserve Bank. The Secretary agreed it was a good idea, but the department director had serious reservations. Ultimately I think the bureaucrats were suspicious of any new ideas and it was perhaps easier to say 'no'. Whatever the case, at that time the bureaucrats had the power to block initiatives, and they chose to do just that.

As a result, we had to borrow in rupees, which was more expensive, and then convert the loan into foreign exchange. We obtained the loan from Citibank in Bombay, issued a letter of credit to Tata Inc. in New York who purchased the machine and then exported it to us. But we incurred extra costs all the way. We also had to enter into a forward contract to protect ourselves against a devaluation of the rupee during the five-year term of the bank loan. It was the most inefficient way of doing things, but the government insisted we do it that way if we wanted the import licence.

It fell to Jayant to make all these applications. He had to learn things which nobody knew. The most complicated problem he faced was that nobody knew what the import duty on a new computer should be. Under India's import customs tariff nomenclature there was no mention of 'computers'. Oddly enough it did not come under 'machines' either, even though a computer was formally called an electronic data-processing (EDP) machine.

Instead computers came under Section 76 which was for 'electronic appliances and apparatus not specified elsewhere'. That meant a gigantic mainframe computer that required a room to house it and air conditioning to keep it from overheating was lumped together with mixer-grinders, toasters and electric razors. Since it was classified as an apparatus, it also attracted a higher rate of duty. An apparatus was considered to be a non-essential luxury item and attracted a 60 per cent import tax rather than the 40 per cent that applied to machines which were meant to be used for industrial purposes.

Ironically there was a different nomenclature in place for excise duty. Excise duty was charged by the Central government on the value of equipment manufactured in India, before sales tax. When something was imported, in order to protect the domestic industry, the government added the equivalent of excise duty which was called countervailing duty (CVD) to the import tax. To figure out the correct CVD rate we had to refer to the excise manual which followed the Brussels nomenclature and classified computers as machines. So a computer was a machine for CVD purposes and an apparatus for the purposes of import duty.

Over and above this, there were cascading duties as well: if the import duty was less than 40 per cent, the importer paid auxiliary duty at a 2 per cent rate; over 40 per cent the auxiliary duty was 5 per cent. Then you had to add the CVD of 15 per cent. We added all the numbers up and thought the total duty would be about 75 per cent.

But when we went to the customs and excise department at the airport to verify the calculations we were told that the CVD was applied on the ad valorem amount after the import duty and auxiliary duty were calculated, which meant the total duty payable on an imported mainframe computer was 101.25 per cent—although this was not actually written down anywhere.

This new and shocking development had to be communicated to Kohli[2] so Jayant[3] drove to a public phone booth outside the airport and called him. Jayant got through to Kohli's assistant and gave him the news but the assistant said, 'You had better tell him yourself in person.' No one wanted to be the harbinger of bad news. The drive from Santa Cruz up north to the Air India building in south Mumbai was the longest ever for Jayant who was chosen to deliver this bit of news. So what would have been a hot drive in a non-air-conditioned car became an even hotter one. In his inimitable style though, Jayant stood through Kohli's dressing-down on why the calculations were so off track.

The system itself cost $340,000 but we ended up paying more than twice that, and losing out on the exchange rate too.

Burroughs also needed a licence to export equipment from the US because the mainframe was considered a strategic item and it needed approval from the US defence department. So we had to provide a statement about what we would do with the computer.

The whole process took between nine months and a year. We started in 1973 and we finally imported the computer in 1974. Later on, it sometimes took two years because the process became even more complicated when the government decided that we were a Monopoly Restricted Trade Practice and our licence applications had to be approved by multiple committees.

The complicated processes, which often defied reason, forced us to become very creative in finding ways to work around the challenges. For example, we found out that we could import the equipment under a special customs bond that enabled us to move it from the airport and open it for inspection by customs at our own

---

[2] Faqir Chand Kohli is erstwhile CEO of TCS, Ramadorai's predecessor.
[3] Jayant Pendharkar was one of the earliest recruits of TCS; he joined the company around the same time as Ramadorai.

offices rather than at the airport warehouse where equipment damage was more likely.

We managed to persuade the customs authorities to agree to a bond which involved the customs officers at the airport wrapping each of the equipment boxes with wire and putting a lead seal on them. Then the boxes were loaded onto two or three trucks which came in a convoy escorted by customs officers to our offices in the Air India building in Bombay.

When we got to our office at the Air India building and offloaded the trucks the customs officials decided they were tired so we took them to the Taj for dinner, served copious quantities of beer and gave them taxi fare to get home. They said they would return early the next morning to clear the equipment.

Next day we arrived at the office very early to make sure the documentation was in order. To our horror we discovered that the electrician, in his eagerness to help, had removed the seals, 'so the boxes could be opened easily'!

I was with Jayant and a couple of field engineers and we asked ourselves what we should do now. We found all the seals and the wires which were in a dustbin, wrapped all the boxes up again with the wire and threaded the seals on to the end and bent the wire so it looked as though it had not been tampered with. We didn't know what would happen but we were concerned that the customs officials might say we had broken the bond and would therefore confiscate the equipment. We had visions of ourselves languishing in jail.

The customs people turned up soon. As soon as they arrived we said, 'See, here are the seals,' and quickly broke the seals in front of them before they could inspect them too closely. Luckily the strategy worked beautifully.

Our agony was not over. We still had the task of verifying the list of items on the import licence with the invoice—nothing tallied because we had all the model numbers from the marketing literature, the engineering guys had their own part numbers and the finance department which made the invoice had yet another set of numbers.

For example, the import licence was for a B1728 computer but the invoice said 'B Series' and somewhere else it said 'CPU 1728' and also '1700 range'. The customs officers asked us, 'But where does it say B1728?' Suddenly one of us saw there was a table on the underside of the box, scrambled under and quickly scribbled 'B1728' in one of the columns. We then called the officers over and showed them the legend. They said, 'Okay.' Really all they wanted to do was to tick off something that said 'B1728'.

Next time around, in 1976, when we imported a much bigger Burroughs 6748 machine that cost over $1 million, we told the Burroughs guys to make sure the invoice looked just like the sales material and matched the numbers on the equipment.

Each cabinet in that machine weighed over a ton and the dimensions were larger than the inside of the elevator in the Air India building. So we actually considered hoisting the cabinets up, slung from a hook on the underside of the elevator. In the end, however, we removed the internal elevator car railings and then somehow managed to slide the cabinets diagonally into the elevator car.

At our offices in the Air India building we had to create a data centre which involved creating a raised floor so cabling could run underneath. Traditionally the void below would be created like a grid, with slotted angles much like those found in a child's Mecano set. This grid would then be covered with tiles to create the raised floor.

In the case of the B6700, the mainframe also required a cold chamber under it and fans under the computer cabinets which would suck the cold air in to cool the machines. Kohli decided to try out an innovation and suggested that we use 9 x 9 x 9 in. bricks made of coal ash, a by-product of electricity generation at Tata Electric, as fillers.

Columns of these would form the grid, and tiles would be placed above. However the column distances necessitated larger tiles, so they had to be specially ordered and, when we moved the cabinets across the room to position them, the larger tiles sagged much more than the smaller ones, causing them to crack. So the attempted innovation turned out to be more of an irritant. Even so, the attempt to recycle waste material was a cause worth trying out and I am sure it would have met the appreciation of 'green' advocators.

Our frustration was far from over. The day after we installed the new mainframe in the Air India building, the government's annual finance budget was announced and the duty on computers was reduced from the 101.25 per cent we had paid to a total of 60 per cent.

In those days it was hard to predict what the policy changes would be in forthcoming budgets and Kohli had been expediting the import because of concerns about the possible devaluation of the rupee. But at least we stood to benefit in the future.

We had fought with the government for a rationalization of duties and appealed to the tax administrators on the basis that the mainframe had been wrongly classified. But at every stage we lost because the administrators said a complex electronic circuit board could not be defined as a machine because it had no moving parts. So eventually we decided to take the issue to the civil courts.

Finally, in 1980, four years after we launched the first appeal, I went with Jayant to the Bombay High Court and our case was heard. After listening to arguments from both sides the judge ruled that the government had no case and that the computers we had imported had been wrongly classified as 'appliance and apparatus' rather than EDP machines. He ordered a full refund of customs and excise duties, so we got a refund of Rs 65 lakh in 1980. For all our efforts Jayant and I treated ourselves to lunch.

It was an important ruling not just because of the refund, but because it forced the government to create a specific classification for computers. Not only did we help create a policy to import computers, but we helped create the software export industry and we got computers correctly classified for customs duties too.

COPYRIGHT ACKNOWLEDGEMENTS

Extracts from *Business Maharajas* and *Business Legends* by Gita Piramal
Extract from *The Vijay Mallya Story* by K. Giriprakash
Extracts from *TATAlog: Eight Modern Stories from a Timeless Institution* by Harish Bhat
Extract from *Go Kiss the World: Life Lessons for the Young Professional* by Subroto Bagchi
Extracts from *The Creation of Wealth: The Tatas from the 19th to the 21st Century* by R.M. Lala
Extract from *Dare to Dream: The Life of M.S. Oberoi* by Bachi J. Karkaria
Extract from *Aditya Vikram Birla: A Biography* by Minhaz Merchant
Extract from *The Ranbaxy Story* by Bhupesh Bhandari
Extract from *The TCS Story . . . and Beyond* by S. Ramadorai